MIGRATIONS OF THE HOLY

Migrations of the Holy

God, State, and the
Political Meaning of the Church

William T. Cavanaugh

WILLIAM B. EERDMANS PUBLISHING COMPANY
GRAND RAPIDS, MICHIGAN / CAMBRIDGE, U.K.

Published 2011 by
Wm. B. Eerdmans Publishing Co.
2140 Oak Industrial Drive N.E., Grand Rapids, Michigan 49505 /
P.O. Box 163, Cambridge CB3 9PU U.K.

Printed in the United States of America

17 16 15 14 13 12 11   7 6 5 4 3 2 1

Library of Congress Cataloging-in-Publication Data

Cavanaugh, William T., 1962-
Migrations of the holy: God, state, and the
political meaning of the church / William T. Cavanaugh.
p.   cm.
ISBN 978-0-8028-6609-7 (pbk.: alk. paper)
1. Church and state.   I. Title.

BV630.3.C39   2011
261.7 — dc22

2010041787

www.eerdmans.com

Contents

—⁓⁓—

v

Introduction

⟨⟨⟨⟩⟩⟩

It has become common in academic discourse to say that the secularization thesis — the idea that religion has become implausible in the modern era and will gradually fade from view — has been disproved by the global "resurgence" of religion. Whether one thinks that religion continues to fade or has made a comeback, defenders and attackers of the secularization thesis tend to agree that religion, for a time, went away somewhere, at least in the West. This book amounts to an argument that a third option is more plausible: the kinds of public devotion formerly associated with Christianity in the West never did go away, but largely migrated to a new realm defined by the nation-state.

In this sense, this book is a challenge to narratives that present modernity as something entirely new. Mark Lilla's book *The Stillborn God* sees an unprecedented "Great Separation" of politics from theology as the fragile achievement of the West, based on the genius of Hobbes, Locke, Hume, Mill, and others, and now threatened by the kind of human "original sin" that constantly seeks to inflate politics beyond a modest concern with the immanent.[1] In a very different way, Charles Taylor's celebrated book *A Secular Age* points to the optional nature of religion in the modern age as something genuinely new and unprecedented in

1. Mark Lilla, *The Stillborn God: Religion, Politics, and the Modern West* (New York: Knopf, 2007).

1

world history.[2] Christianity is not now publicly true but must be chosen by each individual, in a way that would have been unthinkable to someone living in medieval Europe. As Hent de Vries has pointed out, however, "optionality in the 'secular age' is hardly an option itself."[3] If we cannot opt out of optionality, if liberalism has become the overarching mythos of the modern age, then perhaps secular optionality is the same kind of naiveté that Taylor thinks we have outgrown or lost, and the "secular age" is not such a radical departure from all previously known types of social order that are theologically informed. The politics of the modern age is undoubtedly something different, but rather than simply marking the twilight of the gods, perhaps it might be better understood if we examine it for signs of the age-old sin of idolatry. It is this suggestion that I will try, in various ways, to render convincing — or at least plausible — in the chapters of this book.

To view the state in theological terms might bear fruit, not only theoretically but practically, as we attempt to confront the role of the state in the current situation. For example, the global financial crisis that broke in 2008 and sent the world to the brink of an economic depression has produced calls from all sides for greater state intervention in the market. Indeed, massive state intervention to rescue the banking system has been credited with saving us from a deeper disaster. State intervention in the market is not the bugbear it was just a few short years ago. The state, contrary to predictions of its increasing irrelevance in a globalized world, is looked upon as a kind of savior, the deus ex machina to be invoked whenever crisis hits.

We might, however, have reason to be wary of viewing the state as a savior. With regard to the current crisis, what we have seen in government bailouts is not so much the solution to the deeper problems behind the economic crisis as it is a deferral of the consequences to some later time. Governments have rescued the most reckless of the players in the swaps market with borrowed money after having steadfastly refused to regulate it. And the high-risk world of corporate finance turns out not to be so high-risk after all, because the state is there to pick up the pieces when banks that are "too big to fail" wreak havoc. The state is not so much res-

---

2. Charles Taylor, *A Secular Age* (Cambridge, MA: Harvard University Press, 2007).

3. Hent de Vries, "The Deep Conditions of Secularity," *Modern Theology* 26, no. 3 (2010): 391.

cuer as enabler of the worst kinds of risk. While some types of state intervention can mitigate disaster, we should think twice before expecting the
state to save us. The interests of corporate and state elites have become so
deeply intertwined that we cannot expect the state to protect us from corporate interests. The current expansion of the size and reach of the state
will only augment the combined power of these elites.

Why use the language of salvation when discussing the state? I don't
believe that the state can be understood without theology. Carl Schmitt
was right to say that all modern concepts of the state are secularized theological concepts if by "secularized" one means "covert." The story of the
death of the sovereign God and his rebirth in the sovereign state is not a
story of the progressive stripping of the sacred from some secular remainder. It is instead the transfer of care for the holy from church to state. We
not only expect the state to provide technical solutions to market imbal-
ances. In a deeper sense, we want the state to absorb the risk involved in
living a mortal human life. We want the state to defer the consequences of
our actions to some undefined future. In other words, we want the state to
help us cheat death.

I wrote the essays that became the chapters of this book between
2004 and 2007. They do not address the financial crisis directly; rather,
they explore some underlying problems with the way the state has colonized the political imagination of Christians. We have too often assumed
that the nation-state defines the boundaries of a unitary common space
and promotes the common good within that space. We have allowed
those borders to define identity and belonging, and have turned those attachments into a kind of ersatz religion with its own ersatz liturgy. We
have expected salvation from those identities, and resorted to violence to
defend them. And we have thereby obscured our identities as members of
a different body, the body of Christ.

My purpose in this book is to help Christians and others to be realis-
tic about what we can expect from the "powers and principalities" of our
own age, and to urge them not to invest the entirety of their political presence in these powers. In these chapters I try to unthink the inevitability of
the nation-state, and to show that it is not simply natural but one contingent and relatively recent way of organizing bodies in space. The way it or-
ganizes bodies into one unitary "society," policed by a sovereign authority, is also not inevitable. Despite claims of liberal nation-states to
embrace pluralism, I argue that any unitary society will always regard plu-

ralism as a threat. Therefore, I argue for a more radical pluralism, one that does not oscillate between individuals and the state, but allows for a plurality of societies, a plurality of common goods that do not simply feed into a unitary whole. This complex political space would privilege local forms of community, but it would also connect them in translocal networks of connectivity.

As in my previous writings, I argue here that the church in its eucharistic life is just such a network of local "political" spaces connected translocally. The church itself has its own political presence. But this contention is subject to a host of misunderstandings that I will try to allay from the outset.

To say that the church has a political presence is not thereby to reject the separation of church and state. Given my critique of the state in these pages, that point should be obvious. But perhaps it is less obvious because, though I accept the separation of church and state as a liberation of the state from the wielding of coercive power, I nevertheless reject the separation of "religion" from "politics." As I have argued at length in my book *The Myth of Religious Violence,* the idea that Christianity belongs to some special, nonempirical realm of "religion," cordoned off from some other essentially distinct realm of human behavior called "politics," is an invention of the early modern era that facilitated the expansion of civil over ecclesiastical power. The separation of religion and politics helps to promote the separation of one's loyalty to the church from one's loyalty to the nation-state, and thus the "migration of the holy" — to borrow a phrase from historian John Bossy — from church to state.[4]

Though there may be good reasons for limiting the kinds of power that ecclesiastical authorities wield in material matters, there is no basis for seeing Christianity as essentially restricted to an ethereal "spiritual" life. Any incarnational theology is aware of how deeply implicated is the everyday life of the material in our journey to God. Power over the things our bodies use is not a science essentially distinct from the science of the soul. Only an utterly anachronistic reading of the Gospels could divide religion and politics. When Jesus suggests that God and Caesar each be rendered his due, he does not thereby envision a division of labor between two divine beings. There is no realm of life called "politics" that is only in-

---

4. John Bossy, *Christianity in the West, 1400-1700* (Oxford: Oxford University Press, 1985), pp. 153-71.

directly under God's providential care. Once one renders to God what is God's — "The earth is the Lord's and all that is in it" (Ps. 24:1) — there is nothing left that belongs properly to Caesar.

Strictly speaking, the world is a theocracy: it is ruled by God. When Samuel relays the Israelites' request for a king, the Lord complains that "they have rejected me from being king over them" (1 Sam. 8:7). Any talk of theocracy must be immediately qualified, however, by the recognition that the church is not God. The church's many sins have often been a direct result of the wielding of coercive power. Church resistance to violence should not be based on a view of the church as a perfect society, but rather on the penitential recognition that we are incapable of using violence justly. Nevertheless, I do think that, precisely because it is capable of doing penance in ways that the state is not, the church needs to take its own political presence seriously. By this I do not mean active involvement in party politics. In my own context, I am wary of some American bishops' recent forays into electoral politics, often implying support for Republican Party candidates based on mostly empty promises to support the bishops' legislative agenda. Not only are such gambits often counterproductive — the church's own recent scandals have left the bishops with little credibility among the population at large — but they tend to assume that the only solution to any given cultural problem is state enforcement. The church must be wary of nostalgia for Constantinianism. A Christian should feel politically homeless in the current context, and should not regard the dreary choice between Democrats and Republicans, left and right, as the sum total of our political witness.

In this book I point to church practices that resist the colonization of the Christian imagination by a nation-state that wants to subordinate all other attachments to itself. It is necessary, in doing so, to complexify political space: to create forms of local and translocal community that disperse and resist the powers invested in the state and corporation. This book, I hope, contributes to a kind of Christian micropolitics that comes first and foremost from grass-roots groups of Christians.

The first three chapters of this book examine pathologies of the modern state. Chapter 1 examines the history of the modern state and modern nation-state, arguing that neither state nor nation is natural or essential for the promotion of the common good. Chapter 2 examines the dynamics of unity and pluralism in the modern nation-state, and argues, on the basis of the "two cities" concept of St. Augustine, for a more radical political pluralism. Chapter 3 analyzes how mobility and identity are regulated by the state in a globalized world, confronting the figures of migrant and tourist with those of pilgrim and monk in an attempt to suggest a positive Christian response to globalization.

Chapters 4 and 5 address the particular context of the United States of America, showing how a liberal social order can create its own secular gods. Chapter 4 shows how Enlightenment and Christian themes have been combined in the United States to create a messianic nation, which displaces the church. Chapter 5 briefly discusses torture in the War on Terror and how the myth of the Inquisition can be used to justify disciplinary power by the liberal state.

The final four chapters address the church as a public, political space. Chapter 6 contrasts the liturgy of the nation-state with the liturgy of the church, arguing that the Christian liturgy needs to break out of its confinement to a private, sacred space. Chapter 7 argues for the church as a political body. Chapter 8 addresses the sinfulness of the church, arguing that the true visibility of the church as a political body can be found only in repentance for its sin. Chapter 9 deals with Stanley Hauerwas's theological engagements with democratic theorists in an attempt to articulate more precisely how the church can imagine its own political presence in ways that make tangible the receptive generosity of Christ on the cross.

A fully developed political theology and practice is not within the scope of this book. Nevertheless, I intend this book to give Christians and others some critical tools with which to turn the despair of modern politics toward real hope.

CHAPTER ONE

"Killing for the Telephone Company": Why the Nation-State Is Not the Keeper of the Common Good

—⁓—

In Christian social ethics the assumption is often made, with a minimum of examination, that the responsibility for promoting and protecting the common good falls to the state. In this chapter I want to examine that assumption. All too often, Christian social ethics begins from ahistorical and idealized assumptions about the state as protector and benefactor. They are ahistorical because they assume that the state has been with us since biblical times. The state, as Charles Curran says, is "natural and necessary" and "based on creation."[1] It takes different forms — polis for Aristotle, *regimen principum* for Aquinas — but these different terms refer to the same essential reality: all historical forms of political community are conflated into the term "state."[2] These accounts are also idealized because they assume that society is prior to the state and broader than the state. Human society is represented as a pyramid: the family is at the base, other groups and associations are in the middle, and the state is at the top to coordinate and protect. The base has "ontological priority" to the state and calls forth the state to be at its service. Furthermore, "[s]ociety is broader than the state and includes much more." The state is

---

1. Charles E. Curran, *Catholic Social Teaching, 1891-Present: A Historical, Theological, and Ethical Analysis* (Washington: Georgetown University Press, 2002), pp. 138-39.

2. Curran writes of the "state or political order" and the "state or the political community" as if they were simply interchangeable (p. 138).

just one limited part of society, but is established in nature with an important role to play: "the end or purpose of the state or government [is] the pursuit of the common good."[3]

What I find unhelpful about such accounts is the way they float free from any empirical testing of their theses. Christian ethicists will commonly recognize that, in a sinful world, particular states always fall short of the ideal. Nevertheless, the ideal is presented not merely as a standard for Christian political practice but as a statement of fact: the state in its essential form simply is that agency of society whose purpose it is to protect and promote the common good, even if particular states do not always live up to that responsibility. This conclusion is based on a series of assumptions of fact: that the state is natural and primordial; that society gives rise to the state and not vice versa; and that the state is one limited part of society. These assumptions of fact, however, are often made without any attempt to present historical evidence on their behalf.

This may be because such evidence is lacking. In this chapter I will examine the origins of the state and the state-society relationship according to those who study the historical record. I will argue that the above assumptions of fact are untenable in the face of the evidence. I will examine these three assumptions in order. First, unless one equivocates on the meaning of "state," the state is not natural, but a rather recent and artificial innovation in human political order. Second, the state gives rise to society, and not vice versa. Third, the state is not one limited part of society, but has in fact expanded and become fused with society. The primary burden of this chapter is negative: in arguing these three points, I will attempt to present the case against seeing the state as the promoter and protector of the common good. Only in the conclusion will I make some brief comments on what this implies positively for Christian thinking and practice.

A preliminary comment is necessary: my analysis of the development and current condition of the state and nation-state is based on Western models — that is, primarily Europe and the United States. The state and nation-state are Western inventions. They have been exported to the rest of the world with varying degrees of success. In many Southern lands, the reality of the state and the sense of the nation are tenuous at best, and are mixed with other forms of political organization, such as tribal structures. I take most of my examples from the United States, though insofar

---

3. Curran, *Catholic Social Teaching*, pp. 141-44.

as the nation-state has taken root elsewhere, we can see similar dynamics in other contexts.

The State Is Not Natural, but Artificial

History of the Term

The word "state" is sometimes used loosely to refer to the political form through which a stable group of people is organized. Nomadic groups are usually the only kind of political community excluded from this definition, since the term implies some form of geographical stability. The state is thus treated, as Engels says, as a necessary and ancient "product of society at a certain stage of development."[4] Thus questions of "church and state," for example, are perennial questions.[5] In more precise usage, however, "state" refers to a more limited development characteristic of modernity. The state emerged in Europe amidst the late Renaissance and Reformation. As Bruce Porter puts it, "The state as we know it is a relatively new invention, originating in Europe between 1450 and 1650."[6] In this more precise sense, the state is a political form based on the distinctly modern concept of sovereignty, which may be defined as "supreme authority within a territory." As formulated by Bodin, Hobbes, and other lesser figures of the early modern period, the state claims legitimate authority — as opposed to mere coercion — a supreme authority that no lesser authorities within a recognized set of geographical borders may legitimately oppose. Sovereignty is a departure from earlier forms of governance, in which people's political loyalties were based not necessarily on territoriality but on feudal ties, kinship, and religious or tribal affiliation.[7] If a stranger committed a crime on someone else's land, it would be necessary to find out to whom he or she owed loyalty in order to know what law applied.

4. Friedrich Engels, "The Origin of Family, Private Property, and State," in *The Marx-Engels Reader,* ed. Robert C. Tucker, 2nd ed. (New York: W. W. Norton, 1978), p. 752.

5. For example, Hugo Rahner, SJ, *Church and State in Early Christianity,* trans. Leo Donald Davis, SJ (San Francisco: Ignatius Press, 1992).

6. Bruce D. Porter, *War and the Rise of the State: The Military Foundations of Modern Politics* (New York: Free Press, 1994), p. 6.

7. Daniel Philpott, *Revolutions in Sovereignty* (Princeton, NJ: Princeton University Press, 2001), pp. 16-17.

It is perfectly acceptable to use the term "state" in the looser sense, provided one is clear that it is not being used in the stricter sense. Confusion is produced when, as in the case of Curran above, the two senses are intermingled. It should be made clear that, although political community in some form may be natural and ancient, the sovereign state as we know it is not. One could claim that the modern state is just one more variation on the theme of the state, but that would be extremely misleading. In the first place, the term *status* began to appear in a political context only in the late fourteenth century, and until the sixteenth century it was used either to refer to the state of the ruler himself (*status principis* or *status regalis*) or to the current condition of the realm (*status regni*). The emphasis was on a personalized kind of rule embodied in the prince. Only in the sixteenth century does there arise the concept of an abstract "state" that is independent of both ruler and ruled. Machiavelli is a transitional figure in this regard: he used the term *stato* to refer both to the prince's powers and position and to an abstract apparatus above prince and people. By the mid-sixteenth century, the abstract usage had won out in French and English legal writing.[8]

In the second place, to treat the sovereign state as just one more variation on the ancient "state" is to misrepresent the radical nature of the modern state. As is often the case in the history of language, large etymological shifts followed profound changes in social organization. New vocabulary was needed to describe a radically new situation. To treat the modern state as simply a variation in the history of societies is to ignore the fact that there were no such things as societies in the sense of clearly bounded and unitary systems of interaction until the birth of the modern state. As Anthony Giddens says, traditional social systems are composed not of one society but of many "societies"; the modern unitary society that originated in Europe is highly exceptional.[9]

8. Quentin Skinner, *The Foundations of Modern Political Thought* (Cambridge: Cambridge University Press, 1978), vol. II, pp. 352-58.

9. Anthony Giddens, *The Nation-State and Violence* (Berkeley, CA: University of California Press, 1987), pp. 1-2, 52-53. Ernest Gellner discusses the transition from traditional social orders to unitary societies in terms of language: "In a traditional social order, the languages of the hunt, of harvesting, of various rituals, of the council room, of the kitchen or harem, all form autonomous systems: to conjoin statements drawn from these various disparate fields, to probe for inconsistencies between them, to try to unify them all, this would be a social solecism or worse, probably blasphemy or impiety, and the very endeavour

This brings us to the term "nation-state," which designates an even more recent development in the history of political organization. As the hyphen implies, the nation-state is the result of the fusion of the idea of the nation — a unitary system of shared cultural attributes — with the political apparatus of the state. Nations are most commonly united by some combination of shared ethnicity, language, or history, but nationality is not simply "natural" or "objective," since ethnicity, language, and history are all themselves the result of contingent historical construction. The construction of a national sense is a matter of "common feeling and an organized claim."[10] Historically, this claim is first organized by the state. It is only after the state and its claims to territorial sovereignty are established that nationalism arises to unify culturally what had been gathered inside state borders. National claims tend to construct historical myths of origin stretching back into antiquity, but Carlton Hayes and Hans Kohn established in the 1930s and 1940s the majority opinion that nationalism first appeared in the eighteenth century.[11] The nation-state first arose in the eighteenth century and became prevalent only in the nineteenth century and following.[12]

---

would be unintelligible. By contrast, in our society it is assumed that all referential uses of language ultimately refer to one coherent world, and can be reduced to a unitary idiom." Ernest Gellner, *Nations and Nationalism* (Ithaca, NY: Cornell University Press, 1983), p. 21. While Giddens is keen to emphasize the radical break that the modern state represents, he nevertheless uses the term "state" to include traditional class-divided social groups; for Giddens, the crucial transition is marked by the rise of the "absolutist state" and subsequently the "nation-state."

10. "Nationalism," in *The Blackwell Encyclopedia of Political Thought,* ed. David Miller (Oxford: Blackwell, 1987), p. 354.

11. Carlton J. H. Hayes, *The Historical Evolution of Modern Nationalism* (New York: R. R. Smith, 1931), and Hans Kohn, *The Idea of Nationalism: A Study in Its Origins and Background* (New York: Macmillan, 1944). E. J. Hobsbawm refers to Hayes and Kohn as the "founding fathers" of the study of nationalism; he says that their dating of nationalism has not been successfully challenged. E. J. Hobsbawm, *Nations and Nationalism since 1780: Programme, Myth, Reality* (Cambridge: Cambridge University Press, 1990), p. 9.

12. See, for example, Hendrik Spruyt, *The Sovereign State and Its Competitors* (Princeton, NJ: Princeton University Press, 1994), p. 195n2, where Spruyt distinguishes between the state and the more recent phenomenon of the nation-state. See also Benedict Anderson, *Imagined Communities: Reflections on the Origin and Spread of Nationalism* (London: Verso, 1991); and "Nation-state," in *The Dictionary of World Politics,* ed. Graham Evans and Geoffrey Newnham (New York: Simon and Schuster, 1990), p. 258.

Origins of the State

The above suggests something of the wide temporal gap between the modern nation-state and the context in which language of the common good originated. With that caution registered, there is no question that the ground was prepared for the modern state in the medieval period. In his work on medieval political structures, Joseph Strayer locates the turning point toward greater administrative centralization somewhere around the beginning of the twelfth century. Although Strayer acknowledges that once the state did not exist, he sees the embryonic "state" in the increasing bureaucratization of civil authority in the twelfth century and after.[13] Hendrik Spruyt says that Strayer overstates the early origins of the state, but contends that, in the case of France if nowhere else, the basis of the state had been laid by the beginning of the fourteenth century.[14]

In his *On the Medieval Origins of the Modern State*, Strayer narrates the gradual accretion of power to royal courts beginning in the twelfth century. The first permanent functionaries were estate managers hired to centralize, regularize, and keep account of the extraction of revenues from the lands and populations subject to the king.[15] Next to develop were royal courts of law. Courts of law were originally simply royal courts, that is, the "great men" who surrounded the king and made up his household. In the twelfth and thirteenth centuries they were increasingly called upon to settle disputes, frequently by knights and lesser landholders asking for protection against the wealthier nobles. The royal courts that developed were thus important to the king's struggle for power with the nobility. In general, the law became the principal tool of centralization and bureaucratization. By the fourteenth century, the governing apparatuses sur-

---

13. Joseph R. Strayer, *On the Medieval Origins of the Modern State* (Princeton, NJ: Princeton University Press, 1970), pp. 15-27. If Strayer is looser with the term "state" than other historians, he is also looser with the term "sovereignty," seeing it existing in fact but not in theory in the fourteenth century (p. 9); what he means by medieval "sovereignty," however, is simply the right of the king to be the court of last resort in judging the law, whereas the early modern idea of sovereignty includes making the law (p. 102). Strayer also gives an early origin for nationalism, saying that there are "some signs of what might be called nationalism" in England, France, and Spain in the seventeenth century (p. 109).

14. Spruyt, *The Sovereign State*, p. 79.

15. Strayer, *On the Medieval Origins*, pp. 28-29, 69. Hereafter, page references to this work appear in parentheses in the text.

rounding the king had "acquired their power largely by developing their judicial institutions and by protecting the property rights of the possessing classes" (p. 61). By the fourteenth century, war had made royal courts increasingly reliant on taxation, which in turn required inviting representatives of the propertied classes to give their consent in occasional non-voting assemblies. Such assemblies generally succeeded in shifting the tax burden more heavily onto the unrepresented classes (pp. 58-68).

What is significant for our purposes is that Strayer's account leaves little room for the pursuit of the common good as a historical explanation for the rise of the state. According to Strayer, the development of regularized systems of revenue extraction and accounting, law courts, and assemblies were undertaken with reference to its advantages for particular parties, namely the royal household and the propertied classes, and without reference to anything like a common good. The common people came into the purview of the emerging bureaucracy almost exclusively as a resource for revenue extraction. At the same time, the very definition of what is "common" had begun a gradual transformation. The centralization of royal power involved a transfer of rights from local bodies that had previously been the primary referents of communal life. Legal right and the administration of justice was not created by royal power but was usurped from manorial lords, churches, and communities. If Strayer is accurate, this process took place to serve the particular interests of dominant groups, and not as the expansion of common space.

At this early stage, the ascendant civil bureaucracy did not yet refer to a unitary "common." In the absence of the sovereign state, there was no "society" to which a common good could be imputed. Europe was still a complex of multiple *societates* with a very weak level of integration among them. The administrative reach of even the most bureaucratized royal courts was short and rarely touched the lives of the great majority of people. Significant elements of military power lay outside the control of the central apparatus. Political power was still a matter of the personal disposition of the ruler, and his or her rule was diffused into a jumble of overlapping jurisdictions and loyalties. Strayer characterizes the situation of kingly rule in the fourteenth century with this example:

> A king of France might send letters on the same day to the count of
> Flanders, who was definitely his vassal but a very independent and un-

ruly one, to the count of Luxemburg, who was a prince of the Empire but who held a money-fief (a regular, annual pension) of the king of France, and to the king of Sicily, who was certainly ruler of a sovereign state but was also a prince of the French royal house. In such a situation one could hardly distinguish between internal and external affairs. (p. 83)

This distinction between internal and external would eventually get sorted out, but only in the establishment of sovereign borders through the coercive aggrandizement of royal power. The state does not arise as the establishment of a uniform system of common good and justice on behalf of a society of people; rather, a society is brought into being by the centralization of royal power.

The agent of this change is war. Strayer says that the increased intensity of war in the fourteenth century and following was necessary to distinguish inside and outside, and he regards the process of state-building after 1300 as inevitable (pp. 57-58). However, Charles Tilly argues against Strayer that there was nothing natural or inevitable about the rise of the state. In 1300, Tilly says, there were still five possible outcomes open:

(1) the form of national state which actually emerged; (2) a political federation or empire controlled, if only loosely, from a single center; (3) a theocratic federation — a commonwealth — held together by the structure of the Catholic Church; (4) an intensive trading network without large-scale, central political organization; (5) the persistence of the "feudal" structure which prevailed in the thirteenth century.[16]

Tilly also faults Strayer for too little emphasis on the coercive aspects of state-building (p. 43). Tilly's larger contention is that there was nothing natural or inevitable about the rise of the state; it triumphed in Europe because of its superior ability to extract resources from the local population.

Tilly and eight other scholars changed the focus of the study of the genesis of the state with the publication of *The Formation of National States in*

---

16. Charles Tilly, "Reflections on the History of European State-Making," in *The Formation of National States in Western Europe*, ed. Charles Tilly (Princeton, NJ: Princeton University Press, 1975), p. 26. Hereafter, page references to this essay appear in parentheses in the text.

Western Europe (1975). Previous approaches tended to posit the problem in terms of whether or not political managers successfully directed socio-economic change — or "modernization" — toward desirable outcomes, including the survival of the political apparatus itself. As Tilly says, the problem thus put reproduces the worldview of the high administrative official: the world is "out there" to be dealt with and transformed by means of government. For Tilly and associates, the question of which political forms would survive to become a sovereign, national state is best answered in terms of "whether the managers of the political units undertook activities which were expensive in goods and manpower, and built an apparatus which effectively drew the necessary resources from the local population and checked the population's efforts to resist that extraction of resources" (p. 40). Building a state depended on the ability of state-making elites to make war, and the ability to make war in turn depended on the ability to extract resources from the population, which in turn depended on an effective state bureaucracy to secure those resources from a recalcitrant population. As Tilly puts it, "War made the state, and the state made war" (p. 42).

Gabriel Ardant looks carefully at the empirical financial conditions of state- and nation-building, and finds them intimately connected to the ability to make war. He shows how, in the period of European state-building, the greatest changes in fiscal burdens imposed on a population occurred because of war. At the same time, the most serious precipitant to violence, and the greatest spur to the growth of the state, was the attempt to collect taxes from an unwilling populace. Finally, the efforts at nation-building in the nineteenth century, including the efforts to broaden political participation, were due to the demands of war.[17]

The element of popular resistance contradicts the modernizing narrative that sees in the growth of the state the progressive increase of political rights. In the crucial period of state formation, the state either absorbed rights previously resident in other bodies (guilds, manors, provinces, estates) or eliminated them altogether, as in the enclosure of common lands (Tilly, pp. 37-38). Close analyses of the history of taxation,[18]

---

17. Gabriel Ardant, "Financial Policy and Economic Infrastructure of Modern States and Nations," in Tilly, *The Formation of National States*, pp. 164-242. On war and nationalism, see also Hobsbawm, *Nations and Nationalism since 1780*, p. 83.

18. Rudolf Braun, "Taxation, Sociopolitical Structure, and State-Building: Great Britain and Brandenburg-Prussia," in Tilly, *The Formation of National States*, pp. 243-327.

policing,[19] and food supply[20] indicate that popular resistance to state-building was deep, broadly based, frequent, and violent. In England alone, the crown put down by force popular rebellions in 1489, 1497, 1536, 1547, 1549, and 1553, all responses to the centralizing efforts of the Tudors. Those asked to surrender men, crops, labor, money, and land to the emerging state did not do so without a fight. Tilly says: "The state-makers only imposed their wills on the populace through centuries of ruthless effort" (pp. 22-24). However, we should underscore the fact that state-making was not the motivating intention of state-making elites. The state was largely an unintended byproduct of these elites' pursuit of their own ends.[21]

In a 1985 article entitled "War Making and State Making as Organized Crime," Tilly suggests the analogy of the protection racket for the formation of the Western state. The claim that emerging states offered their citizens protection against violence ignores the fact that the state itself created the threat and then charged its citizens for reducing it. What separated state violence from other kinds of violence was the concept of legitimacy, but legitimacy was based on the ability of state-makers to approximate a monopoly on violence within a given geographical territory. In order to pursue that monopoly, elites found it was necessary to secure access to capital from the local population, which was accomplished in turn either by the direct threat of violence or the guarantee of protection from other kinds of violence. The variations in the states produced are explicable in terms of variations in the difficulty of collecting taxes, the cost of military technology used, the force available to competitors, and so on. In sum, Tilly suggests that "a portrait of war makers and state makers as coercive and self-seeking entrepreneurs bears a far greater resemblance to the facts than do its chief alternatives: the idea of a social contract, the idea of an open market in which operators of armies and states offer services to willing customers, the idea of a society whose shared norms and expectations call forth a certain kind of government."[22]

---

19. David H. Bayley, "The Police and Political Development in Europe," in Tilly, *The Formation of National States*, pp. 328-79.

20. Charles Tilly, "Food Supply and Public Order in Modern Europe," in *The Formation of National States*, pp. 380-455.

21. Charles Tilly, "Western State-Making and Theories of Political Transformation," in *The Formation of National States*, pp. 633-38.

22. Charles Tilly, "War Making and State Making as Organized Crime," in *Bringing the*

This view of state-formation has gained wide acceptance. It builds on the early twentieth-century work of Otto Hintze,[23] and is confirmed by the more recent work of Perry Anderson,[24] Hendrik Spruyt,[25] Anthony Giddens, Victor Burke,[26] and others. In his survey of state-making studies over the last three decades, Thomas Ertman is able to say that "it is now generally accepted that the territorial state triumphed over other possible political forms (empire, city-state, lordship) because of the superior fighting ability which it derived from access to both urban capital and coercive authority over peasant taxpayers and army recruits."[27] As for explaining variations within the dominant form of the sovereign state, Ertman says that "the work of Hintze, Tilly, Mann, Downing, and Anderson has already conclusively established that war and preparations for war tended to stimulate the creation of ever more sophisticated state institutions across the continent," and that war was the "principal force" behind the expansion and rationalization of state apparatuses.[28]

In a recent book, Michael Howard sums up the evidence bluntly: "The entire apparatus of the state primarily came into being to enable princes to wage war."[29] The word "primarily" suggests that violence was not the only factor in the creation of the modern state. All of the authors mentioned acknowledge a variety of other interrelated factors, including the rise of capital markets, technological innovations, geographical position, the introduction of Roman law, and urbanization. Perhaps the best

---

State Back In, ed. Peter B. Evans, Dietrich Rueschemeyer, and Theda Skocpol (Cambridge: Cambridge University Press, 1985), p. 169.

23. Otto Hintze, *The Historical Essays of Otto Hintze,* ed. Felix Gilbert (New York: Oxford University Press, 1975).

24. Perry Anderson, *Lineages of the Absolutist State* (London: New Left Books, 1974).

25. Spruyt, *The Sovereign State and Its Competitors.*

26. Victor Lee Burke, *The Clash of Civilizations: War-Making and State Formation in Europe* (Cambridge: Polity Press, 1997).

27. Thomas Ertman, *Birth of the Leviathan: Building States and Regimes in Medieval and Early Modern Europe* (Cambridge: Cambridge University Press, 1997), p. 4.

28. Ertman, *Birth of the Leviathan,* pp. 26, 4. Ertman's project builds on this consensus in offering what he says is a better account of the factors that predict whether or not a state will have an absolutist or constitutional framework. Ertman contends that Hintze, Tilly, Downing, and Mann do not adequately account for the "nonsimultaneity" of the process, that is, that not all states were affected by war-making at the same time (pp. 15, 26-27).

29. Michael Howard, *The Invention of Peace: Reflections on War and International Order* (New Haven: Yale University Press, 2000), p. 15.

way to express it, with Bruce Porter, is that war was the catalyst and sine qua non mobilizing the other factors in the formation of the state.[30] One need not romanticize the medieval period to conclude that the state, at least in its origins, is not appropriately categorized as that agency of society that has responsibility for the common good. Those who study the origins of the state would find such a categorization rather remote from the empirical evidence.

The State Is Not a Product of Society, but Creates Society

The conceptual leap that accompanies the advent of the state in the sixteenth century is the invention of sovereignty, a doctrine that asserts the incontestable right of the central power to make and enforce law for those people who fall within recognized territorial borders. Giddens contrasts borders with traditional frontiers, peripheral and poorly marked or poorly guarded regions in which the power of the center is diffuse. In premodern Europe, authority was often marked by personal loyalties owed in complexly layered communal contexts. In the state, by contrast, borders mark out a unitary space in which the individual is subject directly to the center, which has the right to enforce its will through a monopoly on the means of legitimate violence within those borders.[31]

As an example of the complex premodern situation, Giddens cites the province of Sedan in the mid-seventeenth century.

> Sedan is often regarded as a distinct realm. But others have seen it as a boundary province of the larger state of France, in which the monarch was not able to sustain more than minimal authority. The hesitations of historians are not particularly surprising, reflecting in some part those current at the time. The dukes of Bouillon held direct lordship over the area, but owed some of their possessions to the bishops of Liege, who in turn were princes owing allegiance to the French crown. The ducal family relinquished Sedan in exchange for certain other areas in France. On occasion, this has been regarded by historical writ-

30. Porter, *War and the Rise of the State*, pp. 7, 24, 60-61.
31. Giddens, *The Nation-State and Violence*, pp. 49-51, 85-89.

ers as the annexing of previously foreign territory, by others as the consolidation of royal power over French lands.[32]

What takes place in the modern era — not complete in some places until the late nineteenth century — is a reconfiguration of space that is much more profound than the creation of an expanded common space through the gathering up and coordination of formerly scattered elements into one. What happens is a shift from "complex space" — varied communal contexts with overlapping jurisdictions and levels of authority — to a "simple space," characterized by a duality of individual and state.[33] There is an enfeebling of local common spaces by the power of the center and a simultaneous parochialization of the imagination of Christendom into that of the sovereign state. To say that the state "creates" society is not to deny that families, guilds, clans, and other social groups existed before the state. Rather, the state "creates" society by replacing the complex overlapping loyalties of medieval *societates* with one society, bounded by borders and ruled by one sovereign to whom allegiance is owed in a way that trumps all other allegiances.

The early modern theorists of sovereignty saw this dynamic clearly. As first formulated by Jean Bodin, sovereignty is the triumph of the one over the many, the creation of a unified simple space. As such, the sovereign must be "absolute" and alone, which means above all to be able to give law without being subject to law. The laws of the sovereign, "although they be grounded on good and lively reasons, depend nevertheless upon nothing but his mere and frank good will."[34] Because law is based on will, the sovereign cannot be subject to his own laws. The unity of the republic depends on the absolute singularity of the sovereign, who creates a simple space through his power.[35] Bodin thus unblinkingly asserts that sovereignty, and therefore the state, is created not by contract, custom, or natural right, but by sheer power. All other kinds of association are subject for their very existence on the recognition of the sovereign.

Hobbes, too, derives sovereignty from will, though he attempts to

---

32. Giddens, *The Nation-State and Violence*, p. 89.

33. I adopt the language of complex and simple space from John Milbank, "On Complex Space," in *The Word Made Strange: Theology, Language, Culture* (Oxford: Blackwell Publishers, 1997), pp. 268-92.

34. Jean Bodin, *The Six Bookes of a Commonweale*, ed. Kenneth McRae (Cambridge, MA: Harvard University Press, 1962), book I, chap. 8, p. 92 (translation modified).

35. Bodin, *The Six Bookes*, book VI, chap. 6.

found legitimacy in the implied consent of the people. For Hobbes, the sovereign is the representative of the people, their own creation: it is from this that legitimacy derives and this that makes Hobbes the founder of liberalism, despite the absolutist form his government would take. The foundation of the state in Hobbes is not a common good but rather a shared evil: the fear of death. Each person is possessed of a "perpetual and restless desire of power after power, that ceaseth only in death."[36] Individuals in the state of nature do not occupy a common space, for each has a *jus in omnia*, a right over everything, and that makes them enemies, locked in the war of all against all. The only way out of this condition is for each to surrender his or her will to the sovereign, who gathers up the many into one. Despite Hobbes's derivation of legitimacy from representation, therefore, it is the state that first gathers people into society with one another.

This creation of a unitary space requires the church's absorption into the sovereign and the absorption of any other bodies that would threaten the unity of Leviathan. Sovereignty is absolute for Hobbes because the *jus in omnia* that each individual transfers to the sovereign is unlimited. If each individual is possessed of an inviolable will that is his or hers alone, then the only way such a will could be transferred or represented is by the encounter with another irresistible will. Yet for Hobbes, the individual is not oppressed but liberated by Leviathan. In his view, the state is not enacted to realize a common good or common *telos*, but rather to liberate the individual to pursue his or her own ends without fear of interference from other individuals. In the peculiar new space created by the state, the individual members do not depend on one another; rather, they are connected only through the sovereign — as spokes are to the hub of a wheel. Cardinal Bellarmine has written, as Hobbes reports, that "the members of every commonwealth, as of a natural body, depend on one another." Hobbes replies: "It is true, they cohere together; but they depend only on the sovereign, which is the soul of the commonwealth; which failing, the commonwealth is dissolved into a civil war, no one man so much as cohering to another, for want of a common dependence on a known sovereign; just as the members of a natural body dissolve into the earth, for want of a soul to hold them together."[37] Hobbes sees clearly that it is the state that enacts civil society, and not vice versa.

36. Thomas Hobbes, *Leviathan* (New York: Collier Books, 1962), p. 80.
37. Hobbes, *Leviathan*, p. 418.

English liberalism would appear to fork into two paths, one of which dead-ends with Hobbes's absolutism and the other of which bears fruit in Locke and his followers among the framers of the U.S. Constitution. Locke, however, is dedicated to the same basic reconfiguration of space as is Hobbes. Commentators usually assume that Locke had an abrupt change of mind somewhere between his earlier absolutist writings, especially the *Two Tracts on Government* (1660-62), and his later, more liberal writings, notably the *Letter Concerning Toleration* (1689) and *Two Treatises of Government* (1690). His thinking did certainly shift, but not regarding the fundamental importance of subordinating the church and other social groups to the state for the sake of public peace and order.[38] What Hobbes accomplished by absorbing the church into the state, Locke accomplished by privatizing the church. Peace would never be attained if essentially undecidable matters such as the end of human life were left open to public debate. What is common is therefore re-defined as follows: "The commonwealth seems to me to be a society of men constituted only for the procuring, preserving, and advancing their own civil interests. Civil interests I call life, liberty, health, and indolency of body; and the possession of outward things, such as money, lands, houses, furniture, and the like."[39] A. J. Conyers suggests that, for Locke, "[w]hat is left to discuss in the public arena, therefore, is not the common good that creates society at the level of common affections and common goals, but merely the resolution of differing material interests."[40]

The political space imagined by Locke has two poles, the individual and the state. The state is enacted immediately from the need of the solitary individual to protect his person and possessions. The world belongs to all humankind in common, but it is quickly withdrawn from the common by human labor. Even the "wild Indian" who "knows no enclosure, and is still a tenant in common" establishes an exclusive individual right to whatever he appropriates from nature by his labor.[41] Here Locke breaks

38. Robert Kraynak points to the underlying continuity in Locke's development in "John Locke: From Absolutism to Toleration," *American Political Science Review* 74 (1980): 53-69.

39. John Locke, *A Letter Concerning Toleration* (Indianapolis: Bobbs-Merrill, 1955), 17.

40. A. J. Conyers, *The Long Truce* (Dallas: Spence Publishing, 2001), p. 130. See also C. B. Macpherson's classic *The Political Theory of Possessive Individualism: Hobbes to Locke* (Oxford: Oxford University Press, 1962), pp. 194-262.

41. John Locke, *Two Treatises of Government* (New York: Dutton, 1978), p. 129 [Bk. II, chap. 5].

with tradition, for which property is social according to its use. Aquinas says: "In this respect [of their use] man ought to possess external things, not as his own, but as common, so that, to wit, he is ready to communicate them to others in their need."[42] For Locke, by contrast, property is a strictly individual natural right, and the basis of the state, for the purpose of the state is to establish and enforce laws that clearly separate what is mine from what is thine. However, Locke combines this emphasis on individual property rights with a curious sort of utilitarian justification of the system of political economy as a whole. Locke says that no one may appropriate from nature more than he or she can use, because it would then spoil. With the invention of money, however, perishable goods may be translated into imperishable goods, allowing the legitimate accumulation of great wealth. Thus the advent of an exchange economy also means that the legitimate owner of any goods is not necessarily the one whose labor produced the wealth, provided that all exchanges leading to such ownership were free. However, the system as a whole is beneficial for each because wealth is increased through labor and exchange, such that, Locke tells us, even the day laborer in England enjoys one hundred times the material conveniences of an American Indian.[43]

The "society" that Locke's state enacts is coterminous with the market, to which individuals come to contract for certain goods, both material and political. Locke's simplification of political space into the oscillation between individual rights and state sovereignty (what Conyers calls Locke's "bipolar disorder") relegates all other forms of common life — those based on biology, locality, common blood, common tasks, or common calling — to the status of the essentially private "voluntary society." What is common is common only by contract. Besides the Catholic Church, which he explicitly excepted from his principles of toleration, Locke's simple space could find no place for Native American tribes. Locke refers to the "inland vacant places of America," the Indians already having been theoretically eliminated by the stark simplicity of Locke's jus-

---

42. Thomas Aquinas, *Summa Theologiae* II-II.66.2.

43. Locke, *Two Treatises of Government*, 131-41. On this point, see Pierre Manent, *An Intellectual History of Liberalism*, trans. Rebecca Balinski (Princeton, NJ: Princeton University Press, 1994), pp. 39-52. Manent argues that, as a result of Locke's justification of exchange as beneficial for all of society, there can be no concept of "social justice." Hayek is the true heir of Lockean liberalism. Justice is not subject to debate, but is "*always already realized* as long as property is guaranteed and protected" (p. 46).

tification of sovereignty. "Thus, in the beginning, all the world was America," he says, common but waiting to be appropriated to private use and exchange for the benefit of each and all.[44] The untranslatability of American Indians into American law and their consequent destruction is not simply the result of judicial malice but is inscribed in the very nature of state sovereignty. Simple space cannot accommodate the tribal structure. The formal equality of individuals before the law pits individual rights against the traditional tribal sense that the tribe, not the individual, is the bearer of rights.

The classical sixteenth- and seventeenth-century theories of sovereignty that gave definition to the state do not yield much in the way of the common good. The foundational anthropology is strictly individual, such that the goal of the state is to secure the noninterference of individuals with each other's affairs. A new kind of space is invented in which individuals relate to each other through the mechanism of contract, as guaranteed by the center. Public and private interest is seen to coincide, but the discourse thus shifts from good to will and right. The body politic does not pursue a common good, but instead seeks to liberate the individual to pursue his or her own ends. Contrary to Christian anthropology, the sovereign individual is presented here as the natural — not merely postlapsarian — condition of humankind. In fact, however, sovereignty is not the mere gathering of the many into one, but the creation of sovereign individuals related through the sovereign state.

The nation-state presents itself as a way of reconciling the many into one, *e pluribus unum*, and thus serving the common good. However, this reconciliation only comes after the creation of a prior antagonism, the creation of a novel form of simple social space that oscillates between the individual and the state. However, simple space is a dangerous fiction because, as John Milbank puts it, "no action can be perfectly self-contained, but always impinges upon other people, so that spaces will always in some degree 'complexly' overlap, jurisdictions always in some measure be competing, loyalties remain (perhaps benignly) divided." If this is the case, then

> . . . the issue of the common good most pointedly surfaces, not in the
> more abstract deliberations of governments, where, on the contrary,

44. Locke, *Two Treatises*, pp. 134, 140.

its reduction to utilitarian calculus or promotion of free choice will seem most seductively plausible, but rather in the ever re-encountered "boundary disputes" and occasions for collective action in the everyday lives of citizens. These disputes and occasions need somehow to be mediated, and where the reality of "community" fades, the attempt is made to more and more do so by the extension of merely formal regulation of human transactions (with its utilitarian and more predominantly liberal individualist presuppositions). More of life becomes economized and legalized, as legislation seeks — hopelessly — to catch up with every instance of "overlap," and institute more detailed rules of absolute ownership, whether by individuals, or legally incorporated groups: so much and no more for you; so far and no further for you.[45]

The result is not the common good, but an (ultimately tragic) attempt to ward off social conflict by keeping individuals from interfering with each other.

The State Is Not a Limited Part of Society, but It Absorbs Society into Itself

Civil Society

At this point I would expect to encounter both agreement and disagreement from John Courtney Murray, still the dominant voice in U.S. Catholic social thinking about the state and common good. Murray agrees that the state is not the agency within a social order that has responsibility for the common good. The state concerns itself with the much more limited role of vigilance for public order. Murray would disagree in that his distinction between public order and common good follows his sharp distinction of state from civil society.[46] According to Murray, the state is the

45. Milbank, "On Complex Space," pp. 281-82.

46. Murray uses the term "society" to denote what today is most commonly referred to as "civil society," that realm of spontaneous social life beyond the direct reach of the state. To avoid confusion, I follow current usage. John Courtney Murray, "The Problem of Religious Freedom," in *Religious Liberty: Catholic Struggles with Pluralism*, ed. J. Leon Hooper, SJ (Louisville: Westminster John Knox Press, 1993), p. 144.

creation of civil society and is meant to serve it. The state possesses the coercive power necessary to maintain peace and order, but the real life of a social order takes place in civil society, the realm of freedom outside the direct purview of the state. Murray says: "The pursuit of the common good devolves upon society as a whole, on all its members and on all its institutions. . . . Public order, whose care devolves upon the state, is a narrower concept." Public order includes important public goods, but not the common good as such.[47]

This distinction follows from Murray's understanding of the United States' liberal constitutional framework. The state in liberalism does not pursue the good, but rather secures peace among varying conceptions of the good. According to Murray, the American state does not, therefore, try to impose uniformity on the many, but limits itself through mechanisms of consent and checks and balances, so that the many may flourish. Here the many are not merely individuals but rather all those varying types of communal life Murray calls "conspiracies," that is, spaces where people "breathe together." He has in mind especially churches and synagogues, but the principle applies to all those associations that intermediate between individual and state, all of which make for a strong civil society and the pursuit of the common good. Sovereignty derives from the people and is not, as in Hobbes, alienated from them into a transcendent state. Sovereignty remains "immanent" to the people; power remains in the hands of the multitude through mechanisms of consent and checks and balances in government. In this view, liberalism is that constitutional regime that frees the intermediate associations of civil society by limiting the state. Unity exists strictly at the level of political conversation, and does not destroy the underlying pluralisms of civil society.[48] The state, therefore, does not have direct responsibility for the common good; nevertheless, it makes the pursuit of the common good possible.

This view of the state paints an attractively balanced picture; unfortunately, it bears very little relationship to empirical studies of how "inter-

47. Murray, "The Problem of Religious Freedom," pp. 144-45. The three public goods included in public order are peace, public morality, and justice. The inclusion of public morality in this list indicates that Murray envisioned a more significant role for the state than more libertarian types of liberalism would allow.

48. John Courtney Murray, *We Hold These Truths: Catholic Reflections on the American Proposition* (Kansas City, MO: Sheed and Ward, 1960), pp. 45-78, 5-24.

mediate associations" have fared under the state.[49] The rise of the state is the history of the atrophying of such associations. As Robert Nisbet makes plain, the state is not a limited agency arising out of — and created for the service of — local communities, families, and tribes: "[I]f we look not to imaginary beginnings in the never-never-land of ethnological reconstruction" but to the historical evidence, it becomes clear that "the rise and aggrandizement of political States took place in circumstances of powerful opposition to kinship and other traditional authorities."[50] The fundamental conflict of modernity, says Nisbet, is not between state and individual, but between state and social group (p. 109). The history of the state is the creation of an increasingly direct relationship between state and individual by the state's absorption of powers from the groups that comprise what has come to be called "civil society" (p. 104). In other words, the state is not simply local government writ large. The state is qualitatively different: it is precisely that kind of government that does not grow organically out of the self-government of social groups.

Prior to the rise of the state, central authority was weak and associations strong. Rights, honors, immunities, and responsibilities were attached to communities, and not to individuals. The family, the village, the church, the guild, the university were held to precede the individual both in origin and in right. Associations did not depend on royal authority for recognition. Such associations could, of course, be oppressive, and often were. The point here is not to romanticize the medieval period, but simply to show the relative strength of local association over against central authority. Central authority, where it existed, was severely limited in its ability to override local custom and law. The most significant law was not positive law given by a legislator but the customs and rules that provided the inner order of associations (pp. 80-85, 110-12).

The state grew by absorbing the rights and responsibilities of this plurality of social groups. The state came to be seen as the sole source of

---

49. Political scientist Michael Budde comments, "Murray's theory of the state, such as it is, can only be described as naïve, almost a direct transferal from civics texts to political description." Murray's conviction that the American people govern themselves through free consensus leads Budde to observe that "no testing of reality seems to have affected his assessment of American political institutions." Budde, *The Two Churches: Catholicism and Capitalism in the World-System* (Durham, NC: Duke University Press, 1992), p. 115.

50. Robert Nisbet, *The Quest for Community* (London: Oxford University Press, 1969), p. 100. Hereafter, page references to this work appear in parentheses in the text.

law, and as the guarantor of property and inheritance rights; it took over many of the civil functions formerly belonging to the church, such as the system of ecclesiastical courts; it claimed a monopoly on the means of coercion and facilitated the enclosure of common lands; and it claimed that the lesser association itself was, in effect, a creation of the state, a *persona ficta*. In many places Roman law, especially the Justinian Code, provided the legal vocabulary necessary to reenvision social relationships as essentially contractual and subject to a sovereign lawmaker above the law (pp. 104, 112-13).[51] In all places, war was the principal means by which the growth of the state advanced. Nisbet writes: "If there is any single origin of the institutional State, it is in the circumstances and relationships of war. The connection between kinship and family, between religion and Church, is no closer than that between war and the State in history" (pp. 100-101). War requires a direct disciplinary relationship between the individual and the state, and so has served as a powerful solvent of the loyalties of individuals to social groups other than the state.

The absorption of civil society by the state is manifested in at least three different ways in contemporary America. First is the exponential and continuous growth of the state. Bruce Porter has documented this growth, and he concludes that war has been the primary impetus behind it. All but five cabinet departments and the majority of smaller federal agencies have come into being during wartime.[52] World War I produced a 1000 percent increase in federal spending; the increase in government during World War II was three times that of the New Deal, the majority of it in the nonmilitary sector. After World War II, the large bureaucratic state became a permanent feature of the landscape. Under the supposedly "anti-big government" Ronald Reagan, the federal government continued to grow, even in the nonmilitary sector.[53] Today, in response to the "War on Terrorism," such growth is represented by the 170,000 employees of the new Office of Homeland Security, the second largest government institution behind the Pentagon. Another recent example is the Pentagon's Total Information Awareness program, which will gather information on

51. See also Robert Nisbet, *Twilight of Authority* (New York: Oxford University Press, 1975), pp. 166-71.

52. Porter, *War and the Rise of the State*, pp. 291-92. This figure includes the first five years after major wars. The total number of years that fall into this category add up to only one-fifth of the total of American history.

53. Porter, *War and the Rise of the State*, pp. 269, 278-80, 294-95.

every American citizen from databases of credit-card transactions, health records, ticket purchases, housing records, academic grades, and so on.[54]

Nisbet points out that the "absolutist" state of early modernity was in reality much less powerful than the contemporary nation-state, which has succeeded in establishing a direct relationship to every individual within its borders. Nisbet quotes Walter Lippmann to this effect:

> It does not matter whether the right to govern is hereditary or obtained with the consent of the governed. A State is absolute in the sense which I have in mind when it claims the right to a monopoly of all the force within the community, to make war, to make peace, to conscript life, to tax, to establish and dis-establish property, to define crime, to punish disobedience, to control education, to supervise the family, to regulate personal habits, and to censor opinions. The modern State claims all of these powers, and, in the matter of theory, there is no real difference in the size of the claim between communists, fascists, and democrats.[55]

When Lippmann wrote those words in 1929, even he could not have imagined the astonishing growth of state influence in the United States into the twenty-first century.

The second contemporary manifestation of the withering of civil society is the progressive enervation of intermediate associations. As Nisbet, Robert Bellah,[56] Robert Putnam,[57] and many others have documented, what exists is not Murray's free space of robust "conspiracies" but a soci-

---

54. According to congressional officials, Homeland Security is blessed with "unprecedented power for a federal agency to organize itself as it chooses, without congressional oversight." Homeland Security includes a new secret court before which the government is the only party allowed to appear. The Total Information Awareness project is headed by John Poindexter, convicted on six counts of masterminding the secret Iran-Contra connection under Reagan and lying to Congress about it. See Michael Ventura, "Weapons of Mass Deception," *Austin Chronicle*, November 29, 2002. In response to citizen concerns about privacy, the Pentagon has changed the name of the program to Terrorism Information Awareness — without changing the program itself. Michael J. Sniffen, "Anti-terror surveillance system name changed," *St. Paul Pioneer Press*, May 21, 2003, p. 4A.

55. Walter Lippmann, *A Preface to Morals*, quoted in Nisbet, *The Quest for Community*, p. 102.

56. Robert Bellah et al., *Habits of the Heart* (San Francisco: Harper and Row, 1985).

57. Robert Putnam, *Bowling Alone* (New York: Simon and Schuster, 2000).

ety of individuals alienated from substantive forms of common life. Intermediate associations such as the church, unions, and the family still exist, but they are expected to convey identities, virtues, and common ends in a context in which their relationships to production, mutual aid, education, and welfare have been absorbed into the state and the market.[58] Although potential solutions to the problem are hotly contested, the empirical fact of the decline of intermediate associations is not. The Council on Civil Society, for example, which includes such diverse figures as Francis Fukuyama and Cornel West, William Galston and Mary Ann Glendon, is able to treat the disintegration of "civil society" as a given.[59]

The third contemporary manifestation of the absorption of civil society is the symbiosis of the state and the corporation that signals the collapse of separation between politics and economics. As Charles Lindblom wrote in his landmark *Politics and Markets* (1977), "the greatest distinction between one government and another is in the degree to which market replaces government or government replaces market."[60] We live under the former type, according to Lindblom, in which corporate leaders not only buy influence over politicians, regulators, and public opinion, but the business executive him- or herself becomes a type of public official.[61] Lindblom could scarcely have imagined the extent to which the state now treats corporations as its clients. This is hardly surprising given the revolving door between government and industry. A brief glance at George W. Bush's appointees finds that the number-two person at the Environmental Protection Agency was a lobbyist for the chemical giant Monsanto; the chief counsel to the IRS was a corporate tax attorney who won several high-profile cases defending corporate tax havens against IRS enforcement; the deputy secretary of the Interior De-

---

58. Nisbet, *The Quest for Community,* p. 54. Nisbet explicitly disavows any nostalgia for some bygone era. He believes that the existence of genuine community is empirically verifiable, and that it has been eroded in the modern era. However, he does not think that all community is good in and of itself; communities can be corrupt and stifling. Nor does he want to return to past forms of community, but rather to ask what new forms of community are viable today (pp. viii, 31, 106).

59. Council on Civil Society, *A Call to Civil Society* (Chicago: Institute for American Values, 1998).

60. Charles E. Lindblom, *Politics and Markets: The World's Political Economic Systems* (New York: Basic Books, 1977), p. ix.

61. Lindblom, *Politics and Markets,* pp. 170-233.

partment was a lobbyist for the oil, gas, and coal industries — and on and on, ad nauseam.[62]

The point of these examples is that the state does not simply stand over against civil society as its oppressor. Indeed, the point of the transition from state to nation-state is the fusion of state and civil society. The nation-state fully realizes the claim merely articulated by the absolutist state to have direct access to governance of everyday life within a defined territory. Giddens declares: "The nation-state is a power container whose administrative purview corresponds exactly to its territorial delimitation." For this reason, Giddens does not use the term "civil society" with reference to the nation-state; the nation-state is simply what sociologists mean when they say "society" in contemporary life. There is no "civil society" that stands outside the administrative and symbolic system ordered by the state.[63] With respect to origins, there is no unitary and organically preexisting civil society that gives rise to the state. Hegel was empirically correct in positing the state as the ground of civil society.[64] The state creates a unitary space that enacts a single system of social interaction, or society. It is not simply that government has gotten big, and economic and social transactions of every kind must pass through the organs of the state. It is also that the state itself — as well as churches, schools, unions, and other associations — has been colonized by the logic of the market. Marx predicted that the state would wither away. What has in fact happened, as Michael Hardt says, is that civil society has withered, or, more accurately, has been absorbed into the state.[65]

Nisbet thinks that the absorption of civil society in the United States is not systemic, but is due to the importation of the unitary idea of democ-

---

62. These are just a few of the examples cited in Molly Ivins, "Fox-and-chicken-coop comparison might not say it all," *South Bend Tribune*, August 26, 2001. Another kind of example of the fusion of state and civil society comes from the recent prowar rallies organized by radio stations across the United States. Most of the stations are owned by Clear Channel, whose chairman and vice chairman have close business ties to President Bush. In 1998, the vice-chairman, Tom Hicks, purchased the Texas Rangers in a deal that made Mr. Bush $15 million on a $600,000 investment. Paul Krugman, "Channels of Influence," *New York Times*, March 25, 2003.

63. Giddens, *The Nation-State and Violence*, pp. 21-22, 172.

64. G. W. F. Hegel, *The Philosophy of Right*, trans. T. M. Knox (Oxford: Clarendon Press, 1952), paras. 256-57.

65. Michael Hardt, "The Withering of Civil Society," *Social Text* 14, no. 4 (Winter 1995): 27-44.

racy from the Continent that, beginning in the late nineteenth century, has choked out the native species of pluralist democracy.[66] Others, however, have more convincingly argued that there exists a deeper problem endemic to the modern notion of sovereignty. Popular sovereignty is supposed to miraculously solve the problem of the one and the many by subsuming the many of civil society into the one state as the unitary representative of the multiplicity of wills. The problem, as Pierre Manent says, is this:

> If civil society is what is natural, and if the state is only its instrument, why is the state detached from society in such a definite way? Why does civil society not simply take it over again, bringing an end to this "alienation"? Conversely, if the body politic exists only through the Representative, then the Representative is more than a mere representative; he gives consistency to civil society and is the source of social existence. The distinction between civil society and the state, and their union through the idea of representation, sets off a natural oscillation between two extreme possibilities: the "withering away" of the state on the one hand, the absorption of civil society by the state on the other. It is a distinction that calls out for negation, a negation that can benefit only one of the two terms.[67]

In fact, civil society is not the natural source of the state, but both society and state are enacted artificially "from above." The spontaneous life of traditional social groups from below tends to be delegitimated because such groups tend not to be representative, that is, based in consensus. Interests from below will always need to be channeled through the state to achieve legitimacy, as only the state can gather the diversity of interests into a transcendent unity.[68] The state is the source of social life. In the absence of a

---

66. Nisbet, *The Quest for Community*, pp. 248-54. Although the basic contours of Nisbet's sociological and historical analysis of the weakening of associations are, in my opinion, entirely convincing, Nisbet's analysis of the rise of the state is incomplete and often idealist because of his neglect of economic factors. In other words, the dissolution of community is laid on the state as cause, without much analysis of the solvent effects of capitalism. Nisbet ended his career as an ideologue of neoconservatism at the American Enterprise Institute in the 1980s.

67. Manent, *An Intellectual History of Liberalism*, pp. 26-27.

68. Manent, *An Intellectual History of Liberalism*, pp. 50-52, 62-63. This is why, according

common good or *telos*, the state can only expand its reach, precisely in order to keep the welter of individuals pursuing their own goods from interfering with each other. Where there is a unitary simple space, pluralism of ends will always be a threat. To solve this threat, the demand will always be to absorb the many into the one. In the absence of shared ends, devotion to the state itself as the end in itself becomes ever more urgent. The result is not true pluralism but an ever-increasing directness of relationship between the individual and the state as foundation of social interaction.

The fusion of state and civil society is, then, a consequence of the unitary space created by sovereignty, not an accidental feature of modernity. As the early twentieth-century English pluralists saw, a limited state can only be one that does not enact a single society. A limited state could only exist where social space was complexly refracted into a network of associations, that is, where associations were not "intermediate associations," squeezed between state and individual, at all. In the view of John Neville Figgis, there is no single entity called "society." The state should be a *communitas communitatum*. "This is the true meaning of our word Commons; not the mass of common people, but the community of the communities."[69] For Figgis, common good is promoted only by communities of people united for a permanent end. Such communities have corporate personality that is independent of recognition from the state. They are publics in their own right. The pluralists thus rejected the reduction of such a diversity of publics to a single sovereign will.

G. D. H. Cole regards the claim of a unitary sovereign to gather the diversity of wills into one as a ridiculous fiction. It is, in fact, the hijacking of legitimacy by a small fraction of the whole, and it can only be made plausible by the subsumption of difference to state power. Representation should be, at most, the choice of personnel, and not the transfer of will to a

---

to Manent, Lockean liberalism tends toward a monarchical executive power, despite Locke's explicit wishes that the legislative power be supreme.

69. John Neville Figgis, *Churches in the Modern State* (Bristol: Thoemmes Press, 1997), p. 80. For Figgis, the state exists only to provide some minimal regulation of interaction between such publics. The English pluralists should not be confused with American pluralists, such as Robert Dahl, who place great emphasis on intermediate associations but see such associations as conflicting competitors for influence over the state, which remains a neutral and unitary staging ground. See Paul Q. Hirst's "Introduction," in *The Pluralist Theory of the State: Selected Writings of G. D. H. Cole, J. N. Figgis, and H. J. Laski*, ed. Paul Q. Hirst (London: Routledge, 1993), pp. 3-4.

sovereign power.[70] Whether or not Figgis's and Cole's positive recommendations for restructuring the state are possible is not my concern here. What is important is their recognition that unitary sovereignty or simple space is incompatible with a limited state. If this is correct, then the sovereign state can only be hostile to the common good, as John Courtney Murray defined it, as the spontaneous life of the various "conspiracies" built around common ends.

The Nation-State

In the West, the state becomes the nation-state in the nineteenth century, when the vertical relationship of state and individual is opened to include a horizontal relationship among individuals, an increasingly cohesive mass relationship.[71] In the liberal nation-state, the flows of power are not simply from civil society to state, as in Murray, nor from state to civil society; the flows of power are multidirectional. In other words, when state becomes nation-state, it represents the fusion of state and society. The state precedes the idea of the nation and creates it, promoting the imagination of a unitary space and a common history. But in contrast to the absolutist state, the nation-state does not merely enforce its will through coercion. In order fully to realize the doctrine of territorial sovereignty and extend governance to every individual within its borders, the nation-state finds the participation of the many in a unitive project to be essential. Nationalism becomes a popular movement founded on consent.

Since Kohn and Hayes, scholars of nationalism have emphasized that "nation," like society, is not a natural or "ontologically prior" reality, but one that is invented by the state. E. J. Hobsbawm puts it this way: "Nations do not make states and nationalisms but the other way round."[72] Most

---

70. G. D. H. Cole, *The Social Theory*, in Hirst, *The Pluralist Theory of the State*, pp. 82-90.

71. Nisbet, *The Quest for Community*, pp. 101-2.

72. Hobsbawm, *Nations and Nationalism since 1780*, p. 10. This fact was recognized even by some of the great nationalist politicians. Colonel Pilsudski, "liberator" of Poland, said: "It is the state which makes the nation and not the nation the state." Quoted in Hobsbawm, pp. 44-45. To say that nations are invented is not necessarily to say that they are simply therefore "false." Benedict Anderson criticizes Hobsbawm and Gellner for implying falsity. Anderson prefers to see nations in a more neutral way as being "imagined." See Anderson, *Imagined Communities*, p. 6.

scholars agree that nations are only possible once states have been invented, and that nations, even seemingly "ancient" ones, are the product of the last two centuries. Until the nineteenth century, states lacked the internal cohesion necessary to be nations. One way this can be illustrated is by looking at the use of language. As late as 1789, only 50 percent of the citizens of France spoke French, and only 12-13 percent did so "correctly." At the moment of the creation of Italy (1860), only 2.5 percent of the people used Italian for everyday purposes. Italian patriot Massimo d'Azeglio expressed it this way: "We have made Italy, now we have to make Italians."[73]

Nineteenth-century elites promoted nationalist sentiments by various means. The first was the increasing influence of the state over education, by means of which a common history and common myths of origin were told.[74] The second was the spread of standardized language by means of print media. Sicilians and Venetians might not be able to understand each other's speech, but they were beginning to read mass-produced Italian media, which had a significant impact on the creation of Italy.[75] Finally, war had a profound influence on the rise of nationalism. The United States became a nation-state only after the crisis of the Civil War, and nationalism took a quantum leap in the massive mobilization of society for World War I.[76] The questions of language and war are often intertwined: a language is just a dialect with an army, as the saying goes.

In the field of nationalism studies, a minority of scholars, some of them identified as "ethno-symbolists," want to press the origins of nations further back by studying the ethnic identities that are precursors of the modern nation. Liah Greenfeld, for example, dates the sense of "nationness" in England to the sixteenth century, though she claims it was the only nation in the world for the next two centuries.[77] Anthony D. Smith claims

73. Hobsbawm, *Nations and Nationalism since 1780*, pp. 60-61, 44.

74. See, for example, Patrick J. Geary, *The Myth of Nations* (Princeton, NJ: Princeton University Press, 2002). Geary shows how the "science" of European history was invented in the nineteenth century as a tool of nationalist ideology, especially in the case of Germany. Ancestors such as the "Visigoths" were invented to stretch the origins of the nation back to the dissolution of the Roman Empire, and this history was disseminated through state control of education.

75. Benedict Anderson, "Nationalism," in *The Oxford Companion to Politics of the World*, ed. Joel Krieger (New York: Oxford University Press, 1993), p. 617.

76. Porter, *War and the Rise of the State*, pp. xvi, 12-14, 247.

77. Liah Greenfeld, *Nationalism: Five Roads to Modernity* (Cambridge, MA: Harvard University Press, 1992), p. 14.

that the origins of nationalism can be traced back in some European countries to the fifteenth and sixteenth centuries. Ethno-symbolists argue that nations were invented not out of nothing but out of preformed ethnic experiences and consciousness. The difference between previous cultural formations and modern nations is one of degree, not of kind. Once formed, ethnic identities are remarkably stable over generations and centuries.[78]

The ethno-symbolists have been criticized for defining the nation so broadly that all kinds of cultural groupings qualify. Smith, for example, has been criticized for attributing fully developed group consciousness to premodern groups that had only vague ideas of what differentiated them from others. Smith also fails to give due weight to the lack of institutional basis for such groups, such that they did not and could not make claims to territory, autonomy, or independence. Most importantly,

> nationalism is not simply a claim of ethnic similarity, but a claim that certain similarities should count as the definition of political community. For this reason, nationalism needs rigid boundaries in a way that pre-modern ethnicity does not: "Nationalism demands internal homogeneity throughout the putative nation, rather than gradual continua of cultural variation or pockets of subcultural distinction." Most distinctively, nationalists generally assert that national identities are more important than other personal or group identities (such as gender, family, or ethnicity) and link individuals directly to the nation as a whole. In stark contrast to this, most ethnic identities flow from family membership, kinship or membership in other intermediate groups.[79]

In other words, nationalism demands the simple space that only state sovereignty can provide. As Geoff Eley and Ronald Suny argue, ethnic identities may be the raw materials with which the state works, but they are not simply precursors that develop in a linear fashion toward the nation. The nation represents a rupture in the history of social organization.[80]

78. Anthony D. Smith, *The Ethnic Origins of Nations* (Oxford: Blackwell Publishers, 1986), p. 16.

79. Umut Ozkirimli, *Theories of Nationalism: A Critical Introduction* (New York: St. Martin's Press, 2000), p. 185. The internal quote is from Craig Calhoun, "Nationalism and Ethnicity," *Annual Review of Sociology* 19: 229.

80. Geoff Eley and Ronald Suny, "Introduction," in *Becoming National: A Reader,* ed. Eley and Suny (New York: Oxford University Press, 1996), p. 11.

The idea of the nation does not remain an elite idea, but becomes gradually more powerful among the lower classes in the nineteenth and twentieth centuries. Why were common people willing to sacrifice their lives for nations their grandparents had never heard of, as Benedict Anderson asks?[81] Ernest Gellner answers this question by drawing a direct link between the weakening of smaller kinds of association and the growth of the idea of the nation. The loosing of individuals from traditional forms of community created the possibility and need of a larger, mass substitute for community. Loyalties are gradually transferred from more local types of community to the nation.[82] At the same time, there is a gradual opening of the sphere of participation to the masses of people of whom the state had previously taken only sporadic notice.

The rise of rights language goes hand in hand with the rise of the nation-state, because political and civil rights name both the freeing of the individual from traditional types of community and the establishment of regular relationships of power between the individual and the state. Marx was wrong to dismiss rights as a mere ruse to protect the gains of the bourgeois classes.[83] Nevertheless, individual rights do greatly expand the scope of the state because political and civil rights establish binding relationships between the nation-state and those who look to it to vindicate their claims. The nation-state thus becomes something of a central, bureaucratic clearinghouse in which social claims are contested. The nation-state is fully realized when sacrifice on behalf of the nation is combined with claims made on the state on the basis of rights.[84]

Alasdair MacIntyre refers to this dual aspect of the nation-state in the following memorable quote:

> The modern nation-state, in whatever guise, is a dangerous and unmanageable institution, presenting itself on the one hand as a bureau-

---

81. Anderson, "Nationalism," p. 615.

82. Gellner, *Nations and Nationalism*, pp. 63-87.

83. Karl Marx, "On the Jewish Question," in *Karl Marx: Selected Writings*, ed. David McLellan (Oxford: Oxford University Press, 1977), pp. 39-57, esp. 52-56. Marx was right, however, to describe the solvent effect of rights. Marx sees that the "rights of man" are not available to Jews unless they lose their ties to the Jewish community and consent to being treated as "self-sufficient monads" (p. 53).

84. Giddens, *The Nation-State and Violence*, pp. 205-6, 220-21; Tilly, "Reflections on the History of European State-Making," pp. 36-37.

cratic supplier of goods and services, which is always about to, but never actually does, give its clients value for money, and on the other as a repository of sacred values, which from time to time invites one to lay down one's life on its behalf.... [I]t is like being asked to die for the telephone company.[85]

MacIntyre thinks that the nation-state can and does promote certain goods of order, but he also contends that it is incapable of promoting the common good. Integral to the political common good is a distribution of goods that reflects a common mind arrived at by rational deliberation. Rationality, in turn, is contingent on our recognizing our fundamental dependence on one another. According to MacIntyre, the nation-state is an arena of bargaining among different group interests. In the absence of any generally agreed-upon rational standard to adjudicate among such interests, decisions on the distribution of goods are made on the basis of power, which is most often directly related to access to capital. The sheer size of the nation-state precludes genuine rational deliberation; deliberation is carried on by a political elite of lawyers, lobbyists, and other professionals.[86] For the same reason, the unitive community that the idea of the nation offers is an illusion. The nation-state is not a genuine community, a functioning rational collectivity whose bonds make possible the "virtues of acknowledged dependence" necessary for the common good. MacIntyre says: "The shared public goods of the modern nation-state are not the common goods of a genuine nation-wide community and, when the nation-state masquerades as the guardian of such a common good, the outcome is bound to be either ludicrous or disastrous or both."[87]

The influence of money over deliberation to which MacIntyre refers has never been a merely accidental feature of the nation-state. One of the functions of the idea of the nation is to short-circuit the conflict of classes by subsuming both forces of production and domination into one. In-

85. Alasdair MacIntyre, "A Partial Response to My Critics," in *After MacIntyre: Critical Perspectives on the Work of Alasdair MacIntyre*, ed. John Horton and Susan Mendus (Notre Dame, IN: University of Notre Dame Press, 1994), p. 303.

86. Alasdair MacIntyre, *Dependent Rational Animals: Why Human Beings Need the Virtues* (Chicago: Open Court, 1999), pp. 129-33, 141-42; see also MacIntyre, "Toleration and the Goods of Conflict," in *The Politics of Toleration in Modern Life*, ed. Susan Mendus (Durham, NC: Duke University Press, 1999), pp. 139-44.

87. MacIntyre, *Dependent Rational Animals*, p. 132.

stead of the overtly class-based rule of absolutist states, the nation-state invites all classes to participate in a unitary project. This requires the imagination of a common space in which internal differences are minimized and external differences maximized.[88] Class analysis is considered divisive and subversive to the national project. So, for example, in the public forum, both sides of the NAFTA debate asked, "Will this treaty be good or bad for America?" Only a few marginal voices on the losing side were able to suggest that NAFTA would be good for some Americans and bad for others, namely, good for capital and bad for labor. Claims for the interests of groups must be justified in terms of national interests, but the wealthier classes are far more effective at presenting their interests as being national interests.[89] This is why tax cuts for the rich in 2002 and 2003 could be passed off as an "economic stimulus package" meant to get laid-off workers back to the plant, and why dissent from this legislation could be criticized by the House majority leader as sowing divisiveness at a time of national crisis.[90]

If the nation-state tends to elide actually existing internal differences, it tends simultaneously to accentuate external differences. National identity becomes one's primary loyalty, and that highlights what separates one's nation from all others. In terms of law, sovereignty assumes a condition of anarchy among states, and nationalism heightens general consciousness of this condition. What is "common" is reduced to what fits

88. Tilly comments sharply on this process: "Hence the plausibility of doctrines of national self-determination to nineteenth-century Europeans — just so long as they were not dealing with their own ethnic/religious minorities." Tilly, "Reflections on the History of European State-Making," p. 79.

89. See Giddens, *The Nation-State and Violence*, p. 221. For those who need a reminder of the influence of money over governance in the United States, William Greider's *Who Will Tell the People? The Betrayal of American Democracy* (New York: Simon and Schuster, 1992) is breathtaking. Greider chronicles in painstaking detail exactly how corporations and wealthy individuals get what they want in Washington, and how common people are ignored and manipulated.

90. The fate of the Social Security trust fund is an especially egregious example of how this dynamic works. Over the last seventeen years, income taxes have been repeatedly cut, while the U.S. Treasury has "borrowed" $1.1 *trillion* from Social Security payroll taxes, 53 percent of which are paid by people who earn less than $20,000 a year. As economist Dean Baker says, "that's a huge transfer of wealth from low- and moderate-income people, who paid the payroll taxes, to people at the high end, who pay the bulk of individual and corporate taxes." Miles Benson, "Politicians must cure $1.1 trillion headache," *St. Paul Pioneer Press*, August 6, 2001, p. 3A.

into national borders, and what is good can be purchased at the expense of what is good for other nation-states. The development of the nation-state in the nineteenth and twentieth centuries can be summed up as the completion of the contradictory process of alienation from local community and simultaneous parochialization of what is common to the borders of the nation-state. Neither movement facilitates the pursuit of a genuine common good.

Globalization

Understanding this apparently contradictory double movement is crucial to understanding the relationship of the nation-state to the process that has come to be called globalization. The accelerated worldwide economic and cultural universalization that has marked the move to post-Fordist types of production since the early 1970s is said to be trampling the borders of the nation-state and making sovereignty increasingly irrelevant. In some ways this is true, but it is important to see that the nation-state has been one of the primary promoters of this process. Globalization is, in part, the hyperextension of the triumph of the universal over the local, on which the nation-state is founded.

Capitalism and the state arose simultaneously as, respectively, the economic and political logic of the same movement. The state produced a centralized and regularized legal framework to make mechanisms of contract and private property rights possible; it sanctioned the enclosure of common lands to private use, thus "freeing" landless peasants to become wage laborers; it directly promoted international trade; and it universalized and guaranteed money, weights, and measures to facilitate exchanges.[91] Taxation became centrally organized under the state, which effectively signified the decline of the land-owning aristocracy and the ascent of the bourgeoisie. Above all, the state contributed, as we have seen, to the creation of "possessive individualism," the invention of the universal human subject liberated from local ties and free to exchange his or her property and labor

91. Michael Perelman's excellent study *The Invention of Capitalism: Classical Political Economy and the Secret History of Primitive Accumulation* (Durham: Duke University Press, 2000) shows how Smith, Ricardo, Steuart, and other classical economists abandoned their laissez-faire principles when it came to advocating government policies that forced peasants off their land and into factories.

with any other individual.[92] The advent of the nation-state and popular sovereignty has only reinforced the close relationship between the nation-state and capitalism. Enormous outlays of "corporate welfare" are only one manifestation of this fundamental cooperation. More fundamentally, as we have seen, the nation-state serves to subsume class conflict and advance the interests of capital as national interests. As Michael Hardt and Antonio Negri observe, even conflicts between individual capitalists and the nation-state work for the health of capitalism as a whole.[93]

The advance of globalization has indeed eroded the nation-state's sovereignty on several fronts. This may eventually open up interesting possibilities for the reimagination of more complex political spaces. For the moment, however, corporations are the primary beneficiaries. Capital is now more mobile than ever, and nation-states have very little power to contain the flow of money and information across their borders. Corporations have become increasingly transnational, discarding loyalties to any particular locations or communities and moving to wherever cheap labor and unrestrictive environmental laws can be found. One might expect that the nation-state and globalization would be mortal enemies, but that is not, in fact, the case. Capital is free to move where it wants, but labor is not. The profitability of shutting down plants in Wisconsin and reopening them in northern Mexico depends on the national border — and border guards — that stands, in some cases, just a few hundred feet north of the *maquiladoras*.

More striking is the fact that the nation-state regularly advances quite deliberately its own apparent loss of sovereignty. The surrender of sovereignty over tariffs, trade regulations, and environmental laws in the creation of the World Trade Organization (WTO) was promoted by the governing elites of nation-states, and nation-states remain the only bearers of legitimate violence to enforce such international agreements. The U.S. Commerce Department and USAID encourage and subsidize the movement of factories to overseas locations.[94] The 2002 "economic stimulus" package included $21 billion in incentives for U.S. corporations to

92. Giddens, *The Nation-State and Violence*, pp. 148-60; Nisbet, *The Quest for Community*, pp. 104-5.

93. Michael Hardt and Antonio Negri, *Empire* (Cambridge, MA: Harvard University Press, 2000), pp. 304-5.

94. For example, "Losing Our Shirts," *The Independent* (Durham, NC), April 6, 1994, on grants, loans, and advertising by USAID to encourage textile corporations to relocate factories overseas.

use tax shelters in the Bahamas and other Caribbean countries. These examples are inexplicable if one assumes that the nation-state and globalization are simply opposed. What is happening is perhaps best described as the hyperextension of the state's subsumption of the local under the universal. Just as the state enacted a unitary national market, so now a global market is taking its place. Government has not disappeared; rather, it has become decentralized and partially deterritorialized.

The fusion of politics and economics has gone beyond national boundaries, and national governments are increasingly integrated into a transnational system of power distribution of which transnational corporations and supranational organisms like the WTO are other significant components. Saskia Sassen criticizes those who "reduce what is happening to a function of the global-national duality: what one wins, the other loses. By contrast, I view deregulation not simply as a loss of control by the state but as a crucial mechanism for handling the juxtaposition of the interstate consensus to pursue globalization and the fact that national legal systems remain as the major, or crucial, instantiation through which guarantees of contract and property rights are enforced."[95]

If this is the case, then looking to the nation-state to defend the common good against the often-brutal consequences of globalization does not appear promising. This is true not merely because the nation-state is increasingly powerless to oppose globalization, but because the nation-state at a fundamental level is not opposed to globalization. Nation-states may be resources for ad hoc resistance to the process of globalization, but in the long run, the prospects for resistance are undermined by the lack of autonomy of the political in the governance of nation-states.

Conclusion

The nation-state is neither community writ large nor the protector of smaller communal spaces; rather, it originates and grows over against truly common forms of life. This is not necessarily to say that the nation-state cannot and does not promote and protect some goods, or that any nation-state is entirely devoid of civic virtue, or that some forms of ad hoc

---

95. Saskia Sassen, *Losing Control? Sovereignty in an Age of Globalization* (New York: Columbia University Press, 1996), pp. 25-26; see also Hardt and Negri, *Empire*, pp. xi-xvi, 304-9.

cooperation with the government cannot be useful. It is to suggest that the nation-state is simply not in the common good business. At its most benign, the nation-state is most realistically likened, as in MacIntyre's apt metaphor, to the telephone company, a large bureaucratic provider of goods and services that never quite provides value for money.

The problem, as MacIntyre notes, is that the nation-state presents itself as so much more, as the keeper of the common good and repository of sacred values, so that it demands sacrifice on its behalf. The longing for true communion that Christians recognize at the heart of any truly common life is transferred onto the nation-state. Civic virtue and the goods of common life do not simply disappear: as Augustine perceived, the earthly city flourishes by producing a distorted image of the heavenly city. The nation-state is a simulacrum of common life, where false order is parasitical on true order. In a bureaucratic order whose main function is to adjudicate struggles for power between various factions, a sense of unity is produced by the only means possible: sacrifice to false gods in war. The nation-state may be understood theologically as a kind of parody of the church, meant to save us from division.[96]

The urgent task of the church, then, is to demystify the nation-state and to treat it like the telephone company. At its best, the nation-state may provide goods and services that contribute to a certain limited order; mail delivery, for example, is a positive good. The state is not the keeper of the common good, however, and we need to adjust our expectations accordingly. The church must break its imagination out of captivity to the nation-state; it must constitute itself as an alternative social space, and not simply rely on the nation-state to be its social presence; and the church must, at every opportunity, "complexify" space, that is, promote the creation of spaces in which alternative economies and authorities flourish.

The theological rationale for such a move is founded on the biblical account of how salvation history interrupts and transforms human space and time. The word the earliest church used to describe itself was *ekklesia*. In the Septuagint, *ekklesia* was used for the assembly of Israel for various public acts, such as covenant-making (Deut. 4:10), dedication of the temple (1 Kings 8:14), and dedication of the city (Neh. 8).[97] In calling itself

96. I make this argument at length in my book *Theopolitical Imagination* (Edinburgh: T. & T. Clark, 2002).

97. Peter J. Leithart, *Against Christianity* (Moscow, ID: Canon Press, 2003), p. 30.

ekklesia, the church was identifying itself as Israel, the assembly that bears the public presence of God in history. In Greek usage, *ekklesia* named the assembly of those with citizen rights in a given polis. In calling itself *ekklesia,* the church was identifying itself as fully public, refusing the available language for private associations (*koinon* or *collegium*). The church was not gathered like a *koinon* around particular interests, but was concerned with the interests of the whole city, because it was the witness of God's activity in history.[98] At the same time, the church was not simply another polis; instead, it was an anticipation of the heavenly city on earth, in a way that complexified the bipolar calculus of public and private.

The medieval synthesis, though fused with static social hierarchies, at least preserved the biblical sense that the church was not a private association that mediated between the putatively universal state and the sovereign individual. Therefore, when modern Catholic social teaching has insisted on the need for complex space, it should not be dismissed solely as nostalgia for medieval hierarchy. Pope Leo XIII's *Rerum Novarum* noted that the "ancient workmen's Guilds were destroyed in the last century, and no other organization took their place." As a result, working people have been left "isolated and defenseless."[99] The solution, according to Leo, is the proliferation of associations along the lines of the medieval guilds, in complete independence from the state, and under the auspices of the church.[100] Critics have noted the vagueness and nostalgia of Leo's cure, but his diagnosis is insightful: the source of injustice is the modern creation of simple space, the individual cut loose from community and left isolated. Pope Pius XI's *Quadragesimo Anno* also advanced an elaborate scheme calling for a proliferation of labor, religious, and professional vocational groups and "corporations" not under the direct supervision of the state. The principle of subsidiarity was meant as well to keep the state from distorting from above the organic life of community from below.[101]

---

98. Dieter Georgi writes: "Paul chose [*ekklesia*] to indicate that the assembly of those who followed Jesus, the assembly called together in a particular city in the name of the biblical God, was in competition with the local political assembly of the citizenry, the official *ekklesia.* The world is meant to hear the claim that the congregation of Jesus, gathered in the name of the God of the Bible, is where the interests of the city in question truly find expression." Georgi, *Theocracy in Paul's Praxis and Theology* (Minneapolis: Fortress Press, 1991), p. 57.

99. Pope Leo XIII, *Rerum Novarum,* para. 2.

100. Pope Leo XIII, *Rerum Novarum,* paras. 36-43.

101. Pope Pius XI, *Quadragesimo Anno,* paras. 31-40, 79.

Unfortunately, the contemporary church often ignores the possibility that the church itself could encourage the formation of alternative social bodies, and treats the state as the potential solution to any given social ill. An anecdote from political scientist Michael Budde captures this problem:

> Once upon a time, I was hired as a consultant for a public-policy arm of a state-level Catholic bishops' conference. The bishops, according to the institution's staff people, wanted to engage in rededicated efforts to confront the realities of poverty in their state.
>
> What the church bureaucracy had in mind was something on the order of a new lobbying initiative in the state legislature or perhaps an experts conference on poverty in the state.
>
> I told them that they should attempt to take every Catholic in their state on an intensive retreat, with follow-up programs upon their return. Nothing the Church could do would benefit poor people more, I argued, than to energize, inspire, and ignite the passion of larger numbers of the faithful. Without attempts to "convert the baptized," in William O'Malley's phrase, the stranglehold of self-interest, isolation, and religious indifference would continue to throttle church attempts to deal seriously with poverty in a global capitalist order.
>
> My advice, to put it gently, was unappreciated. I was fired. They had an experts conference. As far as I can tell, poverty in their state remained indifferent to their efforts.[102]

The bishops in this case were unable to imagine that the common good could mean the creation by the church itself of authentically common spaces among the haves and have nots — as opposed to advising the state on technocratic solutions to poverty.

The problem is not limited to liberal Christians who rely on the welfare state; it captivates conservative Christians as well, but in a different way. In seeing the nation-state as responsible for the common good, the church mutes its own voice in such crucial moral matters as war and peace, and it is pushed to the margins. Just-war reasoning becomes a tool of statecraft, most commonly used by the state to justify war, rather than a

102. Michael Budde, *The (Magic) Kingdom of God: Christianity and Global Culture Industries* (Boulder, CO: Westview Press, 1997), p. 1.

moral discipline for the church to grapple with questions of violence. The church itself becomes one more withering "intermediate association" whose moral reasoning and moral formation are increasingly colonized by the nation-state and the market. To resist, the church must at the very least reclaim its authority to judge if and when Christians may kill, and not abdicate that authority to the nation-state.[103] To do so would be to create an alternative authority and space that does not simply mediate between state and individual.

How is this appeal "common" and not particular and divisive? In the first place, if the analysis of this chapter is correct, then the nation-state is simply not the universal community under whose umbrella the church stands as one particular association. Not only does the nation-state carve the world up into competing national interests, but, internally as well, it is destructive of forms of commonality that do not privilege the sovereignty of narrow individual self-interest. In the second place, the church is not a merely particular association, but participates in the life of the triune God, who is the only good that can be common to all. Christians, especially through the Eucharist, belong to a body that is not only international — and constantly challenges the narrow particularity of national interests — but is also eternal, the body of Christ that anticipates the heavenly polity on earth. Salvation history is not a particular subset of human history; it is simply the story of God's rule, not yet completely legible, over all of history. God's activity is not, of course, confined to the church, and the boundaries between the church and the world are porous and fluid. Nevertheless, the church needs to take seriously its task of promoting spaces where participation in the common good of God's life can flourish.

103. I examine this issue, and Novak's and Weigel's arguments, in greater detail in my essay "At Odds with the Pope: Legitimate Authority and Just Wars," *Commonweal* 130, no. 10 (May 23, 2003): 11-13.

CHAPTER TWO

From One City to Two:
Christian Reimagining of Political Space

———◦/◦/◦———

There is a profound longing for unity in the Christian tradition, a re-
claiming of primordial unity among human beings — and between
them and God. At the same time, resistance toward this gathering is a reality until the *eschaton*. The context of this opposition is crucial to Jesus' address in John 17, where the "world" *(kosmos)* simply is that reality of mutual
antagonism and opposition to redemption. So Jesus says:

> I gave them your word, and the world hated them, because they do not
> belong to the world any more than I belong to the world. I do not ask
> that you take them out of the world but that you keep them from the
> evil one. They do not belong to the world any more than I belong to
> the world. Consecrate them in the truth. Your word is truth. As you
> sent me into the world, so I sent them into the world. And I consecrate
> myself for them, so that they also may be consecrated in truth. I pray
> not only for them, but also for those who will believe in me through
> their word, so that they may all be one, as you, Father, are in me and I
> in you, that they also may be in us, that the world may believe that you
> sent me. (John 17:14-21 [NAB])

I want to note two things about this passage. First, unity has its basis
in the participation of human beings in God's life. Second, the final consummation of that unity of all still awaits, for Jesus' followers are not re-

moved from the world, though Jesus' prayer is that even the world will come to believe.

In this chapter I will consider what becomes of the longing for unity when the longing for participation in God and the eschatological framework is lost. In Christian thought, the gathering of the many into one is not accomplished by an act of binding one to another. In the body of Christ, the many are gathered into one by means of each one's participation in the head of the body, who is Christ. The body of Christ has a transcendent reference, which, according to Paul, allows for diversity within unity (1 Cor. 12), since the interval between each one and God allows for a diversity of ways of participation in God's life. How will a modern liberal nation-state resolve the question of the one and the many in the body politic if participation in Christ is no longer the common goal? Liberalism is said to allow for a greater pluralism of ends: there are no longer two cities — the followers of Christ and the "world" — but one city with a diversity of individuals, each with the freedom to choose his or her own ends, whether to worship no god, one god, or twenty. But the longing for unity persists, along with the fear that diversity will produce conflict and tear the body politic apart. In the absence of a transcendent *telos*, plurality is not simply a promise but a threat, one that must be met by an even greater pull toward unity. But what could be the source of unity in a nation-state of diverse ends without a transcendent reference to participation in any single god? It can only be that the nation-state becomes an end in itself, a kind of transcendent reference needed to bind the many to each other.

Christianity fits awkwardly into this scheme, as evidenced by the many commentaries about the dangers of "religion" for public life. Martin Marty, for example, cites the case of the Jehovah's Witnesses, who in the 1940s were violently abused by ardent nationalists throughout the United States for refusing to salute the American flag. For Marty, this is an illustration, not of the dangers of nationalism, but of the hazards of "religion" in public.[1]

Marty has two ways of explaining the problem that at first seem directly opposed to each other. On the one hand, Marty accuses "religion" of

---

1. Martin E. Marty, with Jonathan Moore, *Politics, Religion, and the Common Good: Advancing a Distinctly American Conversation About Religion's Role in Our Shared Life* (San Francisco: Jossey-Bass Publishers, 2000), p. 23. Hereafter, page references to this work will appear in parentheses in the text.

being divisive. "Once a particular group considers itself as divinely chosen and draws sharp boundaries between itself and others, the enemy has been clearly identified, and violence can become actual" (pp. 27-28). Marty expands on these ideas in a section entitled "Religion Divides": "Those called to be religious naturally form separate groups, movements, tribes, or nations" (p. 25). The sacred privilege with which these groups feel endowed leads to negativity toward others. On the other hand, however, the problem with "religion" seems not to be that it breaks up a desirable uniformity, but that it works against a healthy pluralism: "Religion in its intense forms can grasp people who would otherwise have multiple commitments and exact complete and exclusive expressions of their loyalty, 'even unto death'" (p. 29). Religion demands one overriding commitment, a potentially lethal subordination of the many to the one.

Given this analysis, it is difficult to see why the antagonists in the opening scenario end up where Marty puts them. The Jehovah's Witnesses are clearly guilty of "religion": they have claimed an exclusive loyalty to Jesus Christ. They have provoked the violence, even though they suffered rather than committed it. What is not clear is why their persecutors are not also guilty of "religion" for demanding an equally exacting "complete and exclusive expression of their loyalty, 'even unto death.'"

The answer seems to lie in the way Marty divides political space. In his terms, America consists of one nation-state, with one "public square" and one "common good." There are, however, two kinds of public space within the one nation-state: in the one, unity is essential; in the other, pluralism is desirable. Marty wishes to embrace pluralism in religious commitment, and he does so not by simply privatizing religious belief. He believes that the solution to the subordination of the many to the one in religion is to encourage religious people to take part in an open and civil conversation about the common good of the nation. Marty says, "A republic prospers when many voices speak," and he argues that religion is an important voice for the vitality of the public conversation (p. 162). Pluralism, however, only works on the level of civil society. Pluralism of religious goods is inevitable and even laudable, but when it comes to the temporal goods of national life, pluralism must give way to consensus about the common good of the nation. At the higher level of the state, there must be a higher unity to keep the nation-state from dissolving. Multiple commitments regarding religious goods at the level of civil society are to be celebrated. It is when multiple commitments at the level of the state are introduced that religion turns dangerous. Marty's solution to the problem of pluralism, then, is a tempering of an individual's particular religious commitment by his or her commitment to the nation-state, a more inclusive reality at the level of the temporal common good.

Marty's solution is common in contemporary Christian social ethics. The basic assumption is that the nation-state is one city, within which there is a division of goods and a division of labor, and these follow certain well-worn binaries: civil society and state, sacred and secular, eternal and temporal, religion and politics, church and state. In the next section of this chapter, I will turn to John Courtney Murray's influential proposal, on which Marty draws, for this division of political space (pp. 16-17). I will explore some deficiencies in construing political space in this way. As in the example of Marty and the Jehovah's Witnesses, when space is configured this way, the unity of the one city will tend to overtake the multiple commitments of civil society, and the division of goods between eternal and temporal will not hold. The nation-state itself becomes a kind of religion.

For a more adequate construal of political space, I turn to Augustine, who speaks not of one city but two. For Augustine, there is no division of goods: both cities use the same finite goods, but use them for different ends. The two cities compete for the same goods; both are practices of binding, alternate practices of *religio*. At the same time that Augustine is more clear-eyed about the opposition of two alternate practices of *religio*, however, he also allows us to avoid simple dichotomies of church versus state. The two cities are not two institutions but two performances, two practices of space and time. For an illustration of this idea, I turn in the final section of this chapter to the Strauss opera *Ariadne auf Naxos* as an analogy for a Christian performative imagination of politics.

E Pluribus Unum

John Courtney Murray is the most influential American Catholic theorist of the solution to the problem of the one and the many in the life of the nation. Like Marty, Murray acknowledges a robust pluralism of different religious voices in the public conversation. According to Murray, what distinguishes American liberalism from its Jacobin counterparts on the Continent is a commitment to a limited government that allows pluralism to flourish. "The unity asserted in the American device 'E pluribus unum'

. . . is a unity of limited order." Murray is keenly sensitive to the tendency of the one to overtake the many, so he emphasizes that the state is not the realization of the common good, but merely the agency that maintains the public order that allows the common good to flourish. The locus of the common good is society, where a vigorous and civil conversation takes place amongst the various "conspiracies" — Protestant, Catholic, Jewish, and secularist.

> The one civil society contains within its own unity the communities that are divided among themselves; but it does not seek to reduce to its own unity the differences that divide them. In a word, the pluralism remains as real as the unity. Neither may undertake to destroy the other. Each subsists in its own order. And the two orders, the religious and the civil, remain distinct, however much they are, and need to be, related.[2]

The religion clauses of the First Amendment are thus not articles of faith but articles of peace; they create a religiously neutral civil sphere that imposes only a limited unity on the plurality, to maintain peace among the many (p. 49).

According to Murray, there are four basic principles that serve to limit the power of the government. Here Murray undertakes the crucial division of goods and division of labors on which the peace of the one city depends. The first is the distinction between sacred and secular, a distinction that follows the above distinction between the religious and the civil. The government "is not man's guide to heaven," and has no stake in judging transcendent truth or serving the church. The second distinction is between society and state. The state is just one limited order in the larger society, though it is that uppermost part of society responsible for the use of coercion. Here Murray's use of "society" corresponds to the current usage of "civil society." Murray says that this distinction develops out of the medieval distinction between *ekklesia* and *imperium*. The imperial power played the limited role within Christendom that the state now plays. The third principle is the distinction between common good and public order. The state is responsible for the latter, but not the former, although public

---

2. John Courtney Murray, *We Hold These Truths* (Kansas City, MO: Sheed and Ward, 1960), p. 45. Hereafter, page references to this work will appear in parentheses in the text.

order creates the conditions under which the common good can flourish. The fourth principle is that of "freedom under law." The law exists only to facilitate freedom, not to direct action.[3] The reconciliation of the one and the many is thus accomplished by a series of binary distinctions that divide one space into two "distinct orders" — sacred and secular, society and state, common good and public order, freedom and law — in which the latter term in each binary has a protective, but strictly limited, power over the former.

In theory, we have achieved a balance between unity and plurality, where, as Murray says, "[n]either may undertake to destroy the other." The problem, as Murray recognizes, is that there is an inherent instability in the relationship of state and civil society. Although neither "may" try to destroy the other, they seem to want to. Pluralism remains a threat. Murray describes the "structure of war that underlies the pluralistic society": it is a "crisis that is new in history" (p. 24).

> The fact is that among us civility — or civic unity or civic amity, as you will — is a thing of the surface. It is quite easy to break through it. And when you do, you catch a glimpse of the factual reality of the pluralist society. I agree with Prof. Eric Vogelin's thesis that our pluralist society has received its structure through wars and that the wars are still going on beneath a fragile surface of more or less forced urbanity. What Vogelin calls the "genteel picture" will not stand the test of confrontation with fact. (pp. 18-19)

Murray's solution to this problem is to articulate a public consensus that can replace this structure of war with a peaceful pluralism of conspiracies locked in rational argument, not battle. Murray posits the urgent need for an "American consensus" based on natural law thinking that can provide a moral foundation for such a conversation to take place. The American consensus "would be no less sharply pluralistic, but rather more so, since the real pluralisms would be clarified out of their present confusion. And amid the pluralism a unity would be discernible — the unity of an orderly conversation" (p. 24).

Unfortunately, Murray ruefully admits, such a consensus once ex-

---

3. John Courtney Murray, *Religious Liberty: Catholic Struggles with Pluralism*, ed. J. Leon Hooper, SJ (Louisville: Westminster/John Knox, 1993), pp. 144-46.

isted but is now dead. In response to Murray's call for rational debate on the moral limits of warfare, Julian Hartt countered that America is not a community capable of embodying the tradition of reasoned discourse on warfare. Murray responds:

> I am compelled regretfully to agree that he is right. Such is the fact. It may even be that the American community, especially in its "clerks," who are the custodians of the public philosophy, is not the repository of the tradition of reason on any moral issue you would like to name. This ancient tradition lives, if you will, within the Catholic community; but this community fails to bring it into vital relation with the problems of foreign policy. (p. 291)[4]

Murray concludes: "It would seem, therefore, that the moral footing has been eroded from beneath the political principle of consent, which has now come to designate nothing more than the technique of majority opinion as the guide of public action — a technique as apt to produce fatuity in policy and tyranny of rule as to produce wisdom and justice" (p. 293). Murray tries to deal with the problem by appealing ever more strongly to a lost tradition of reason and the limited state, but a heavy sense of resignation settles over his work at this point. State and civil society seem locked in a perpetual war over the same space. The many always threaten to overtake the one, but Murray cannot increase the power of the one without doing damage to the ideals of a limited state and a flourishing of pluralism. Pluralism seems to be a tragic reality: it is both goal and threat. All Murray can do is appeal to the ideal of a peaceful, rational consensus that seems tragically to have failed.

What actually happens in Murray's America when rational moral consensus fails? Does America disintegrate into warring conspiracies? Do the various groupings of civil society wax stronger and overtake the enfeebled, limited state? Empirical evidence suggests that the answer to the latter two questions is an emphatic no. While there is plenty of evidence that whatever moral consensus in sexual issues that may have existed in the past has been eroded to an extent that Murray could not foresee, the American nation-state has not disintegrated, and the state itself has grown

---

4. See Michael J. Baxter, "John Courtney Murray," in *The Blackwell Companion to Political Theology,* ed. Peter Scott and William T. Cavanaugh (Oxford: Blackwell, 2004), pp. 150-64.

immensely powerful and omnipresent in civil society. The Department of Homeland Security is but one example. Far from the state withering or being overtaken, it is civil society that has withered or been absorbed into the state.[5] The associations of civil society — churches, unions, families, and so on — still exist, but they have lost much of their independent authority. They now convey identities and meanings within the overriding symbol system managed by the twin realities of state and market. The decline of the intermediate associations of civil society is taken as a given by groups of scholars such as the Council on Civil Society.[6] In short, Murray's world of robust conspiracies and limited state has simply not come to pass. The one has largely overtaken the many, just as Wal-Mart has overtaken small family businesses.

My analogy to Wal-Mart is deliberate, for certainly capitalism has had a significant homogenizing effect. While choices have proliferated, there is very little dissent from the ideology of free choice itself. However, I am primarily interested in the political solution to the "structure of war" underlying pluralism. What Murray does not seem to realize is that the American nation-state has found its solution to the problem of pluralism in devotion to the nation itself. The nation-state is made stronger by the absence of shared ends, and the absence indeed of any rational basis on which to argue about ends. In the absence of shared ends, devotion to the nation-state as the end in itself becomes ever more urgent. The nation-state *needs* the constant crisis of pluralism in order to enact the *unum*. Indeed, the constant threat of disorder is crucial to any state that defines its indispensability in terms of the security it offers. Pluralism will always be a crisis for the liberal state, and the solution to the crisis of pluralism is to rally around the nation-state, the locus of a mystical communion that rescues us from the conflicts of civil society. Though the American consensus as a natural law tradition of reasoning is dead, as Murray ruefully admits, another kind of American consensus is alive and well. It is the

5. See Michael Hardt, "The Withering of Civil Society," *Social Text* 14, no. 4 (Winter 1995): 27-45.

6. See Council on Civil Society, *A Call to Civil Society* (Chicago: Institute for American Values, 1998). I cite this work as evidence of the withering of civil society, not because I agree with the solution put forward. I think the authors fail to grasp the extent to which American liberalism itself is destructive of the intermediate associations of civil society. For a more detailed exposition of the way that the modern nation-state is hostile to civil society, see chap. 1 above.

consensus that America is, as former Secretary of State Madeleine Albright put it, "the indispensable nation."[7]

The fundamental incoherence of the nation-state is sublimated by devotion to the nation-state itself, especially its organization of killing energies. There is thus a necessary connection between the two seemingly contradictory faces of the nation-state that Alasdair MacIntyre identifies. On the one hand, the state is a clearing-house for goods and services in which decisions are made between competing interests based on power, not rational deliberation about shared ends. MacIntyre goes beyond Murray in saying that the public discourse of the nation-state not only does not but cannot be conducted on the basis of common norms of rational inquiry in the Aristotelian-Thomist sense, in part because of the sheer size of the modern nation-state. Decisions are based on money and power, not reason, and thus conflict — especially between classes — is endemic. On the other hand, the nation-state presents itself as a repository of sacred value that requires its citizens to be ready to kill and die on its behalf. Despite Murray's protest that the state is not to be the agent of the common good, the nation-state itself becomes the sham common good. Of the nation-state masquerading as the guardian of the common good, MacIntyre says:

> For the counterpart to the nation-state thus misconceived as itself a community is a misconception of its citizens as constituting a *Volk*, a type of collectivity whose bonds are simultaneously to extend to the entire body of citizens and yet to be as binding as the ties of kinship and locality. In a modern, large-scale nation-state no such collectivity is possible and the pretense that it is is always an ideological disguise for sinister realities.[8]

The primary "sinister reality" that must be disguised is violence. Carolyn Marvin argues that "nationalism is the most powerful religion in the United States," and it is a religion that produces unity through blood sacrifice in war.[9] It has been pointed out many times that the country is most

7. Madeleine Albright, quoted in Andrew J. Bacevich, *American Empire: The Realities and Consequences of U.S. Diplomacy* (Cambridge, MA: Harvard University Press, 2002), p. x.

8. Alasdair MacIntyre, *Dependent Rational Animals: Why Human Beings Need the Virtues* (Chicago and LaSalle, IL: Open Court, 1999), p. 132.

9. Carolyn Marvin and David W. Ingle, "Blood Sacrifice and the Nation: Revisiting Civil Religion," *Journal of the American Academy of Religion* 64, no. 4 (Winter 1996): 768.

unified in times of war. In Randolph Bourne's memorable dictum, "War is the health of the State."[10] According to Marvin, this fact points to the inherently religious nature of American nationalism, for religion as she defines it — following, in different ways, Durkheim and Girard — is bound up with blood sacrifice to defuse crises of group identity. It is crucial, however, that we deny the religious nature of nationalism. Why?

> Because what is obligatory for group members must be separated, as holy things are, from what is contestable. To concede that nationalism is a religion is to expose it to challenge, to make it just the same as sectarian religion. By explicitly denying that our national symbols and duties are sacred, we shield them from competition with sectarian symbols. In so doing, we embrace the ancient command not to speak the sacred, ineffable name of god. The god is inexpressible, unsayable, unknowable, beyond language. But that god may not be refused when it calls for sacrifice.[11]

And so we return to Martin Marty's problem at the beginning of this chapter. "Religion" in public is dangerous because it tries to impose unity on plurality. At the same time, however, religious and lethal devotion to the unity of the nation-state itself is assumed to be a normal part of one's civic duties. Plurality is desirable only at the level of civil society and only as long as it does not interfere with the sacred duty to stand together at the level of the state. There is only one temporal city. The church may jealously guard its sacred space within that city, but it may not demur from the state's monopoly on violence.

From One City to Two

The problem of the one and the many will be insoluble from a theological point of view as long as there is only one city within which the church must contend for space. Murray and his successors were trying to find a way for the church to move beyond an outdated Constantinianism that re-

---

10. Randolph Bourne, "The State," in *War and the Intellectuals: Collected Essays, 1915-1919*, ed. Carl Resek (New York: Harper and Row, 1964), p. 71.

11. Marvin and Ingle, "Blood Sacrifice," p. 770.

quired the coercive power of the state to be wielded on behalf of the church's interests. In doing so, however, Murray attempts a division of labor between two realms — sacred and secular, infinite and finite — each with its proper goods and proper functions. In separating the sacred and the secular orders, however, Murray left open the possibility that the former would be rendered increasingly "extraterrestrial": "The whole of man's existence is not absorbed in his temporal and terrestrial existence. He also exists for a transcendent end. The power of government does not reach into this higher sacred order of human existence."[12] The visible church is inevitably entangled in terrestrial life, but insofar as it is, the church and the government inhabit the same terrestrial city. The nation-state is simply a given, within which the church and the government must maneuver for space.

The Constantinian solution to the problem of church and state is for the church to use the state to rule the city. The "sectarian" solution is for the church to renounce the state and live apart from the city. Murray's and Marty's solution is for the church to locate itself within the city but outside of the state, and for the state to take a strictly limited role in ruling the city. All of these solutions share an imagination of one earthly city within which the political life of a people takes place. There is one polis that the church can seek to rule, flee, serve, advise, or transform. The heavenly city refers to different goods than those of temporal politics.

We can see the problem when we consider the difference between Augustine's "two cities have been formed by two loves"[13] and Pope Gelasius I's famous and influential dictum, "Two there are . . . by which this world is ruled." For Augustine, church and coercive government represent two cities, two distinct societies that represent two distinct moments of salvation history. There is not one society in which there is a division of labor. In Gelasius's words, a half century later, there is one city with two rulers, "the consecrated authority of priests and the royal power."[14] The eschatological reference is not absent: for Gelasius, the distribution of power between priest and king is a sign that Christ's coming

---

12. Murray, *Religious Liberty*, p. 144.

13. St. Augustine, *The City of God*, trans. Marcus Dods (New York: Modern Library, 1950), XIV.28.

14. Pope Gelasius I, "Letter to Emperor Anastasius," in *From Irenaeus to Grotius: A Sourcebook in Christian Political Thought*, ed. Oliver O'Donovan and Joan Lockwood O'Donovan (Grand Rapids: Eerdmans, 1999), p. 179.

has put a check on human pride. Nevertheless, the element of time has been flattened out into space. The one city is now divided into "spheres," and, as Gelasius says, "each sphere has a specially qualified and trained profession."[15] It is this flattening out that allows Murray to map the modern distinction of state and civil society onto the medieval distinction of *imperium* and *ekklesia*.

The centuries following Gelasius would see the two powers often locked in a struggle for dominance over the one city, Christendom. Carolingian and Ottonian emperors would assert their control over ecclesiastical affairs — in Carolingian times it was common to amend Gelasius's dictum so that there were two by which the *church* was ruled, until the Investiture Controversy reasserted clerical control over church affairs. Oliver O'Donovan put it this way: "The history of the Christendom idea shows differentiation being sacrificed to equilibrium, the two offices turning into each other's shadows; and it shows us one establishing hegemony over the other as attention falls on the difference between 'temporal' authority and 'spiritual.'"[16]

The current revival of Augustine's political thought (Rowan Williams, John Milbank, Oliver O'Donovan, et al.) owes much to the way the two cities concept configures space and time. Augustine has no theory of church and state, no spatial carving up of one society into spheres of influence. There is no sense that there is a single given public square in which the church must find its place. Augustine complexifies space by arguing that the church itself is a kind of public; indeed, it is the most fully public community. The city of God has to do with ordering matters that are considered public, because the city of God makes use of the same temporal goods as does the earthly city, but in different ways and for different ends.[17] There is no division between earthly goods and heavenly goods, secular and sacred; there is no sphere of activities that is the peculiar responsibility of the earthly city. The city of God, therefore, is not part of a larger whole, but is a public in its own right. Indeed, the city of God is the

---

15. Pope Gelasius I, "The Bond of Anathema," in O'Donovan and O'Donovan, *From Irenaeus to Grotius*, pp. 178-79.

16. Oliver O'Donovan, *The Desire of the Nations: Rediscovering the Roots of Political Theology* (Cambridge: Cambridge University Press, 1996), p. 204. On priest and king as shadows of one another after the Investiture Controversy, see also Ernst Kantorowicz, *The King's Two Bodies* (Princeton, NJ: Princeton University Press, 1957).

17. Augustine, *City of God*, XVIII.54.

only true "public thing," according to Augustine, as pagan Roman rule had failed to be a *res publica* by refusing to enact justice and serve God.[18]

It follows that the earthly city is not a neutral, common space, bounded by "articles of peace," where the various "conspiracies" meet, as in Murray's scheme. For Augustine, the earthly city is not religiously neutral, but its members share a common end: "the love of self, even to the contempt of God."[19] John Milbank suggests that, for Augustine, "the ends sought by the *civitas terrena* are not merely limited, finite goods, they are those finite goods regarded without 'referral' to the infinite good, and, in consequence, they are unconditionally *bad* ends."[20] There is a unity in the earthly city, but it is a false unity, one based on the *libido dominandi*. Augustine is not averse to calling this false unity a *religio*, as he notes that the word *religio* applies not only to the worship of God but to "the observance of social relationships" in general.[21] Love of self lends itself to a dissipating individualism, but the love of glory and public praise that issue from self-love restrains the centrifugal effects of the *libido dominandi*. Civic unity is also maintained by the pursuit of war, uniting a fractious populace against a common enemy (V.12). Augustine sees — as Murray does not — that the "structure of war that underlies the pluralistic society," in Murray's words, has a tendency to be resolved by appeal to unity of the earthly city in war against external enemies. To do so, however, produces not real unity and order, but a false order, a restraint of vice through vice (XIX.25). The earthly city, therefore, is a tragic reality, doomed to dissolution, yet the

18. Augustine, *City of God*, XIX.21-5.

19. Augustine, *City of God*, XIV.28. Robert Markus has famously posited Augustine as the first Christian theorist of the secular, "religiously neutral civil community," a reading that has been rightly rejected by Williams, Milbank, O'Donovan, and others. See R. A. Markus, *Saeculum: History and Society in the Theology of St. Augustine* (Cambridge: Cambridge University Press, 1970), pp. 166-78.

20. John Milbank, *Theology and Social Theory: Beyond Secular Reason* (Oxford: Basil Blackwell, 1990), p. 406.

21. Augustine, *City of God*, X.1. (Hereafter, references to this work will appear in parentheses in the text.) The Dods translation reads: "The word 'religion' might seem to express more definitely the worship due to God alone, and therefore Latin translators have used this word to represent *thrēskeia*; yet, as not only the uneducated, but also the best instructed, use the word religion to express human ties, and relationships, and affinities, it would inevitably produce ambiguity to use this word in discussing the worship of God, unable as we are to say that religion is nothing else than the worship of God, without contradicting the common usage which applies this word to the observance of social relationships."

city of God uses the order the earthly city produces to its benefit as it sojourns through this world (XIX.26). The two cities have this temporary earthly peace in common, but it is not a kind of common political space or state. As O'Donovan says, for Augustine, "[o]nly the 'earthly peace' . . . is common to both communities, not an institution but simply a condition of order. Each community makes, as it were, its own peace out of it."[22]

It is often thought that Augustine does not identify the church with the city of God. This is true in one respect and inaccurate in another. It is true that Augustine does not simply identify the city of God with the visible church on earth, which is so notoriously filled with both the wheat and the chaff. However, Augustine does identify the church with the city of God in at least one place: he refers to Old Testament figures that "are to be referred only to Christ and His church, which is the city of God" (XVI.2). Later, Augustine says, "the Church even now is the kingdom of Christ, and the kingdom of heaven," because it contains the righteous within it (XX.9). As Christ's body, the church is ontologically related to the city of God, but it is the church not as visible institution but as a set of practices. The city of God is not so much a space as a performance. Likewise, the earthly city is a particular tragic performance of the *libido dominandi*. It is true that the city of God and the earthly city are ideal moral communities whose actual performance in time is, for Augustine, the history of Israel and the church, on the one hand, and the history of the Babylonian and Roman empires, on the other.[23] But what we are not given is anything like a theory of church and state, or civil society and state. There is no division of sacred and secular, private and public, no division of labor between the things that are Caesar's and the things that are God's for, as Dorothy Day once commented, if you give to God what is God's, there is nothing left for Caesar.

Augustine does not map the two cities out in space, but rather projects them across time. The reason that Augustine is compelled to speak of two cities is not because there are some human pursuits that are properly terrestrial and others that pertain to God, but simply because God saves in time. Salvation has a history, whose climax is in the advent of Jesus Christ,

---

22. Oliver O'Donovan, "The Political Thought of *City of God* 19," in Oliver O'Donovan and Joan Lockwood O'Donovan, *Bonds of Imperfection: Christian Politics, Past and Present* (Grand Rapids: Eerdmans, 2004), p. 59.

23. Oliver O'Donovan, "The Political Thought of *City of God* 19," pp. 56-57.

but whose definitive closure remains in the future. Christ has triumphed over the principalities and powers, but there remains resistance to Christ's saving action. The two cities are not the sacred and the profane spheres of life. The two cities are the *already* and the *not yet* of the kingdom of God.

Because of the persistence of sin, Augustine accepts the use of the coercive means of the earthly city by the city of God to restrain evil and provide some order while we await the eschaton. Augustine is misunderstood, however, if sin takes on the status of a given reality that then necessitates the violence of a permanent, natural political sphere — the state. Where this move is made, it is common either to de-historicize the *already* of the kingdom of God, such that it stands, as it did for Reinhold Niebuhr, "at the edge of history," beckoning us to a better relative justice or to acknowledge the salience of the *already* in history, but to argue for a proper "balance" or "tension" between the *already* and the *not yet*.[24] For Augustine, however, the *already* is not a transcendent principle but a reality to which the church witnesses in history. And the *already* and the *not yet* are not to be "balanced" any more than the city of God and the earthly city are to keep each other in check. The reality of the *already* and the *not yet* is not a kind of Stoic admonition to seek moderation, a middle course between the contrasting passions of optimism and pessimism.

The advent of the kingdom of God is not balanced by any countervailing principle; Christ has definitively triumphed, and the powers and principalities are passing away. The reason that the kingdom is not yet fully consummated is not that God is holding back, as if God would want the kingdom to be revealed only partially, in anticipation. As Gerhard Lohfink remarks, "We cannot say such things any more than we can say that God was revealed in Jesus, but only in anticipation, only partially, and certainly not entirely and definitively."[25] The *not yet* results not from God holding

---

24. Reinhold Niebuhr, *An Interpretation of Christian Ethics* (New York: Seabury Press, 1963), pp. 62-83. For Niebuhr, the underlying problem of social and political life is something like Murray's "structure of war" underlying civil society, and Christ's kingdom has no immediate relevance: "The ethic of Jesus does not deal at all with the immediate moral problem of every human life — the problem of arranging some kind of armistice between various contending factions and forces. It has nothing to say about the relativities of politics and economics, nor of the necessary balances of power which exist and must exist in even the most intimate social relationships" (p. 23).

25. Gerhard Lohfink, *Does God Need the Church? Toward a Theology of the People of God* (Collegeville, MN: Liturgical Press, 1999), p. 138.

back, but from humans holding back. And there is nothing "natural" or fated about human sin. Indeed, the story of the Fall makes clear that human sin is not the way it is meant to be, nor indeed the way that it really is.

For Augustine, the Fall is not simply to issue in a generic pessimism to balance the optimism afforded by the advent of Jesus Christ. The Fall, after all, is not a tragic or pessimistic doctrine. To the contrary, the Fall indicates that sin is not simply a given; sin is a contingent reality, a falling away from an original goodness (*City of God*, XIV.11). Augustine repeatedly stresses that evil is not a created reality, but lives as a parasite off the good. The enemies of God oppose God by a perverted will, not by nature (XII.3). Unlike the Babylonian creation myth, the world is not created out of the need to restrain an original violence. The world is created in peace: goodness, not violence, is the way things really are. Rome, by contrast, was founded in an original act of violence, the murder of Remus by his brother Romulus. Augustine notes "no difference between the foundation of this city and of the earthly city" (XV.5), for the earthly city is founded in violence that conquers a previous violence, vice that restrains a previous vice. The "sickliness" of the earthly city is therefore "not nature, but vice" (XV.6).

For Augustine, then, coercive government is not natural, but is the result of the Fall. From creation, God "did not intend that His rational creature, who was made in His image, should have dominion over anything but the irrational creation — not man over man, but man over the beasts." It is only sin "which brings man under the dominion of his fellow" (XIX.14-15).[26] For Augustine, coercive government is essentially a tragic reality, not part of God's original intention for creation, but a means of keeping sin in check by sin. There is also no sense in Augustine that the earth is divided up *by nature* into different "earthly cities" or nations, each with its own government. As Augustine reads the story of Babel, the world was divided into separate peoples as a consequence of sin. Christ, in contrast, is the one who gathers the many into himself.[27] The earthly city has no way of solving the problem of the one and the many; pluralism for the earthly city remains tragic. The city of God is the universal reality, while the earthly city is partial and particular. The city of God, "while it

---

26. The interpretation of these passages is not uncontroversial. In an appendix to his book, Markus examines the evidence and shows — conclusively, I think — that Augustine held that government is not natural, but is the result of sin; see Markus, *Saeculum*, pp. 197-210.

27. See Augustine, *The Trinity*, trans. Edmund Hill (Brooklyn: New City Press, 1991), IV.11.

sojourns on earth, calls citizens out of all nations, and gathers together a society of pilgrims of all languages" (*City of God*, XIX.17), thus reversing the effects of the Fall. In doing so, "far from rescinding and abolishing these diversities . . . it even preserves and adapts them" (XIX.17).

For Augustine, government is part of God's providential ordering of history, but as part of the earthly city, "which shall not be everlasting" (XV.4), civil government is a temporary reality; because Christ has triumphed over sin, the earthly city is passing away, receding into the city of God. As the word implies, the *temporal* is not a space or a sphere of reality, but is a kind of rule that is temporary. And it is not merely slated for destruction once God finally gets around to fully installing the kingdom in some far-off future. The principalities and powers have already met their end in the triumph of Christ. This is not to "overemphasize" the *already* at the expense of the *not yet*; there is no question of "realized eschatology," faith in the moral progress of humankind. Rather, it is simply to acknowledge the ontological priority of the *already* over the *not yet*. The *already* is what really is, and violence is not simply one of the given data with which Christian ethics must deal.

This kind of imagination of the political may seem like an irresponsible refusal to take seriously the effects of sin, but this is not the case if we take the cross and resurrection of Jesus Christ as the key to reading history. On the cross, the effects of the *not yet* are made clearly visible on the body of Christ. The public effects of sin and violence are there for all to see. And yet Paul describes the cross as strength and victory (1 Cor. 1:18-25). Though sin persists after the resurrection, death has been robbed of its power (1 Cor. 15:55). The "tension" between the *already* and the *not yet* comes from the drama of suffering — and, as sinful human beings, committing — the present evil; the tension is not because we do not know which side is going to win out. Paul is quite confident of both present suffering and the fact that God has absorbed that suffering once and for all. Again, there is no question of "realized eschatology." The *not yet* remains clearly visible in the deaths of the martyrs who imitate Christ, but in the light of a larger story, their deaths are called "victories" over the demons and powers that conspire against the city of God. Augustine calls the martyrs the means by which the false religion of the earthly city is exposed and the true religion is made known (VIII.27). The effects of sin are apparent in martyrdom, but the martyr confronts death as if it has lost its sting, as if it no longer ultimately matters. Because the kingdom is already present, Christ's victory over death is the only reality. The *already* and the *not yet* are not balanced in martyrdom; rather, the violence of the *not yet* is exposed as belonging to a type of rule that is passing away. In their imitation of Christ, the martyrs and not the violent become the key to reading and performing history eschatologically.

Performing the City of God

It is not my present intention to critique Augustine's comments on the use that the city of God makes of the coercive powers of the earthly city. We must at least agree, I think, with Karl Barth's judgment that the state's exercise of violence is an abnormality, an *opus alienum* and not an *opus proprium*.[28] What is important for my present purpose is the way that Augustine's image of the two cities breaks the modern monolithic conception of a single public space, bounded by the nation-state, in which the church must somehow find a place. For Augustine, neither city is a space with clearly defined boundaries, but both are sets of practices or dramatic performances, one tragic, the other comic, broadly speaking. The task of the church is to interrupt the violent tragedy of the earthly city with the comedy of redemption, to build the city of God, beside which the earthly city appears to be not a city at all.

Let me illustrate this idea with Richard Strauss's opera *Ariadne auf Naxos*. The action is set in the house of the richest man in Vienna, who is busy throwing a feast for numerous guests. The host is a man of indiscriminate taste. He has scheduled dinner to be followed by two performances, one a tragic *opera seria* based on the Ariadne legend, and the other a comedy featuring harlequins, nymphs, and buffoons. The pompous composer of the opera is outraged when he discovers that his masterwork is to be followed by such a frivolous offering. The situation becomes much worse for the composer and his prima donna when the major-domo — on orders from his lordship, the master of the house — announces that, in order to leave time for the fireworks display, both the tragedy and the comedy will have to be performed simultaneously, on the same stage.[29]

---

28. Karl Barth, *Church Dogmatics* III/4 (Edinburgh: T. & T. Clark, 1961), p. 456.

29. Richard Strauss, *Ariadne auf Naxos*, trans. Alfred Kalisch (New York: Boosey and Hawkes, 1943), pp. 3-15. I am grateful to Doug Asbury, a student at Seabury-Western Seminary, for calling my attention to this opera during a class discussion of my book *Torture and Eucharist*.

The composer objects to the other actors infiltrating his tragedy, as Ariadne on Naxos "is the symbol of Mankind in Solitude." The major-domo, however, explains that his lordship has watched the rehearsals and "has been greatly displeased that in a mansion so magnificently equipped as his, a scene so poverty-struck as a Desert Island should be set before him" (pp. 15-16). He wants to enliven the tragedy with characters from the comedy. And so Zerbinetta and her troupe of comedians prepare to bring light to the Ariadne story. Zerbinetta, says the dancing master, is "a past mistress of improvisation. As she always plays herself, you see, she is always at home in scenes of every kind" (p. 18).

As the curtain rises on the second act of Strauss's opera, Ariadne is at the grotto grieving her abandonment by her lover, Theseus. Ariadne resolves to await Hermes, the messenger of death, to take her away to the underworld, the realm of death, for in death is peace and the cessation of suffering and corruption. However, Zerbinetta and her troupe of comedians interrupt Ariadne's tragedy and alter the direction of the opera. Zerbinetta tries to convince Ariadne that she wants not death, but a new lover. On the scene comes the rakish young god Bacchus, whom Ariadne at first mistakes for the messenger of death. Eventually, however, she is won over by his wooing, and she embraces life instead of death, as he carries her off to the heavens. Bacchus has the last word, proclaiming, "By thy great sorrow rich am I made. . . . And sooner shall perish the stars in their places, than Death shall tear thee from my arms" (pp. 25-48).

In some Christian political imaginings, the one stage is the one earthly city, the nation-state, on which the church is urged to play a supporting role. For Augustine, however, the stage is the world on which the one drama of salvation history is being enacted. The earthly city and the city of God are two intermingled performances, one a tragedy, the other a comedy. There are not two sets of props, no division of goods between spiritual and temporal, infinite and finite. Both cities are concerned with the same questions: What is the purpose of human life? How should human life be ordered to achieve that purpose? The difference is that the city of God tells the story that we believe to be true, that God in Christ through the Spirit has saved us from the tragedy of inevitable violence. Like Zerbinetta and her troupe, the church interrupts the tragedy of the earthly city by enacting the comedy of redemption in Christ. The church does not allow the earthly city to define one public space, but constantly redefines what is truly public. The church is not a separate institution enacting a wholly separate drama, but works with other actors to try to divert trag-edy into the drama of redemption.

Samuel Wells's book *Improvisation* is a wonderful reflection on the drama of Christian ethics. Wells points out that drama as it has been used in Christian ethics is too limited a concept if it means following out a prewritten script. Christian life is better likened to dramatic improvisa-tion, where actors are formed in certain habits — virtues — and then al-lowed to take the action in some unanticipated directions. Wells argues that this kind of improvisation imitates the ways of God with creation. God neither simply accepts nor rejects ("blocks") the sinfulness of the world, as if it were a given, but rather "overaccepts" the sin of the world in the life, death, and resurrection of Jesus. "Overaccepting" is a theatrical term that indicates an improvised reframing of the action of a drama in light of a larger story one wants to tell. Wells cites the example of the con-cert pianist who is interrupted by a child banging on the keyboard. Rather than simply allowing the noise to continue or having the child removed, the pianist puts his hands on either side of the child's and begins weaving a beautiful improvised melody that incorporates the child's discordant notes.[30] Overaccepting is not always so immediately beautiful. Martyr-dom exhibits all the desperate ugliness of violence and death, and yet mar-tyrdom transfigures death by placing it into the larger story of what Christ has done with death.

Christian political ethics is often distorted by treating certain contin-gent realities as givens. Sin and violence are treated as the way things are, at least for now; the *not yet* is detemporalized into a constant feature of life on earth. There is one city, protected from dissolution by the state, a natural institution meant to safeguard those penultimate political goods that re-quire protection by coercion. Our task is to manage history by bringing some order to a more basic chaos. In his reading of Genesis, by contrast, Augustine shows how original goodness is more basic than sin. He shows how God opens up a second city, a new kind of imagination that does not treat sin as a given. As Wells indicates, God is the only true given and the only true giver. Christian ethics is not about managing history, but about

---

30. Samuel Wells, *Improvisation: The Drama of Christian Ethics* (Grand Rapids: Brazos Press, 2004), pp. 59-70, 131-32. Wells emphasizes that improvisation is not about being origi-nal or clever, but about doing the obvious. Being trained well and thinking in terms of the larger story means that the actor should have a good instinct about what comes next (p. 12).

overaccepting the apparent givens of human life and turning them into gifts in the light of God's grace. "Thus is fate (a given) transformed into destiny (a gift) by placing it within a larger story."[31] In Augustine's terms, the city of God is the story enacted in history of the way that God has taken the tragedy of human sin and incorporated it into the drama of redemption.

Envisioning the two cities as performances helps us to avoid some serious problems with the way the church is imagined. The church as God sees it — as the body of Christ — is not a human institution with well-defined boundaries, clearly distinguishable from the secular body politic. The church is not a polis but a set of practices or performances that participate in the history of salvation that God is unfolding on earth. The earthly city likewise is not simply identified with the state as institution; for example, the idea of Christian mail carriers is by no means contradictory! In Augustine's metaphor, both cities are groups of people united by the things they love and by the way they imagine and use them, not primarily by the things we associate with institutions: buildings, equipment, bylaws, and so on.

The church is not a separate enclave, but — as in the *Ariadne auf Naxos* metaphor — it joins with others to perform the city of God. There is no sense that the church's social presence is for the sake of the church, nor must all other kinds of social bodies be shunned as impure. Not only does the church find itself involved with other troupes, but the improvisation that goes on to try to prevent death from having the final word often leaves the boundaries between what is church and what is not church permeable and even ambiguous. Nicholas Healy says this: "The church is sinful and 'worldly,' and the Spirit acts throughout creation; so 'church' and 'world' may often be more prescriptive than descriptive categories within a theodramatic horizon."[32]

Although, for Augustine, the history of the city of God is primarily the history of the church, there is no question that the empirical church is full of sin, and the history of the church must be told in a penitential key. The church is not an ideal community to be celebrated for its moral superiority over the state and other types of association. The ontological *participation* of the church in Christ does not mean a full and simple identifica-

31. Wells, *Improvisation*, pp. 124-26 (quoting from p. 126).
32. Nicholas M. Healy, *Church, World, and the Christian Life: Practical-Prophetic Ecclesiology* (Cambridge: Cambridge University Press, 2000), p. 170.

tion of the church with Christ on earth. The church must acknowledge its sin and always tell the story of salvation penitentially, as the history of the forgiveness of sin — *our* sin.

Nevertheless, in order to tell this story faithfully, we must never allow the acknowledgment of our sin to become an apologia for further Christian complicity in sin. The church's confession of sin can become a kind of resignation to the inevitability of sin, the constancy of the "not yet," which requires, with a fated and regretful sigh, that we take up the sword again to restrain sin with sin. When the acknowledgment of our sin circles back to a tragic view of the world, our humility becomes demonic. A true understanding of eschatology requires neither tragic resignation to sin nor a triumphal declaration that the church is the realized eschaton. It requires a fully penitential "overaccepting" of human finitude and sinfulness by receiving the healing kingdom that God, through Christ and the Spirit, has planted right in the midst of our bloodstained history. The recognition of our sinfulness becomes not recognition of our tragic fate but a humble acknowledgment that we are not in charge of making history come out right by violent means. Our fate has been transformed into our destiny, which is to receive the kingdom of God in humility and thankfulness. The city of God is not the shape of our triumph, but of our repentance.

Conclusion

I will conclude with two brief examples to illustrate what the movement from one city to two might look like in contemporary politics. Both examples have to do with Iraq. The vision of one city can be seen in the arguments by several prominent American Catholic commentators in 2003 that the church was welcome to give its opinion on the impending war, but judgment of this matter belonged to the president.[33] The assumption was that the church is one of many contributors to the one public debate on the war, but when the nation makes up its mind, the church in America should loyally support the war effort. In fact, most American Christians before the war were content to support President Bush's determination to

---

33. George Weigel, "The Just War Case for the War," *America* 188, no. 11 (March 31, 2003): 7-10; Michael Novak, "War to Topple Saddam is a Moral Obligation," *The Times* (London), February 12, 2003.

invade Iraq, despite the emphatic and repeated opposition to the war by the pope and the governing bodies of virtually every major Christian denomination. When the church is viewed as particular — as one of the many in civil society — and the nation-state is viewed as universal — as the larger unifying reality — then it is inevitable that the one will absorb the many, in the putative interests of harmony and peace. Indeed, war becomes a means of furthering the integration of the many into the one: we must all stand together when faced with an enemy.

The enactment of another city would begin with the church striving to create another public performance, a more universal public than America. The church's public role would be to improvise a different drama, one of reconciliation, not war. The efforts of Voices in the Wilderness, a group of both Christians and non-Christians, were exemplary in this regard. During the decade of lethal sanctions against Iraq, Voices in the Wilderness brought medicine, toys, and food into the country — in violation of U.S. law. Such efforts enact a different drama by dismissing national borders as ultimately unreal. In the case of the current war, another city takes shape when the church alongside others refuses to accept an advisory role to the president, and makes its own judgment on the justice of the war. This means not only speaking out against an unjust war, but refusing to fight it. This would, of course, require a significant shift away from the common American Christian imagination of church and state as two parts of a whole. But repentance for our complicity in violence must take the form of fostering an eschatological sense that the earthly city is passing away, and that the church is called to witness in its own public life to a new order of peace and reconciliation.

CHAPTER THREE

Migrant, Tourist, Pilgrim, Monk:
Identity and Mobility in a Global Age

—⟡⟡⟡—

I mages of mobility dominate the literature on globalization. William Greider, for example, depicts globalization as a constantly accelerating machine that reaps as it destroys, trampling down fences and ignoring familiar boundaries. No one is at the wheel; in fact, there is no wheel, no steering mechanism at all. Greider also likens globalization to a storm, a whirlwind that has blown all previously stable order, borders, and identities out of place.[1] For the last few centuries the world has been carved up into clearly bordered nation-states, and the nation has been the primary source of identity. What happens now that national identities are being shaken by the storm? In the new mobility, will there emerge a new cosmopolitan global identity that transcends our old divisions? How is the church affected, and how should Christians respond to the disorder of the new world order?

I will address these questions first by examining the status of borders in a global age, and then by addressing the question of mobility. I will undertake the latter task by examining three kinds of mobility: the mobility of the migrant, the tourist, and the pilgrim. The migrant and the tourist represent two kinds of mobility typical of a globalized world. The pilgrim represents a type of mobility long venerated in the Christian tradition.

1. William Greider, *One World, Ready or Not: The Manic Logic of Global Capitalism* (New York: Simon and Schuster, 1997), pp. 11-26.

Finally, I will turn from mobility to examine a type of stability, that of the monk. I will suggest that the figures of the pilgrim and the monk together are important resources for a Christian response to globalization.

A Borderless World?

The rhetoric of globalism presents globalization as a solvent of borders and of particular identities. The former chair of the U.S. International Trade Commission describes globalization as a "process in which technology, economics, business, communication and even politics dissolve the barriers of time and space that once separated a people."[2] That there could be an identifiable "people" with a particular identity — once all barriers have been dissolved — seems unlikely. The primary bearer of identity over the past two centuries, the nation-state, would appear to be the first casualty of globalization. Kenichi Ohmae's book *The End of the Nation State* (1995) is typical in its confident assertion that nation-states are increasingly irrelevant in a globalized age. According to Ohmae, nation-states have been shown to have been nothing more than "a transitional mode of organization for managing economic affairs."[3] Once necessary for the stability of markets, nation-states now represent a "hardening of economic arteries," as Ohmae says. Markets are the lifeblood of any people; political structures that block the free flow of goods are succumbing to the constant requirement for flexibility and change in order to keep the economy on the move.[4]

Globalist rhetoric about the irrelevance of borders is attractive both for its simplicity and for the catholicity of its vision. A world without borders is a peaceful world, a world where all may be one. In reality, however, the demise of the nation-state has been greatly exaggerated. Since the collapse of communism, twenty-five new nation-states have been created, many of which have built political structures around newly liberated national identities.[5] In Europe, Jacques Le Pen in France, Jörg Haider in Austria, and Gianfranco Fini in Italy have won considerable electoral support

---

2. Alfred Eckes, quoted in John Ralston Saul, *The Collapse of Globalism, and the Reinvention of the World* (Woodstock, NY: Overlook, 2005), p. 19.

3. Kenichi Ohmae, *The End of the Nation State* (New York: Free Press, 1995), p. 149.

4. Ohmae, *End of the Nation State*, pp. 145-49.

5. Saul, *Collapse of Globalism*, p. 234.

for their anti-immigrant style of right-wing nationalism.[6] Much of the ferment in the Islamic world has been attributed to local reactions against the infiltration of foreign products, ideas, and cultures from the West. The United States, especially since the attacks of September 11, 2001, has seen a resurgence of flag-waving nationalism and a rise in suspicion of immigrants and foreigners. At the same time, U.S. government officials who back free trade and small government have established vast new bureaucracies for the surveillance of U.S. residents and have sought to deny rights to foreigners under U.S. control (as at Guantánamo Bay).

These signs of resurgent nationalism are commonly presented as a defensive reaction against globalization. The contest, as Benjamin Barber puts it, is "Jihad vs. McWorld," the struggle of particular identities to survive against the onslaught of universalization.[7] It may be, however, that a strong nation-state is not necessarily incompatible with globalization. Indeed, in some of its manifestations, globalization depends on the maintenance of strong borders and strong identities. For example, the shifting of manufacturing and service jobs from the West to China and India is one of the key manifestations of the new globalized economy. However, China and India have become major players in global trade precisely by pursuing strictly nationalist strategies of development. China maintains an old-fashioned unconvertible, pegged currency and refuses to let it float free on the international currency market. A below-market *yuan* has made Chinese goods and Chinese labor extraordinarily cheap, leading to a booming export economy. The Chinese government still controls half of the country's industry, and it shapes development policy with a heavy hand. Both China and India maintain powerful militaries, and their economic policies are driven not by globalist ideology but by national interest.[8]

In the West, the rhetoric of a smaller state that interferes less in the market has not, in fact, produced a less powerful state. Subjecting an entire society to market logic requires a sustained assault by the state on the intermediate social organizations that stand between the individual and the state (think "No Child Left Behind").[9] Despite the rhetoric of shrinking

---

6. Saul, *Collapse of Globalism*, pp. 248-49.

7. Benjamin Barber, *Jihad vs. McWorld* (New York: Times, 1995).

8. Saul, *Collapse of Globalism*, pp. 165, 205-9.

9. For a similar analysis of Thatcher's England, see Nicholas Boyle, *Who Are We Now? Christian Humanism and the Global Market from Hegel to Heaney* (Notre Dame, IN: University of Notre Dame Press, 1998), pp. 35-55.

government, the ratio of government expenditures to GDP — as well as the ratio of government revenue to GDP worldwide — has not decreased under globalization.[10]

Instead of speaking about the irrelevance of the nation-state to the market, it is more nearly true to say that the state intervenes on behalf of the freedom of increasingly transnational corporations. This may take the form of more overt coercion, such as the intervention of the Nigerian military to protect the interests of the transnational Shell Oil company or, arguably, the intervention of the United States in Iraq to benefit corporate oil interests. Or it may take the form of government subsidies for corporate pursuits, such as ethanol production. It may take the form of the government running enormous deficits, as in the case of the United States, while cutting taxes on corporations. Or it may take the form, most intriguingly, of government promotion of international agreements that actually tie the hands of governments. Examples include agreements stipulating the deregulation of currency markets or the "freeing" of international trade from tariffs or environmental and labor laws. The creation of the World Trade Organization, for example, was negotiated by the representatives of nation-states and is enforceable only because of the coercive power of nation-states. It represents, at the same time, the voluntary surrender of governmental power to regulate the freedom of transnational corporations.[11] This voluntary surrender is incomprehensible unless we see that the nation-state is not so much disappearing as merging its interests with those of the transnational corporation.

Migrant

While governments embracing the ideology of globalism have been eager to facilitate the movement of capital across national borders, this has not been true of labor. No international treaty standardizing the treatment of workers has been signed, and there is little enthusiasm at the level of national governments for such an agreement. Most significantly, capital is

---

10. Saul, *Collapse of Globalism*, p. 202.

11. See Ralph Nader and Lori Wallach, "GATT, NAFTA, and the Subversion of the Democratic Process," in *The Case Against the Global Economy*, ed. Jerry Mander and Edward Goldsmith (San Francisco: Sierra Club, 1996), pp. 92-107.

free to move across national borders, but labor is not. Indeed, the impermeability of borders for laborers accounts for much of what we call "globalization." It is the very fact that workers south of the border can be paid a tenth of what workers a few miles north of the border make that accounts for the phenomenon of factories in the United States shutting down and moving to Mexico. It is the immobility of labor that accounts for the mobility of capital. In other words, the borders of the nation-state are not simply an impediment to globalization; they are also essential to globalization. Moves in the United States to shut down its border with Mexico are currently popular in American politics, not least among candidates of the party that most enthusiastically embraces free global trade. But Ronald Reagan's famous admonition to the Soviets, "Tear down this wall!" was evidently not transferable from Berlin to the Rio Grande.

Yet the immobility of labor is not quite the whole of the story. Migration does occur across international borders. Indeed, the displacement of people has become a major phenomenon of a globalized world. Large populations of refugees and migrants have spilled across borders in all parts of the globe.[12] Millions of "illegal aliens" live and work in the United States, most of them from south of the border. Borders regulate mobility, but they do not prevent it. In fact, it is most accurate to say that the purpose of borders is to control the movement of labor, not to stop it. National borders confer identity on those who are contained within their boundaries or who cross over them. That identity runs the gamut from recognition and protection under the concept of citizenship to the conferral of liminal status on whole groups of people.

The case of "guest workers" in Europe brings this point home. Resurgent nationalism in France and other European countries is largely an anti-immigrant reaction to the presence of millions of workers from outside of Europe. The reason guest workers were imported, beginning in the 1960s, was that advances in social democracy in Europe after World War II had eliminated the availability of a large reserve of cheap, easily exploited labor. The granting of fundamental social rights to a broad range of citizens in European nation-states necessitated the importation of a large new population of people who did not enjoy the rights of citizens. The twentieth-

12. I do not think that a sharp distinction between migrants and refugees is necessary here. While migrants supposedly leave their home countries voluntarily, the overwhelming majority are compelled to do so from economic necessity.

century ideal of citizens' rights and social justice necessitated the importation of a nineteenth-century working class, one not entitled to full citizens'
rights.[13] The same dynamic prevails in the United States. The closing of the
border with Mexico is surely attainable — militarily speaking.

The "problem" of illegal immigration could also be stopped by enforc-
ing stiff penalties against employers of undocumented workers. Instead, enforcement has focused on the immigrants themselves, relying on the largely
ineffectual strategy of deportation. Immigrants can and do find ways to enter, return to, and stay in the United States. What they lack is only official
recognition and the full rights accorded to citizens. The fact that the border
"problem" has gone unfixed for decades should lead us to suspect that the
ongoing problem serves a purpose: the United States needs a readily ex-
ploitable source of cheap labor. The purpose of the border is not simply to
exclude immigrants but to define them, to give them an identity. That identity is a liminal identity, an identity that straddles the border and defines the
person as being neither fully here nor there. The instability and mobility of
identity in a globalized world thus depends on the borders that supposedly
fix identities against the whirlwind of globalization.

The modern nation-state was born of the attempt to protect the
rights of humans as humans. The Declaration of the Rights of Man in 1789
declared all human life as such to be the subject of rights. As Giorgio
Agamben points out, however, the more "life" became the subject of rights
— that is, the more life, liberty, the pursuit of happiness, health, the satisfaction of human needs, and so on, became the subject of rights — the
more "life" became inscribed into the political order and brought under
sovereign control.[14] This process is completed when state sovereignty becomes linked to the *nation* (from *nascere*, to be born). Political life in the
nation-state is not derived from the conscious and free subject, but from
the bare fact of birth. The key political question now takes the form of
"Who is German?" or "Who is American?" and more pointedly "Who is
not?" Migrants and refugees challenge the link between nativity and citizenship. The nation-state may choose to confer citizen status on some migrants and refugees. Unless that takes place, however, migrants retain a
liminal status. The person without a nation-state is what Agamben calls

---

13. Saul, *Collapse of Globalism*, pp. 97-98.

14. Giorgio Agamben, *Homo Sacer: Sovereign Power and Bare Life*, trans. Daniel Heller-
Roazen (Stanford: Stanford University, 1998), pp. 121, 127.

"bare life," whose biological needs may be attended to by humanitarian relief efforts, but whose full identity as the bearer of rights is constantly held in question.

Tourist

A second kind of mobility in a globalized world is identified with the figure of the tourist. If the migrant sees the bordered world from below, the tourist views it from above; the tourist gaze is the cosmopolitan gaze. Unhindered by borders, the tourist scans the globe and imagines herself entering into the experience of otherness in any part of the globe. At the same time, however, borders do not simply disappear, for the maintenance of borders is crucial to the maintenance of the otherness that the tourist seeks. The maintenance of center and periphery remain important for the tourist gaze.

Though the origins of tourism can be found in medieval pilgrimage, the early modern era saw a shift in the reasons for travel from penitence to business and pleasure. The sixteenth through eighteenth centuries saw the rise of the Grand Tour among wealthy Europeans, whose purpose was self-education and pleasure through encounters with the exotic. What we now identify as tourism arises in the twentieth century with the democratization of travel spurred by increasingly widespread access to money and free time in the West. Tourism is linked with the perceived transcendence of class barriers in the twentieth-century and twenty-first-century West. Nicholas Boyle counts this as one of the central illusions of a globalized world:

> What is "the holiday" — arrangements for which have come to dominate the working year — but a temporary pretense that we are capitalists, an annual two-week saturnalia during which the waiters in the hotel are allowed to be its leisured guests? Is it not the same lure we dangle before all the world to draw it on into the global system — "join us and you too can be the tourists, not the waiters," a modern version of the promise of citizenship in the mother country made by our nineteenth-century ancestors and models to their colonial dependents and no more likely to be honored.[15]

15. Boyle, *Who Are We Now?* p. 117.

At the root of tourist mobility is the search for transcendence, of class and of limits more generally. The contrast with previous modes of travel is significant. Eric Leed writes: "For the ancients the journey had value in that it explained human fate and necessity, while the moderns extolled it as a manifestation of freedom and as an escape from necessity and purposiveness."[16] The goal of transcendence of necessity and of the material conditions of life is at the heart of tourism.

Daniel Boorstin's book *The Image* (1961) is often cited as a landmark in the critique of tourism. Boorstin noted that at the heart of tourism was the futile attempt to make the exotic an everyday experience, without its ceasing to be exotic.[17] Exotic experiences must be contrived artificially in order for them to be repeatable at will; tourism is the inauthentic consumption of "pseudo-events."[18] Since Boorstin, however, many studies of tourism have tried to counter his perceived elitism with an appreciation of the spiritual quest that lies behind attempts to transcend everyday life. Dean MacCannell's important book *The Tourist: A New Theory of the Leisure Class*, for example, treats tourism as a substitute for religion, a quest for authenticity: "Sightseeing is a kind of collective striving for a transcendence of the modern totality, a way of attempting to overcome the discontinuity of modernity, of incorporating its fragments into unified experience."[19] MacCannell recognizes that the authenticity served up by tourism is a staged authenticity. But MacCannell criticizes Boorstin for contrasting the tourist with the authentic traveler, thus maintaining a neat distinction between true difference and false difference, as if one could break through the appearances served up by tourism and penetrate into real experience. MacCannell notes that Boorstin thus reproduces the classic tourist posture of complaining about other tourists, to wit, "They are the tourists, I

16. Eric J. Leed, quoted in Luigi Tomasi, "*Homo Viator*: From Pilgrimage to Religious Tourism via the Journey," in *From Medieval Pilgrimage to Religious Tourism: The Social and Cultural Economics of Piety*, ed. William H. Swatos, Jr., and Luigi Tomasi (Westport, CT: Praeger, 2002), pp. 1-24 (quoting from p. 13).

17. Daniel J. Boorstin, *The Image: A Guide to Pseudo-Events in America* (New York: Vintage, 1961), p. 77. Boorstin remarks tartly: "Every bird-watcher knows how hard it is to reconcile oneself to the fact that the common birds are the ones most usually seen and that rare birds are really quite uncommon."

18. Boorstin, *The Image*, p. 103.

19. Dean MacCannell, *The Tourist: A New Theory of the Leisure Class* (Berkeley: University of California Press, 1999), p. 13. MacCannell observes that "tourist attractions are precisely analogous to the religious symbolism of primitive peoples" (p. 2).

am not." For MacCannell, the relationship between surface and depth is much more complex; the only authentic experience of local life not staged for tourists that the tourist is likely to have is to see the locals going about their tourist business in a routine way, having gotten used to the presence of tourists.[20]

The transformation of the tourist in his spiritual quest is often supposed to take place by the encounter of the modern (or hypermodern) subject with the authentic local subject who has been untouched by modernity.[21] As Edward Bruner points out, however, it is often the tourist who remains unchanged, while the natives are forced to change in order to accommodate tourists.[22] Under such circumstances, it is difficult to talk about authentic difference. MacCannell asks: "Is it not possible that any celebration of 'difference' is something insidious: that is, the sucking of difference out of difference, a movement to the still higher ground of the old arrogant Western Ego that wants to see it all, know it all, and take it all in, an Ego that is isolated by its belief in its own superiority."[23] The tourist gaze depends on borders to maintain the kind of difference that it craves. At the same time, however, the tourist gaze destroys difference precisely in its perceived ability to rise above and transcend all borders, to suck difference into the unified experience of the self.

The tourist is more than the man in plaid Bermuda shorts, black socks, and dress shoes snapping pictures of hula dancers. The tourist is, as MacCannell says, "one of the best models available for modern-man-in-general."[24] Tourism is the aesthetic of globalism in both its economic and political forms. Tourism shares the basic structure of Western economic and military expansion. The transnational corporation seeks to transcend all borders, to view all places as ultimately interchangeable locations for either producing or selling products. The disciplines imposed by the International Monetary Fund (IMF) on countries that stray from "free-market"

20. MacCannell, *The Tourist*, pp. 105-7.

21. In this context, at least, I prefer "hypermodern" to "postmodern," because I see globalization as an extension of the modern project, a celebration of the new and different that is unified by the same transcendent ego.

22. Edward M. Bruner, "Transformation of Self in Tourism," *Annals of Tourism Research* 18 (1991): 238-50 (quoting from p. 239).

23. MacCannell, *The Tourist*, pp. xx-xxi (this quote is found in the introduction to the 1989 edition of the book).

24. MacCannell, *The Tourist*, p. 1.

ideology are indifferent to the particularities of place and time. Joseph Stiglitz, former president of the World Bank, has been critical of this kind of approach. It has prevailed, according to Stiglitz, because of its simplicity: "[I]ts policy recommendations could be administered by economists using little more than simple accounting frameworks. . . . Indeed, in some cases economists would fly into a country, look at and attempt to verify these data, and make macroeconomic recommendations for policy reforms all in the space of a couple of weeks."[25] The universal gaze of economic globalism is a kind of mutation of Christian eschatology that promises that all will be one.[26] In the case of globalism, this eschatology promises the freedom of the self to rise above material limits and to have access to an ever-expanding array of products and experiences.

Once again, however, globalization cannot simply aim at a borderless world, and in fact the rhetoric of borderlessness is deceptive. Transnational corporations are not really transnational, for almost all are based in the West. The utopia of limitless and borderless consumption is offered to those who can pay, primarily Westerners of the middle class and above. The globalized economy, like tourism, depends on the maintenance of a center and a periphery. The global consumer, like the tourist, goes in search of the exotic. The consumer seeks to make his own the authenticity of single-malt whiskies from remote Highland distilleries and single-origin cocoa from Ecuadoran tribal lands. The progress of modernity depends on the instability of modern identity and the conviction that reality and authenticity are *elsewhere*. The conquering spirit of globalism — the attempt to turn every other place and thing on the globe into a potentially consumable experience — depends ironically on the maintenance of bordered identities, the preservation of premodern authenticity. The primary boundary, then, that globalization must constantly reinforce is the boundary between the modern and the premodern, the developed and the undeveloped.

This is not, of course, by any means to say that the division between the modern and the premodern is a standoff. The victory of the globaliz-

25. Joseph Stiglitz, "More Instruments and Broader Goals: Moving Toward the Post-Washington Consensus," quoted in Saul, *Collapse of Globalism*, p. 105.

26. For a development of this theme, see Graham Ward's comments on the eschatology of capitalism in his article "Religion and Democracy" in *What Comes After Modernity? Secularity, Globalization, and the Re-enchantment of the World*, ed. James K. A. Smith (Waco: Baylor University Press, forthcoming).

ing subject lies precisely in its ability to situate the premodern and define its identity. The disciplines imposed by IMF economists depend on their ability to *define* certain actors as premodern and undeveloped, and therefore in need of change, to become like us. The very terms "premodern" and "undeveloped" establish non-Western subjects as deficient relative to the Western standard. However, the result is not and cannot be simply the homogenization of the world and the eventual disappearance of the premodern and undeveloped world, for the very dynamic of globalization depends on the modern/premodern and developed/undeveloped dichotomies. Dean MacCannell says: "Interestingly, the best indication of the final victory of modernity over other sociocultural arrangements is not the disappearance of the nonmodern world, but its artificial preservation and reconstruction in modern society."[27] The artificial preservation of local identities is essential to tourism. In other words, the tourist represents both the attempt to transcend all borders and identities and the simultaneous attempt to fix the identities of non-Western subjects within its gaze.

Pilgrim

Does the Christian tradition have resources for addressing the problems of identity in the dynamic of globalism? I believe that the figure of the pilgrim is a good place to start. Here we find a model of mobility that is not dependent on an imperial gaze.

Tourism has precursors in medieval pilgrimage, but there are significant differences. Although the motives for both may be seen in the search for transformation of the self, medieval pilgrimage was situated in a system of penitence largely absent from the modern world. The primary motive of pilgrimage was transformation of the self through the forgiveness of sin. This transformation of the self was not self-transformation as such, because it responded to a discipline that had its source outside the self: God. Pilgrims traveled to obtain indulgences and to complete penances that had been assigned them, meaning that pilgrimages were not always voluntary and self-initiated.[28] Indeed, in contrast to tourists, pilgrims did not travel to assert their freedom from necessity but to respond to the ne-

---

27. MacCannell, *The Tourist*, p. 8.
28. Tomasi, *"Homo Viator,"* pp. 3-12.

cessity of their destiny in God. Humility, therefore, was the essential virtue of the pilgrim. Pilgrimage was a kenotic movement, a stripping away of the external sources of stability in one's life. The pilgrim's way was the way of the cross: "If any want to become my followers, let them deny themselves and take up their cross and follow me" (Mark 8:34). The journey required a disorientation from the trappings of one's quotidian identity in order to respond to a call from the source of one's deeper identity.

The modalities of pilgrimage and tourism also differ. Pilgrims generally traveled on foot. The journey was often arduous, not an exercise in leisure, and the perils of the journey were often considered part of corporal penance. Pilgrimage was not a for-profit industry, and it was available to all members of society, including the poor.[29] A network of sanctuaries, hospices, and monasteries supported pilgrims with acts of charity and hospitality. Finally, medieval pilgrimage was a communal journey. Pilgrimage was a social event, during which many of the ordinary rules of hierarchy and social structure were suspended.[30]

The above account is not meant to idealize medieval pilgrimage. The point is not that medieval pilgrims were necessarily more authentic and more spiritually sincere than modern tourists. The point is rather that medieval pilgrims were enmeshed in a communal system of penitence, and they brought a common framework to their travels. In modernity the only common framework is the search for difference. As Luigi Tomasi points out, there were plenty of pilgrims decried as inauthentic in the medieval period, those who went for base motives or those who went as proxies for someone else.[31] But what is significant is the way that judgments about what defined authenticity differed from such judgments in our time.

The most significant such difference in judgment is that regarding the status of center and periphery, or identity and difference. As Erik Cohen points out, the pilgrim moves toward the center of her world, the tourist toward the periphery. The pilgrim moves toward the source of or-

---

29. In their classic study of pilgrimage, Victor and Edith Turner observe: "In a society which offered scant economic opportunities to leave one's close circle of friends, neighbors and local authorities tied to the land, the only possible journey for those who were not merchants, peddlers, minstrels, jugglers, acrobats, wandering friars or outlaws was a holy journey, a pilgrimage or crusade." Victor Turner and Edith Turner, *The Pilgrimage*, quoted in Tomasi, "*Homo Viator*," p. 7.

30. Tomasi, "*Homo Viator*," pp. 3-7.

31. Tomasi, "*Homo Viator*," p. 9.

der and blessing in her world, toward God, as mediated through particular holy places (usually made so by contact with particular holy persons or their material relics). The tourist, by contrast, desires to escape his world, to remove himself from modern civilization in order to seek authenticity in difference — in the novel and the exotic. For this reason, pilgrims welcome other pilgrims, but tourists regard other tourists with disdain. For the pilgrim, the presence of other pilgrims at a site attests to its authenticity: the more pilgrims, the more powerful a shrine. For the tourist, the presence of other tourists at a site detracts from its authenticity. The tourist seeks to gain authenticity through contrast with others. The more tourists crowd a location, the less likely is one to encounter authentic otherness, thus the need for the tourist to find increasingly peripheral places to encounter difference.[32] The presence of pilgrims hallows a particular place; the presence of tourists hollows it out. The vacation vacates particular locations, so the tourist must constantly be on the move, seeking out the unspoiled, only to spoil it with his presence.

As I am using them here, both "tourist" and "pilgrim" are ideal types. Actual people do not fall neatly into one category or the other. Nor does the pilgrim/tourist binary map onto the religious/secular binary. There is a burgeoning literature on "religious tourism," and other kinds of journey not associated with Christianity or any "traditional religion" — to Elvis Presley's Graceland or to Ground Zero in Manhattan, for example — are treated as pilgrimage.[33] It is not my purpose here to explore all the different types of what is called "pilgrimage." Other traditions have practices of pilgrimage, and other traditions have valuable contributions to make toward responding positively to the challenges of globalization. Here I am only capable of briefly exploring some positive Christian contributions. I am particularly interested in exploring how the history of pilgrimage in Christianity can provide clues for how the church is to live in a globalized world. There can be no direct application, since most of the social condi-

---

32. Erik Cohen, "Pilgrimage and Tourism: Convergence and Divergence," in *Sacred Journeys: The Anthropology of Pilgrimage*, ed. Alan Morinis (Westport, CT: Greenwood, 1992), pp. 47-61.

33. In addition to Swatos and Tomasi, *From Medieval Pilgrimage to Religious Tourism*, already cited, see Ellen Badone and Sharon R. Roseman, eds., *Intersecting Journeys: The Anthropology of Pilgrimage and Tourism* (Urbana: University of Illinois, 2004); see also William H. Swatos, Jr., ed., *On the Road to Being There: Studies in Pilgrimage and Tourism in Late Modernity* (Leiden: Brill, 2006).

tions under which medieval pilgrimage flourished have vanished. Christendom is long gone, replaced by a world that values plurality above all. The church itself now finds itself located not at the center of culture but on the periphery, both in the West — where church attendance and Constantinian arrangements decline — and in the world at large, where the church's center of gravity is increasingly located in the Southern Hemisphere, at the periphery of the world market. If the church can practice pilgrimage today, it will be in a very different context.

To embrace the identity of pilgrim now is first of all to embrace a certain kind of mobility in the context of globalization. The church has been unmoored and should joyfully take leave of the settledness of Constantinian social arrangements that gave it privilege and power. To accept our status as pilgrims on our way back to God is, as Augustine saw, to accept the provisional nature of human government. Our status as pilgrims makes clear that our primary identity is not what is defined for us by national borders. The pilgrim seeks to transgress all artificial borders that impede the quest for communion with God and with other people.

Loyalty to the nation-state is not eclipsed by a simple cosmopolitanism, however, for like the migrant and unlike the tourist, the pilgrim travels on foot and does not enjoy a commanding view of the globe from above. Again, humility is the key virtue of the pilgrim. A church that desires to be a pilgrim does not claim the power to treat every location as interchangeable and impose global solutions on the world. As it was before, pilgrimage today is a kenotic movement. The church on the periphery finds itself in solidarity with the migrant and with other people whose identity is liminal. The pilgrim church is itself a liminal reality, occupying the border between heaven and earth. The term *peregrinus*, from which "pilgrim" is derived, recognizes this liminal status: the meaning of the term in Latin includes foreigner, wanderer, exile, alien, traveler, newcomer, and stranger.[34] Like the Israelites, whose care for the alien and poor was motivated by remembrance of their own slavery and wandering (e.g., Deut. 10:17-19; 24:17-22), the pilgrim church is to find its identity in solidarity with the migrant who travels out of necessity, not in order to transcend all necessity.

The pilgrim does not constantly seek difference for its own sake but moves toward a center, which in the Christian case is communion with

---

34. Valene Smith, "Introduction: The Quest in Guest," *Annals of Tourism Research* 19 (1992): 1-17, quoting from p. 1.

God. The pilgrim thus rejoices when others join with her on pilgrimage, because communion with God is also communion with other people, all made in the image of God. Though globalism seeks to bring the world together into one global village and celebrate the differences of all, neither union nor difference has in fact been achieved. Globalism has tended to reinforce divisive borders, especially those between the developed and the undeveloped. The cosmopolitan gaze of the tourist seeks to connect with others, but ends up vacating their otherness, and thus destroying the connection. The pilgrim, on the other hand, sees all as potential brothers and sisters on a common journey to God. The pilgrim preserves otherness precisely by not seeking otherness for its own sake, but moving toward a common center to which an infinite variety of itineraries is possible. If God, the Wholly Other, is at the center, and not the great Western Ego, then there can be room for genuine otherness among human beings. The pilgrim church is therefore able simultaneously to announce and dramatize the full universality of communion with God, a truly global vision of reconciliation of all people, without thereby evacuating difference.

As the work of John Zizioulas has so fruitfully emphasized, the source for Christian exploration of communion and otherness is the doctrine of the Trinity, in which otherness is constitutive of unity, not a threat to unity. The tourist is restless because his identity depends on seeking difference, but also differentiating himself from others. The other is ultimately a threat, and so the tourist must constantly depart from others. According to Zizioulas, the Other in patristic thought is conceived of as "ever-moving rest" (*akinētos stasis*), which does not negate particularity in moving from one particular to another.

> Movement and rest are not contradictory, because the otherness of the Other is not threatened but confirmed through relationship and communion: every "other," in moving to and relating with another "other", confirms the particularity of the "other", thus granting it a specific identity, an ontological "rest." In this movement, the ultimate destination of otherness is the Other *par excellence*, who affirms the particularity of every "other" and in whom, in this way, all particulars find their ontological affirmation (= rest) as "other".[35]

35. John Zizioulas, *Communion and Otherness: Further Studies in Personhood and the Church* (New York: T. & T. Clark, 2006), p. 53.

Such a rest in movement can only be affirmed in the context of a teleology, an eschatological movement of the pilgrim toward the One who is calling her home. The tourist perpetually seeks escape; freedom can only mean autonomy. In the Christian tradition, freedom consists in responding to a call to relationship with God and other human beings. The doctrine of creation means that humans are constituted ontologically by a call from the Other. This means that human life has a history, and that history has a goal. The pilgrim does not seek escape, but moves toward a center, heaven, a future in communion with God and others. At the same time, this goal does not negate otherness. The movement toward the future is not a rupture or leaving behind of the past, for in an eschatological ontology, as Zizioulas points out, every "old" receives its significance from the "new." Otherness, therefore, coincides with communion.[36]

Monk

No account of pilgrimage could be complete without an analysis of those upon whom the pilgrim depends. Those who journey as pilgrims are not self-sufficient, but must rely on those who abide along the way, those who remain in place in order to offer hospitality to those who journey. In the medieval period, an extensive network of support for pilgrims developed, and monasteries played a significant role. The Rule of St. Benedict included special directions for the reception of pilgrims (53:1): "All guests who present themselves are to be welcomed as Christ, for he himself will say: *I was a stranger and you welcomed me* (Matt. 25:35)."[37] It is worth noting that the word *xenos* Matthew attributes to Jesus here can also be translated "alien" or "foreigner."[38] The Rule directs (53:15) that "[g]reat care and concern are to be shown in receiving poor people and pilgrims, because in them more particularly Christ is received." The abbot himself is to pray with them, eat with them, and wash their feet. Guests are to be greeted with "all humility," either with a bow of the head or complete prostration of the body, because Christ is adored in

---

36. Zizioulas, *Communion and Otherness*, pp. 42-43, 54-55.

37. *The Rule of St. Benedict in English*, ed. Timothy Fry, OSB (Collegeville, MN: Liturgical Press, 1982), p. 73.

38. See Walter Bauer, *A Greek-English Lexicon of the New Testament* (Chicago: University of Chicago Press, 1979), p. 548.

them (53:6-13).[39] Following Matthew 25, the identity of the stranger is located in Christ. In a very concrete way, the particularity of each person is honored in the universality of Christ.

Although Benedict's Rule thus reveres the pilgrim who journeys, it also requires of monks a vow of stability that, in most cases, forbids them to journey. In the first chapter of the Rule, Benedict chastises the *sarabaites,* who form intentional communities based on nothing more than their own wills. Though the sarabaites are the "most detestable kind of monks," somehow the *gyrovagues* manage to outdo them, in Benedict's eyes: "In every way they are worse than sarabaites" (1:11). Gyrovagues "spend their entire lives drifting from region to region, staying as guests for three or four days in different monasteries. Always on the move, they never settle down, and are slaves to their own wills and gross appetites" (1:10-11).[40] Gyrovagues are the tourists of monastic life. Their constant mobility imprisons rather than frees, because there is nothing that is not disposable, and therefore nothing stable and strong enough to break through the illusions of the individual will. The vow of stability is meant to bring the narrow individual will into the broader context of the common mind, through the guidance of the abbot. But obedience will never be possible if the monk can just leave anytime he finds some command disagreeable. Contrary to the attitude of the tourist, the Rule associates broadness with stability and narrowness with mobility. Stability is required to enter into true communion with God and with others, which is a timeful process.

Amidst the hypermobility of a globalized world, there is much to recommend stability. Surely this is part of what Alasdair MacIntyre meant when he said that we await "another — doubtless very different — St. Benedict."[41] MacIntyre endorsed the cultivation of constitutive *local* communities in which virtue could be fostered. And yet, as MacIntyre would no doubt agree, there is nothing inherently superior about stability over mobility, or the local over the global. The *telos* of stability and mobility makes all the difference. A new St. Benedict would try, as the old one did, to discern which forms of stability and mobility are most conducive, within his cultural context, to the goal of universal and personal communion with

---

39. *Rule of St. Benedict,* pp. 73-74.

40. *Rule of St. Benedict,* pp. 20-21.

41. Alasdair MacIntyre, *After Virtue,* 2nd ed. (Notre Dame, IN: University of Notre Dame Press, 1984), p. 263.

God and with those made in the image of God. From within the monastic vow of stability, pilgrims were encouraged and supported. Gyrovagues were not.

What kinds of stability and mobility should the church renounce and embrace in a globalized age? I believe that the church must first take its distance from any artificial segmentation of a truly global concern for all of God's children. This means primarily the relativization of national borders and the active denunciation of all kinds of nationalism that would impede the catholicity of the Christian vision of the planet's common destiny. At the same time, Christians must eschew the kind of imperial cosmopolitanism of globalism that views all people and places from above as interchangeable. The tourist gaze, as I have called it, conquers and coordinates the world's differences into a single consciousness. The military imposition of Western models of economics and politics in the two-thirds world is the most troubling manifestation of such a consciousness.

More positively, the church should embrace its status as pilgrim. Our primary citizenship is in heaven (Phil. 3:20), toward which we journey. We are first members of the body of Christ, a body that crosses and transgresses national borders. We are Christians first, members of an international, not merely national, body. Our pilgrim status makes the church a liminal body in any bordered nation-state. We may renounce the trappings of privilege and power that Constantinianism assured us. At the same time, however, our pilgrim status makes us broader, more global, and more catholic than any merely national identity could.

If we are to take stability seriously, however, our catholicity cannot be mere cosmopolitanism. We are, like both the pilgrim and the monk, to hallow the particular and the local. We need to help — in cooperation with others outside the church — to build strong local communities and cooperative social arrangements deeply rooted in their places. The humility of the pilgrim and the monk are rooted in the humus of a particular place. This stability allows us to practice hospitality, especially for the migrants who must journey out of necessity. To welcome and revere migrants as Christ — to feed them and pray with them and wash their feet — is, in a sense, to turn migrants into pilgrims — and thus to turn fate into destiny.[42]

---

42. I borrow this phrase from Samuel Wells, who describes Christian ethics as the transformation of the apparent givens of life into gifts. God is the only real given. Apparent

An example of this kind of approach is Cardinal Roger Mahony's call for civil disobedience in the face of a proposed crackdown on those aiding undocumented immigrants. H.R. 4437, also known as the "Sensenbrenner Bill," was passed in the U.S. House of Representatives in late 2005, but has not been passed in the Senate. The bill would have made it a felony to shield or offer support to illegal immigrants, thus threatening the church's ministry in places like Mahony's Los Angeles archdiocese, where the church has a well-established system of support for migrants, regardless of their legal status. On Ash Wednesday 2006, Mahony asked Catholics in his archdiocese to devote Lent to fasting, prayer, and reflection on the treatment of immigrants. He also announced that, should H.R. 4437 pass, he would instruct his priests, nuns, and laypeople to defy the law.[43] In a letter to President Bush regarding the bill, Mahony quoted Matthew 25 at length, and announced that "this one example in Matthew's Gospel is foundational to our discipleship of Jesus Christ."[44]

Following Jesus on our pilgrimage through this world clearly relativizes any national borders that define some people as "illegal." Their primary identity is bestowed in Christ; it is Christ we welcome when we welcome the stranger. This position puts the church at the margins of the law and at the margins of any national identity. Before we are Americans, we are Christians. But that marginality is accompanied by a rootedness in the concrete needs of particular people, a rootedness that stands as the basis for hospitality to the migrant poor. The church should respond to globalism by enacting a more truly global story of all things made one in Christ. At the same time, the identity of the universal Christ is found in the one lonely migrant who knocks at the door, looking for rest.

---

necessity is transformed into gift by placing it within the larger narrative of creation and redemption. "Thus is fate (a given) transformed into destiny (a gift) by placing it within a larger story." Samuel Wells, *Improvisation: The Drama of Christian Ethics* (Grand Rapids: Brazos, 2004), p. 126.

43. "The Gospel vs. H.R. 4437," *The New York Times*, March 3, 2006, p. A22.

44. Letter from Cardinal Roger Mahony to George W. Bush, December 30, 2005: http://www.archdiocese.la/archbishop/story.php?newsid=704 (accessed Jan. 11, 2008).

CHAPTER FOUR

Messianic Nation: A Christian Theological Critique of American Exceptionalism

⟨⟨⟨⟨⟩⟩⟩⟩

September 11, 2001, has taken on the status of a *kairos* moment in U.S. history, a decisive hour when, we are told, everything changed. In the New Testament, *kairos* often takes on eschatological significance, a time of crisis, as distinguished from the ordinary calendar time of *chronos*.[1] A kind of eschatological sensibility pervades discourse about "9/11," not necessarily in the sense of an end to chronological time, but rather a suspension of ordinary time. We live in a state of exception, a time when exceptional measures such as torture become thinkable. *Kairos*, however, does not legitimate a generalized state of anarchy in which rules are suspended for everyone. *Kairos* is messianic time (see, e.g., Acts 3:20), a time for one decisive actor to appear on history's stage. In the language of American exceptionalism, that actor is the United States, the "indispensable nation," as Madeleine Albright called it, the one exceptional nation needed for exceptional times.[2]

Although I have been using theological language to describe American exceptionalism, such discourse need not be explicitly theological. I want to distinguish between two broad types of American exceptional-

1. Oscar Cullmann, *Christ and Time: The Primitive Christian Conception of Time and History*, trans. Floyd V. Filson (Philadelphia: Westminster Press, 1950), pp. 39-55.

2. Quoted in Andrew Bacevich, *American Empire: The Realities and Consequences of U.S. Diplomacy* (Cambridge, MA: Harvard University Press, 2002), p. x.

ism, one with Judaeo-Christian roots, the other with its roots in the Enlightenment. There is, of course, much mixing of the two types, but they represent two quite distinct ways of approaching the question. The first explicitly appeals to Christian theological concepts such as the election of Israel and God's providence. The second appeals to Enlightenment language concerning the universal applicability of the American value of freedom. The two would appear to be at odds: the one appeals to a nation under the Christian God, the other to the freedom to have one God, none, or many. I am going to argue, however, that both of them — theologically speaking — end up in the same place, and it is not a good place from the point of view of Christian theology. My basic argument is that, when a direct, unmediated relationship is posited between America and a transcendent reality, either God or freedom, there is a danger that the state will be divinized.

The first two sections of this chapter will offer a brief overview of the two kinds of American exceptionalism. I will then look at one contemporary attempt to combine the two from a theological point of view. In the final section, I will argue that American exceptionalism in both forms is a fundamental distortion of the Christian doctrines of election and providence.

America as the New Israel

In its original form, American exceptionalism is an explicitly theological notion, based in the doctrine of election. Just as God chose the Israelites to accomplish God's special purposes on earth, so God has chosen the United States. The promise to make Abraham a "great nation" includes the promise of a new land (Gen. 12:1-2). The doctrine of election is based in the notion of God's choice of a particular people at a particular moment in history, but it also contains a strong element of universalism. Abraham is promised blessings not only for his own people; his people would, in turn, become a blessing for the whole earth (Gen. 12:3). There is a strongly universalizing missionary impulse at the heart of the doctrine of election. Salvation is not just *for* the Jews, but *through* the Jews, for the sake of the whole world.

Christian interpreters from the New Testament onward saw the church as the fulfillment of Israel. The idea that the doctrine of election could be applied to nations in the modern sense would have to await the creation of nations.[3] In the sixteenth century we find William Tyndale expounding on the idea that England, like Israel of old, stood in a special covenant relationship with God, a relationship that implied not just blessings but responsibilities, and severe punishment for shirking those responsibilities. Tyndale's commentaries that accompanied his English translation of the Bible identified covenant as the central theme of the biblical narrative. Tyndale's translation had a tremendous impact on the Puritans, who would colonize the New World. The other major influence was John Calvin, whose emphasis on election many Puritan leaders imbibed firsthand while in exile in Geneva. The Puritans also absorbed Calvin's ecclesiology, in which civil authority was an arm of the church.[4]

When the Puritans were harried out of England and migrated to the New World, they regarded their journey as an opportunity to reconsider the theme of covenant. Settling in a new land suggested a parallel with the Israelites leaving bondage in Egypt and claiming the Promised Land. In John Winthrop's writings, the theme of the covenant was pervasive. Still, the theme of judgment was prominent: status as God's chosen people meant not just blessing but responsibility. In Winthrop's famous exhortation aboard the *Arbella* in 1630, he used the prophet Amos (3:2) to connect chosenness with judgment: "So He tells the people of Israel, you only have I known of all the families of the earth, therefore will I punish you for your transgressions." Winthrop's famous evocation of the fledgling colony as a "city upon a hill" (from Matt. 5:14) was followed by a dire warning of God's wrath should the colony "deal falsely with our God." The elevated position of the city only exposed it to the greater scrutiny of God and the world. For this reason it was all the more important that civil and ecclesiastical governance be inseparable. In Winthrop's view, "the care of the public must oversway all private respects, by which, not only conscience, but mere civil policy, doth bind us."[5]

---

3. Adrian Hastings argues that the idea of Israel as a nation influenced nascent English nationalism as early as the high Middle Ages, but I tend to agree with critics who argue that what Hastings means by "nation" bears very little resemblance to the modern use of the term. Modern nationalism is only possible once the state makes sovereignty attainable. For Hastings' view, see his *The Construction of Nationhood: Ethnicity, Religion, and Nationalism* (Cambridge: Cambridge University Press, 1997).

4. Richard T. Hughes, *Myths America Lives By* (Urbana, IL: University of Illinois Press, 2003), pp. 19-26.

5. John Winthrop, "A Model of Christian Charity" (1630) at: http://religiousfreedom .lib.virginia.edu/sacred/charity.html.

As long as church and state were closely intertwined, the identification of the colony with a new Israel was less difficult to justify from biblical precedent. The church mediated between God and the civil authority. However, with the shift from Puritan theocracy to the disestablishment of the church in the First Amendment, the theme of the new Israel became an important one in nascent American nationalism. The relationship between God and America was increasingly direct. The church came to mediate, not between God and America, but between the individual and God and between the individual and America. The new Israel was identified not with any church or churches in their manifold diversity, but with America as such. Despite the significant differences between the Puritan narrative and Revolutionary ideals, the new nation found in the Puritan genealogy the only readily available myth for the genesis and destiny of America.[6] The primary difference is that the location of chosenness moved beyond the confines of ecclesiastical structures and embraced the new nation as a whole. America, as the new Israel, became itself a kind of metachurch. And thus was George Washington hailed as a new Moses.[7] Even such foes of organized religion as Thomas Paine could not resist the use of the Puritan genealogy to speak of America's chosen destiny.[8]

The theme of America as the new Israel took on increasing importance in the nineteenth century, though the tone and substance became increasingly different from that of the Puritan narrative. Consider Herman Melville's contention that "we Americans are the peculiar, chosen people — the Israel of our time." Melville links the biblical theme of election to the nineteenth-century theme of progress: "The Past is the text-book of tyrants; the Future the Bible of the free." Americans are "the pioneers of the world," says Melville, "the advance-guard sent on through the wilderness of untried things, to break a new path in the New World that is ours." The world will be blessed through this new Israel, but not through the fear of the Lord.

> Long enough have we been skeptics with regard to ourselves, and doubted whether, indeed, the political Messiah had come. But he has come in *us*, if we would but give utterance to his promptings. And let

---

6. Anders Stephanson, *Manifest Destiny: American Expansion and the Empire of Right* (New York: Hill and Wang, 1995), pp. 15-21.

7. Stephen H. Webb, *American Providence: A Nation with a Mission* (New York: Continuum, 2004), p. 34.

8. Stephanson, *Manifest Destiny*, p. 13.

us always remember that with ourselves, almost for the first time in the history of earth, national selfishness is unbounded philanthropy; for we cannot do a good to America, but we give alms to the world.[9]

Here we see a shift from a nation under God to a nation as God's incarnation on earth, the nation as Messiah. Once the relationship between God and America becomes direct and unmediated, the identification of America's will with God's becomes a readily present temptation. We can see in Melville's quote the blending of the biblical notion of election with American ideas of progress, expansion, and capitalism. Winthrop shades into Adam Smith, where the naked pursuit of self-interest works — by the "invisible hand" of divine providence, through the mechanism of the free market — for the benefit of all. As American expansionism accelerated in the late nineteenth century, it became increasingly common to wed biblical notions of providence to the progress of the world toward American-style democracy and free-market capitalism.[10]

The Empty Shrine

Melville's comments provide an apt transition point to another strand of American exceptionalism, which owes more to Enlightenment thought than to biblical precedents. This kind of exceptionalism is based not on the particularism of the election of Israel by the God of Abraham, Isaac, and Jacob, but in the universalism of certain concepts of freedom and right. In the Enlightenment narrative, the tragedy of religious violence can only be solved by a recognition of the indeterminable nature of the truth about God, at least on a public level. It is this recognition that has given

9. Herman Melville, *White Jacket, or, the World in a Man-of-War* (Evanston and Chicago: Northwestern University Press and Newberry Library, 1970), pp. 150-51.

10. Ernest Lee Tuveson, *Redeemer Nation: The Idea of America's Millennial Role* (Chicago: University of Chicago Press, 1968), pp. 153-65; see also Russel B. Nye, *This Almost Chosen People: Essays in the History of American Ideas* (East Lansing: Michigan State University Press, 1966), pp. 1-42. Max Weber's famous thesis about Protestantism and capitalism would draw a direct line from Puritan Calvinism to American capitalism. I think this thesis is suggestive, but it is not necessary for the purposes of my present argument. See Max Weber, *The Protestant Ethic and the Spirit of Capitalism*, trans. Talcott Parsons (New York: Charles Scribner's Sons, 1958).

priority to the freedom to worship the god of one's choice, or no god at all. The priority of freedom to the good becomes not just a political theme but an economic one as well. This priority of freedom is embodied in democracy and free markets, which hold the key to the happiness of all. The nation that is the vehicle of this hope for the world is exceptional, therefore, not because it was chosen by a particular act of the biblical God but because it is based in something prior and more universal, the freedom of the human will. The United States is not the successor to a past "chosen people," but is, as Colin Powell has said, the first "universal nation," the first to break the bonds of particularity.[11]

This kind of American exceptionalism is not necessarily anti-theological, but it refrains from using theological language out of respect for the human conscience. According to Michael Novak, words like "God," when used in an official capacity by the government, are "like pointers, which each person must define for himself. Their function is to protect the liberty of conscience of all, by using a symbol which transcends the power of the state and any other earthly power." A Christian will fill in the content of symbol with Christian doctrine; an atheist will fill it in with no content at all. What matters is that at the public heart of democratic capitalism there is an "empty shrine," swept clean out of reverence for the transcendent. According to Novak, the emptiness of the shrine is precisely what makes democratic capitalism universal, the key to the wealth and happiness of the nations.[12]

Novak's "empty shrine" is the theological corollary of the idea of "openness." Democracy and free markets are open insofar as they do not try to impose any preconceived goods, but allow the individual to embrace his or her own goods. Freedom is not a substantive good but a formal structure that maximizes the possibility of each person to realize his or her particular goods. What America has discovered, therefore, is not particular to America, but is the key to happiness and peace for the whole world. Nevertheless, as the first realization of this universal truth, America is exceptional and has the obligation to spread its blessings throughout the world — by peaceful means if possible, but by military means if necessary.

As Andrew Bacevich has shown, though "openness" has become a

11. Quoted in Bacevich, *American Empire*, p. 219.

12. Michael Novak, *The Spirit of Democratic Capitalism* (New York: Simon and Schuster, 1982), pp. 50-55.

buzzword for both Republicans and Democrats since the George H. W. Bush administration, the concept goes back to at least the nineteenth century. Openness has meant first and foremost the breaking down of all global barriers to free trade. Banker Charles Conant said this in 1898: "The United States shall assert their right to free markets in all the old countries which are being opened to the surplus resources of the capitalistic countries and thereby given the benefits of modern civilization."[13] The unique role of the United States in expanding the scope of freedom is highlighted here, but also highlighted are the benefits that openness will bring to the entire world. The kind of zeal that Christian missionaries were bringing to distant shores in the nineteenth century was matched by the zeal to bring freedom to the more dimly lit regions of the world, where darkness and savagery were said to reign. Today the flow of Christian missionaries from the United States to other parts of the world has largely abated, but missionary zeal for openness has not. As President George W. Bush's national security strategy expressed it, the United States will use its unique military and economic position not to press for unilateral advantage, but to "extend the peace by encouraging free and open societies on every continent."[14]

Besides a kind of secularized missionary zeal, the Enlightenment strand of American exceptionalism also has a kind of secularized version of providence, which tends to go by the name of "history." From Francis Fukuyama's famous thesis about the "end of history,"[15] to Bill Clinton's, Condoleezza Rice's, and George W. Bush's separate contentions that America has found itself on the "right side of history," a common narrative about the end of the Cold War is being told.[16] The collapse of the Soviet Union has rendered history's unmistakable verdict in favor of democracy and free markets. No viable alternative remains. And America is not simply one exemplar of such freedom; America is *the* vanguard of freedom, *the* force that contained communism and led the way for the rest of the world to follow. America is the destiny of the rest of the world, and thus it stands in an ambiguous position regarding history. On the one hand, history is larger than America; on the other hand, America is the driving force behind history. As Secretary of State Madeleine Albright

13. Quoted in Bacevich, *American Empire*, p. 55.

14. George W. Bush, "The National Security Strategy of the United States of America," September 2002, prologue.

15. Francis Fukuyama, "The End of History?" *National Interest* 16 (Summer 1989): 3-18.

16. Bacevich, *American Empire*, pp. 33, 34, 216, respectively.

said, "We have our own duty to be authors of history."[17] Given the emphasis on human freedom, America is not simply subject to history but is charged with making history come out right.

Although the Enlightenment version of American exceptionalism eschews explicitly theological language, it is not devoid of theological consequences. If God language has been banished in an attempt at modesty, to respect the free human conscience, the exceptionalist rhetoric and the godlike ambitions of America in history have not been tamed. Indeed, because we are the *most modest*, we stand out as the exception to history; because we are the *most open*, we have an obligation to share that openness with the rest of the world, and to use our power to overcome any barriers to openness. Nowhere is this paradox more apparent than in the realm of American military power. By some accounts, the United States spends more on its military than all the other nations of the world combined. The goal is what the Pentagon's *Joint Vision 2010* calls "Full Spectrum Dominance." According to William Cohen, former secretary of defense, "technology now gives the United States an opportunity that no other military has ever had: the ability to see through the fog of war."[18] In other words, omniscience and omnipotence are now within our grasp. This aspiration is expressed in the Pentagon code names for two recent military operations, "Infinite Reach" and "Infinite Justice." As General Tommy Franks has said, the new technology gives U.S. military commanders "the kind of Olympian perspective that Homer had given his gods."[19] The aspiration of America in its position as exception to the nations is to rise above history, to see and act as God sees and acts. We know what is good for everyone, and we have the power to enforce that vision anywhere in the world.

It would be easy to dismiss Franks's comments as a bit of hyperbole, or as merely metaphorical. No one really believes that the American nation-state or the military is a god. I think we would do well, however, to remember jurist Carl Schmitt's famous dictum about the modern state:

> All significant concepts of the modern theory of the state are secularized theological concepts not only because of their historical develop-

---

17. Quoted in Bacevich, *American Empire*, p. 33.

18. Quoted in Bacevich, *American Empire*, p. 133.

19. Quoted in Andrew J. Bacevich, *The New American Militarism: How Americans Are Seduced by War* (Oxford: Oxford University Press, 2005), p. 22.

ment — in which they were transferred from theology to the theory of the state, whereby, for example, the omnipotent God became the omnipotent lawgiver — but also because of their systematic structure, the recognition of which is necessary for a sociological consideration of these concepts.[20]

If we are to understand why the secularized Enlightenment version of American exceptionalism has not cured the idea of its missionary zeal and ambitions to direct history, we should attend to Schmitt, for whom state sovereignty is simply the taking over of the omnipotence and omniscience of God by the political authority. Secularization in Schmitt's sense is not the stripping away of the sacred from some profane remainder. Rather, the state takes over the theological underpinnings of the church, and casts them in terms that are only implicitly theological. Every political structure, according to Schmitt, is undergirded by a "metaphysical image" of the world.[21]

The deepest theological danger inherent in American exceptionalism, then, is that of the messiah nation that does not simply seek to follow God's will, but acts as a kind of substitute god on the stage of history. When the concept of chosenness becomes unmediated by the church and unmoored from the biblical narrative, the danger is that the nation will not only be substitute church but substitute god. When the shrine is emptied of the biblical God and replaced with a generic principle of transcendence, the danger is that we will not come to worship God but will worship our freedom to worship God. The empty shrine is surreptitiously filled. Our freedom itself becomes an idol, the one thing we will kill and die for. This would not surprise Emile Durkheim, for whom all religion is the collectivity's worship of itself. According to Durkheim, religion is the social group's way of representing itself to itself. All religion, in other words, is civil religion.[22] From a Christian theological point of view, this is true only of false religion. True religion is not self-worship but worship of the one true God. How one discerns the difference between true worship

20. Carl Schmitt, *Political Theology: Four Chapters on the Concept of Sovereignty*, trans. George Schwab (Cambridge, MA: MIT Press, 1985), p. 36.

21. Schmitt, *Political Theology*, p. 46.

22. Emile Durkheim, *The Elementary Forms of Religious Life*, trans. Joseph Ward Swain (New York: Free Press, 1963), p. 139.

and idolatry, however, is a matter that requires all the resources of a constitutive tradition and a church that is capable of making such judgments.

Evangelical Enlightenment

If the unmooring of American exceptionalism from its biblical origins has proven to be theologically hazardous, is the answer to reconnect them? According to Stephen H. Webb, the answer is yes. Webb has published the most significant recent theological defense of the idea of American exceptionalism in a book called *American Providence*. According to Webb, if Christians do not learn to read history theologically, they capitulate to the privatization of the biblical God. The secularized version of the Enlightenment has sapped our ability to read history providentially because the modern myth of freedom tells us that we, not God, are in charge of history. The doctrine of providence has taken on a bad odor because it seems to set God up in competition with human freedom.[23] For the biblical authors, on the other hand, God remains active in human history without thereby diminishing human freedom. We must recover the ability to read history as the Bible does, as the unfolding of God's purposes in history in the acts of humankind (pp. 1-9).

According to Webb, this biblical reading of history demands a kind of American exceptionalism. We must discern God's activity not in general but in specific events and specific places. And any reading of recent history must take account of the preponderant role that America has played on the world stage. "While Israel is the key to history, another nation has undeniably moved to the front pages of current affairs and will stay there for the foreseeable future" (pp. 7-8). Webb acknowledges that one should not baptize every American action (p. 8), nor should one think that America is the only nation through which God is working (p. 6). Nevertheless, "that America is doing more than any other nation to spread the kinds of political structures that can best prepare the globe for God's ultimate work of establishing the final kingdom is not theologically insignificant" (p. 8).

The kind of political structures to which Webb refers in this quote are those found in American-style democracy, along with their economic

---

23. Webb, *American Providence*, pp. 21-22. Hereafter, page references to this work will appear in parentheses in the text.

counterpart, the free market. Webb believes that the Christian evangelization of the world will be completed once the world is opened up to American-style freedoms. Webb thus blends biblical language with Enlightenment themes. He rejects the anticlerical French version of the Enlightenment, but embraces the Anglo-Saxon, Lockean version, which he claims was deeply theological (p. 78). Webb believes that the ultimate success of the Enlightenment project of human freedom is part of God's plan to open up the world to the choice of Jesus Christ. Therefore, Webb approves of what he calls George W. Bush's "Evangelical Enlightenment or enlightened Evangelicalism" — he also calls it "evangelical Kantianism" (p. 78).

> Speaking to an audience of Iraqi immigrants in Dearborn, Michigan, President Bush stated an Enlightenment ideal that was worthy of Immanuel Kant: "The desire for freedom is not the property of one culture. It is the universal hope of human beings in every culture." The president can speak with such confidence because he combines the Enlightenment heritage of optimistic humanism with the evangelical fervor of an altar call. (p. 78)

It is not clear here if evangelicalism provides any content — or just "fervor." Webb believes that democracy and free markets are ultimately a product of Christianity, specifically, "the great Protestant theme of freedom."[24] But that freedom is essentially an empty shrine: "there is no wizard behind all the glittering machinery of the new empire" (p. 112). This is good news, however, because it keeps us from repeating the mistakes of past empires. We have no "coherent social vision" to impose on others. "Our very respect for freedom, in other words, both fuels our overseas endeavors and inhibits us from developing the kind of ideology that could result in global domination" (p. 85). America is not a particular social vision but the universal form of freedom. According to Webb, "Everyone can be American while still maintaining something of their national identity" (p. 111). This does not mean that Webb embraces openness and freedom for its own sake. The ultimate purpose of spreading openness is to al-

---

24. Stephen H. Webb, "On the True Globalism and the False, or Why Christians Should Not Worry So Much about American Imperialism," in *Anxious about Empire: Theological Essays on the New Global Realities*, ed. Wes Avram (Grand Rapids: Brazos, 2004), p. 121; see also Webb, *American Providence*, p. 10.

low for the spread of the Christian gospel. "Forcing Muslim nations into democratic political orders can accomplish much good in the world, but it needs to be recognized that this goal is theological as well as political" (p. 139). By this, Webb does not mean that Muslims should be forcibly converted to Christianity. He means that they should be converted to American-style democracy — forcibly if necessary — so that Muslims may have the opportunity to freely choose Christianity. America is not the gospel, but is the vehicle that God has chosen to spread the gospel. American-style democracy provides the empty form for evangelization, but the Christian gospel provides the content.

Webb is certainly right that the doctrine of providence requires Christians to discern God's activity in history. The question is: With what criteria and by what authority are Christians to make such judgments? The danger in locating God's activity in America is that America itself becomes the criterion for locating God's activity in the world. The danger, in other words, is that the form/content relationship becomes inverted. The biblical narrative provides the form — God acts directly in history — without providing the content of that activity. The real content becomes the ideology of American-style democracy and free markets. The criterion for discerning God's activity in history is provided by America, and not by the actual content of the gospel. For Webb, the main criterion for reading current events providentially seems to be what is taking place on a grand scale on the stage of history. Although Webb acknowledges that success is not the only criterion of God's favor (p. 52), he repeatedly holds up the unique rise of America as evidence that God is working through America in a special way.

After the triumph of Western liberalism over communism, Webb says, "we have come to a point where history affords a pretty clear text" (p. 52). God has pretty clearly pronounced in favor of American-style democracy and free markets. Criteria derived from Jesus' activities in the Gospels are largely irrelevant. For example, Webb explicitly rejects the idea of reading history from the underside, that is, from the point of view of the poor majority of the world's population. "God moves nations by working through history, not against it. By definition, the poor are not effective agents of significant historical change" (p. 62). Gandhi had the backing of wealthy friends, and Martin Luther King's movement depended on the middle class. "The poor *are* agents of God's grace (as opposed to being agents of significant historical change) precisely because they are occasions for the nonpoor to open themselves to aiding others" (p. 62). Jesus' preference for the poor and the outcast has nothing to do with reading history. They end up as good moral lessons about individual charity — "charity works best on an individual level" (p. 64) — but charity cannot be the key to the way God is acting in history because it accomplishes nothing on a grand scale. Likewise, Jesus' nonviolence and death on a cross are peripheral to a providential reading of history. Martyrdom can be an individual decision. "Nation-states, however, cannot be founded on the principle of this willingness to die rather than to fight" (p. 159).

As a result of this unwillingness to read providence from the point of view of the cross, Webb does not leave much room for God's judgment to interfere with America's sense of mission. Although he acknowledges that providence is a dialectic of judgment and blessing (p. 25), he tends to dismiss attempts to apply judgment to specific cases of American conduct as "typical bromides of the left" (p. 73). Those who protested the Vietnam War were motivated by "an orgiastic embrace of excessive forms of behavior fueled by utopian political theory" (p. 26). The "leftist critique of globalism is a case of sour grapes." Contemporary European anti-Americanism is "a psychological disturbance along the lines of an obsession" (p. 110). Webb makes no serious attempt to deal with slavery, the genocide of the Indians, or any other inconvenient facts about American power. The problem is not merely that Webb reads American history and sees the glass as half full; the problem is that Webb's providential reading of history leans heavily toward the account told by the victors. If God works through "significant historical change," and the greatest agent of significant historical change on the contemporary scene is America, then America becomes itself the criterion for discerning God's action in the world. America strides godlike across the world stage, moving history forward. As Americans, it becomes our responsibility to make history come out right.

Reading history for signs of God's providential activity is an exercise that Christians must undertake as independently as possible from ideologies of both the right and the left. To do so as Christians requires an account of the church as that body that has the authority, by the power of the Holy Spirit, to discern God's activity in history. The church is itself, as the body of Christ, a significant locus of God's activity in history. The New Testament writers understood the church as the eschatological gathering of Israel, the historical body that mediates God's truth to the world. Unfortunately, Webb's account largely bypasses the church:

How God acts in history cannot be unrelated to the ways in which humans organize themselves to achieve their own ends. This approach suggests that God works in history not only through individuals but also through nation-states, if for no other reason than we are all political creatures, enacting our identities in families, communities, and nations. (p. 7)

Webb jumps from individuals to nation-states without considering the church as a locus of God's work in history. It is not that Webb has no church, but that the church simply cannot be a significant political presence in its own right. For example, Webb applauds René Girard's analysis of Jesus Christ as the divinely innocent victim who shows the way to a future without scapegoating and violence. The church, however, must not simply try to embody this activity of God in history.

If the church should try to embody this peace, it would become one institution among many, with its own enemies, and thus the church would become just another state. The church, in other words, even as it preaches peace, is in need of the balance of powers between nation-states in order to protect it and provide the space for its mission. Only God can bring scapegoating to an end; until then, states are necessary to keep enemies in check. (p. 161)

The violence of the nation-state can be seen as a locus of God's activity in history, but the church cannot try to embody the peace of Jesus Christ in history. God will make the peace of Jesus Christ actual, but only in some vague and distant future. In this view, America, not the church, is where we must look for God's activity in the here and now.

It is extremely significant, I think, that Webb ends his book *American Providence* with a chapter on — of all people — Carl Schmitt. Schmitt had tried to rescue democracy in the Weimar Republic by strengthening the hand of the government to act. His position led him within a few short years to become something of the official jurist of Hitler's government, until falling out of favor with the Nazi party in 1936.[25] Schmitt's brief flirtation with Nazism has not erased his influence, which in the United

---

25. Michael Hollerich, "Carl Schmitt," in *The Blackwell Companion to Political Theology*, ed. Peter Scott and William T. Cavanaugh (Oxford: Blackwell Publishers, 2004), pp. 108-9.

States has largely been channeled through Leo Strauss. Schmitt defined sovereignty as that power that decides on the exception. The mere proceduralism of liberal democracy was incapable of dealing with threats to state order. The sovereign cannot be subject to the law at all times, but must be given the power to rise above the law and decide in exceptional circumstances. Schmitt is useful because, according to Webb, the doctrine of providence requires the ability to discern and act decisively in concrete historical circumstances. For Schmitt, "the exception in jurisprudence is analogous to the miracle in theology."[26]

According to Webb, liberal proceduralism does not allow the intrusion of God into the political system, but absorbs the miraculous into itself (p. 162). Schmitt helps us to see both the necessity of the decisive political actor within American politics — Webb cites George W. Bush in the wake of the 9/11 attacks (p. 167) — and the necessity of America itself to act as global sovereign. "[W]ithout some kind of world religion, global management will have to work through the imposition of power rather than the quest for consensus" (p. 114). America must take its place as the decisive actor that channels the actions of God in the new world order.

"The specific political distinction to which political actions and motives can be reduced is that between friend and enemy," says Carl Schmitt.[27] Webb finds Schmitt's basic distinction useful because it helps to mark out a legitimate autonomy for the political realm. Only the state can decide who is friend and who is enemy, and only the state can decide whom to fight. This dynamic is what gives meaning to national politics. Unfortunately, says Webb, the church has tried to interject itself into this process. Webb echoes Schmitt's insistence that the state, not the church, determine what is or is not a just war.[28] According to Webb, "the problem is not that the church embraces peace but that the church wants to displace the political sphere with its legitimate determination of who is to count as the enemy" (p. 156). The church "wants to usurp the personal authority of the sovereign for the formal rule of law," which, in Webb's terms, is to ban God from direct intervention in history. The church preaches forgiveness, and this may have political application at times, but

26. Schmitt, *Political Theology*, pp. 5-15, 36.

27. Carl Schmitt, *The Concept of the Political*, trans. George Schwab (New Brunswick, NJ: Rutgers University Press, 1976), p. 26.

28. Hollerich, "Carl Schmitt," p. 118.

to dismiss the friend-enemy distinction is to abandon the doctrine of providence. "God's enemies are not necessarily our own, of course, but to be a friend of God is to seek out God's purposes in history, and those purposes are not unrelated to the struggle for freedom, a struggle that involves the tragic necessity of war" (p. 156).

Part of what Schmitt was trying to do was to retain the sense that political authority comes from God, and not from the people who act as God. The problem with democracy, according to Schmitt, is that God is made immanent: in a democracy the people absorbs the transcendent into itself. Schmitt cites with approval Tocqueville's observation that "in democratic thought the people hover above the entire political life of the state, just as God does above the world, as the cause and the end of all things."[29] Webb applauds Schmitt's diagnosis but chides him for subsuming the theological into the political, in effect identifying God with the state. According to Webb, the "outermost sphere" that makes possible all social relations is the kingdom of God, not the state. The kingdom of God, however, is not a political but an eschatological reality, "a theological discourse on violence that can, *no matter how far into the future,* trump the political" (p. 162; italics added). Webb also claims that Schmitt is right about democracy in general, but America is a "stunning exception" to the rule. Americans are democrats who do not reject a transcendent authority, but have translated it into the doctrine of God's providential guiding of America (pp. 163-64). Unlike Europeans, "Americans were never forced into thinking that they had to make a decision for either the state or the church" (p. 163).

In theory, then, Webb has managed to combine the two strands of American exceptionalism — the biblical and the Enlightenment — while avoiding the danger of reducing the Christian faith to mere civil religion, the self-worship of the collective. America's mission of spreading liberalism remains "under God." The violence of the state remains ultimately, "no matter how far into the future," subordinate to the kingdom of God. It may be, however, that Schmitt was more clear-eyed about the nature of the modern nation-state. For Schmitt, it is not enough to solve the question of the relationship of the spiritual and the political orders in the abstract. The real question is, Who decides? Schmitt cites Thomas Hobbes's discussion of the demand that state power be subordinate to a spiritual

---

29. Schmitt, *Political Theology,* p. 49.

power because the latter is of a higher order. Hobbes, says Schmitt, rejects all attempts to "substitute an abstractly valid order for a concrete sovereignty of the state."[30] For Hobbes, power attaches to persons, not to abstract orders such as a "spiritual power," or, we may add, the "kingdom of God." The real question is, Who must obey whom? For Schmitt, as for Hobbes, there can be no doubt: the state has the whole power to decide in matters of politics and matters of war.

Schmitt utterly rejects Bellarmine's idea that the church possesses an "indirect power" in temporal matters. For Schmitt, the decision for either the state or the church at the political level is unavoidable, and America is not an exception. To act decisively in a way that realizes transcendent — and not merely immanent — authority, the modern state must be unitary. Providential action requires the overcoming of what Schmitt calls the "typically Judeo-Christian splitting of the original political unity."[31] As Michael Hollerich observes, Schmitt's words about Hobbes apply equally to himself: Hobbes's absorption of the church into the state has the intention of "rendering harmless the effect of Christ in the social and political sphere; of de-anarchizing Christianity, while leaving it in the background a certain legitimating function."[32]

In order for these words not to apply to Webb's American exceptionalism as well, he will have to ensure that the church provide something more than a legitimating function for civil religion. The danger in this kind of exceptionalism is that of idolatry: the state, which represents both the will of God and the will of the people, will come to identify the two. Webb believes that America has avoided this danger. America is the exception, since belief in the biblical God is still strong here. The problem, in my view, is that the political presence of the biblical God is mediated through the official discourse of America, and not through a distinctively Christian body that stands under the explicit authority of Jesus Christ. The church as mediator between God and America — a church that has the critical distance to pronounce judgment as well as blessing — is in danger of being erased. What has happened in effect is that America has become the new church. When the relationship of America and God is thus direct, there is little to check the identification of God's will with

---

30. Schmitt, *Political Theology*, p. 33.
31. Carl Schmitt, quoted in Hollerich, "Carl Schmitt," p. 118.
32. Hollerich, "Carl Schmitt," p. 119.

America's. America is God's people, the bearer of God's salvation to the world. The "typically Judeo-Christian splitting of the original political unity" into what St. Augustine called the "two cities," the *civitas terrena* and the *civitas dei*, has been absorbed into the omnipotent modern nation-state. Without the irritant of the body of Christ, the body politic is free once again to divinize the political authority, to transfer the sovereignty of God to the sovereign state.

Israel and the Church

What does the "typically Judeo-Christian splitting" of the political order entail? It means first that Israel's election calls a body that does not fit neatly into any existing political order, because obedience to God trumps all other kinds of obedience. God has elected Israel, and not any nation-state, to be the primary agent of God's activity in history. The election of Israel is the primary datum of the biblical theology of providence. Furthermore, Israel is not a nation-state in any modern sense. Israel's experience of what might be called statehood was relatively brief, between David and the conquests by the Assyrians and Babylonians. Israel's prior experience as a tribal confederation, and subsequent experiences as a Temple community and as a federation of synagogues, show that the nation-state is not by any means the most determinative analogue for Israel.[33] Israel is a people, one that stands in a unique relationship to all the nations of the earth, because of its covenant with the God of Abraham, Isaac, and Jacob.

In the Christian theological tradition, the fulfillment of Israel is not any nation-state, but the church. The New Testament church understood itself as the eschatological fulfillment of the gathering of Israel, consummated in the atoning death and resurrection of Jesus Christ. The letter of James addresses Christians as the "twelve tribes in the Dispersion" (James 1:1). Following the ascension of Jesus, the early church found it necessary to choose a replacement for Judas, so that the sign value of the twelve disciples, representing the twelve tribes of Israel, would be maintained (Acts 1:15-26). The New Testament word translated "church" is *ekklesia*, a term

---

33. Gerhard Lohfink, *Does God Need the Church? Toward a Theology of the People of God,* trans. Linda M. Maloney (Collegeville, MN: Liturgical Press, 1999), pp. 106-20.

used in Greek city-states meaning a public assembly of the political community. In the Septuagint, the Scripture of the New Testament authors, *ekklesia* had been used to translate the Hebrew *qahal*, the assembly of Israel before YHWH. The use of the same term for the church indicates a theology of continuity between the church and Israel. Another New Testament term related to *ekklesia* is *tois hagiois*, "the saints" (Acts 9:13; Rom. 15:25), a term used since Daniel 7 to refer to the eschatological people of God.[34] First Peter 2:9 has no qualms about applying other terms used of Israel — "a chosen race, a royal priesthood, a holy nation, God's own people" (Exod. 19:6) — to the church.

The theme of the church as Israel is especially important for understanding Paul. Galatians 6:15-16 presents a summary of Paul's position on the relationship between Jews and Gentiles: "For neither circumcision nor uncircumcision is anything; but a new creation is everything! As for those who will follow this rule — peace be upon them, and mercy, and upon the Israel of God." Here the "Israel of God" refers to the church, both Jewish and Gentile believers in Christ, that is, all those who follow the "rule" of the new creation, for whom circumcision or uncircumcision means nothing. This passage is an expansion of what Paul argues in Galatians 3. For Paul, all who believe in Christ are now the heirs of those chosen in Abraham's election. "Those who believe are the descendants of Abraham. And the scripture, foreseeing that God would justify the Gentiles by faith, declared the gospel beforehand to Abraham, saying 'All the Gentiles shall be blessed in you'" (Gal. 3:7-8). The heirs of Israel are no longer determined by blood but by faith in Jesus Christ. Therefore, "if you belong to Christ, then you are Abraham's offspring, heirs according to the promise" (Gal. 3:29). This accords well with Jesus' saying in Matthew 3:9: "Do not presume to say to yourselves, 'We have Abraham as our ancestor'; for I tell you, God is able from these stones to raise up children to Abraham."

Paul does not believe that Israel had been cast off or replaced by the church. According to Paul's image in Romans 9–11, the branches that had been cut off the root of Israel could be grafted back on. The church is to remain open to Israel, for the eschatological goal is the gathering of the whole of Israel. The nonbelieving Jews are not rejected (Rom. 11:1), but will once again be restored to Israel (Rom. 11:26-27). In the meantime, the be-

---

34. Gerhard Lohfink, *Jesus and Community: The Social Dimension of Christian Faith*, trans. John P. Galvin (Philadelphia and New York: Fortress and Paulist, 1984), pp. 76-77.

lievers in Christ are warned not to boast, for they, too, can be cut off again from Israel, on which they were grafted by the mercy of God (11:17-22).

In Pauline theology, the church, as the body of Christ, reconciles all peoples, regardless of nationality:

> For he is our peace; in his flesh he has made both groups [Jews and Gentiles] into one and has broken down the dividing wall, that is, the hostility between us. He has abolished the law with its commandments and ordinances, that he might create in himself one new humanity in place of the two, thus making peace, and might reconcile both groups to God in one body through the cross, thus putting to death that hostility through it. (Eph. 2:14-16)

Membership in the body of Christ thus creates a new kind of citizenship: "So then you are no longer strangers and aliens, but you are citizens with the saints and also members of the household of God" (Eph. 2:19). According to N. T. Wright, Paul's polemic in Galatians, Romans, and throughout his epistles is not against "works righteousness" but "national righteousness," the belief that fleshly Jewish descent guarantees membership in God's covenant people. For Paul, membership in Israel is broken open and extended to all people worldwide through faith in Christ.[35] The body of Christ is a truly transnational body that does not fit easily within any unitary political order. Wright, Richard Horsley, Dieter Georgi, Neil Elliott, and other major Pauline scholars have argued that Paul's view of the church has deeply political overtones, for it cuts across allegiance to any earthly kingdom or empire.[36] As Wright says, Paul's missionary work

> implies a high and strong ecclesiology in which the scattered and often muddled cells of women, men, and children loyal to Jesus as Lord form colonial outposts of the empire that is to be: subversive little groups when seen from Caesar's point of view, but when seen Jewishly an advance foretaste of the time when the earth shall be filled with the glory of the God of Abraham and the nations will join Israel

---

35. N. T. Wright, "The Paul of History and the Apostle of Faith," *Tyndale Bulletin* 29 (1978): 61-88.

36. See, e.g., the essays by these authors and others in *Paul and Empire: Religion and Power in Roman Imperial Society,* ed. Richard A. Horsley (Harrisburg, PA: Trinity International Press, 1997).

in singing God's praises (cf. Rom. 15:7-13). From this point of view, therefore, this counterempire can never be merely critical, never merely subversive. It claims to be the reality of which Caesar's empire is the parody; it claims to be modeling the genuine humanness, not least the justice and peace, and the unity across traditional racial and cultural barriers, of which Caesar's empire boasted.[37]

After the conversion of the emperor Constantine to Christianity in the fourth century, the position of the church changed from one of subversion to one of privilege. What did not change, however, is the "typical Judeo-Christian splitting" of unitary political authority. Constant conflicts between the church and the civil authority over temporal rule would not subside until the rise of the unitary sovereign state in the modern era. As Schmitt testified, the church would retain an awkward and uncomfortable presence in the political world into the twentieth century.

Conclusion

I hope to have said enough to indicate why American exceptionalism is problematic from a Christian theological point of view. When the relationship between God and America becomes unmediated — either in its explicitly or implicitly theological form — the temptation to civil religion and the divinization of the state becomes difficult to resist. The presence of the church as discerning community is necessary to test loyalty to any nation-state against loyalty to God — not the generic god of civil religion, but the God of Jesus Christ. We need the church to perform its crucial role of judging the powers of this earth by the standards of Christ and his gospel, lest God's will and America's will come to be identified as one.

---

37. N. T. Wright, "Paul's Gospel and Caesar's Empire," in *Paul and Politics: Ekklesia, Israel, Imperium, Interpretation,* ed. Richard A. Horsley (Harrisburg, PA: Trinity Press International, 2000), pp. 182-83.

Chapter Five

How to Do Penance for the Inquisition

—◈—

As a Catholic theologian who has written on the subject of torture, I often face the question of the Inquisition when giving lectures on torture in the modern world. The question often comes in the form of a semi-accusation: "How can you criticize the United States for using torture when the Catholic Church has such a history of torture — you know, the Inquisition and all that?" Behind the question seems to lurk a whole range of common perceptions about Catholicism, medieval society, and about torture itself. Catholicism seems especially identified with the past, with a medieval culture in which no aspect of life was untouched by Christianity, in which, in other words, there was no independent "secular" realm. Medieval society, in turn, is identified with a "Dark Ages," a time of ignorance and superstition in which corporal punishment and torture seem to have found a natural home. It was a time when focus on the sufferings of Christ bled inevitably into such "gothic" excesses as self-flagellation and the Inquisition.

Torture itself, therefore, tends to be identified with the past. When revelations of Abu Ghraib, Guantánamo, and "extraordinary rendition" put torture on the front page, commentators often use the adjective "medieval" to condemn the torture to which the United States, its friends, and its foes resort in the present day. When torture appears in the modern world, it is often seen as an atavism, a relic from the past that belongs properly to the days when Catholicism was inescapable and sadistic cardinal inquisitors extracted confessions from heretics on the rack. Therefore, the solution to torture is thought to be more modernity, more faith in enlightened progress, and greater reinforcement of the boundary between the secular public realm and the dark passions of the religious soul.

The idea that the medieval period was one long witch-hunt, and that torture was the preferred instrument of ecclesiastical discipline, has little purchase with scholars of the period. As Brad Gregory points out, the burning of a man in Orléans in 1022 was the first recorded execution for heresy in Europe in six hundred years.[1] The Inquisition proper was a twelfth-century innovation that used torture in cases of heresy much more sparingly than did civil courts in cases of robbery and forgery. The Inquisition almost never used torture as a punishment, as civil judges often did. Even at its most severe, in its Spanish version, torture was rare; it was largely confined to the first two decades after the establishment of the Spanish Inquisition in 1478. The scholarly consensus holds that the Black Legend propagated by Spain's English and Dutch Protestant enemies beginning in the sixteenth century greatly exaggerated the extent and severity of the Inquisition.[2] Nevertheless, there is no denying that the Catholic Church did sanction the use of torture in the past. The Inquisition is one of the many sins of the church for which Catholics should do penance.

What is most interesting about the popular tale of the Spanish Inquisition, however, is not what it says about the past but what it says about the present. Why is the Black Legend of the Spanish Inquisition so well known among those who may otherwise know very little about the actual history of medieval or early modern Europe? The Black Legend of the Inquisition is part of a larger Enlightenment narrative that celebrates modernity and its institutions as darkness overcome. The Black Legend is so popular because it is a reassuring tale for us in the modern West. It sets up a temporal dichotomy between the past and the present and assures us that we have left barbarism behind. It is a wonderfully progressive story in which we tell ourselves that the present is better than the past. This gives us hope that the future will be better than the present. If leftovers like tor-

---

1. Brad S. Gregory, *Salvation at Stake: Christian Martyrdom in Early Modern Europe* (Cambridge, MA: Harvard University Press, 2001), p. 31.

2. For an analysis of the historical distortions produced by the "Black Legend" of the Inquistion, see Edward M. Peters, *Inquisition* (New York: Free Press, 1988).

ture remain from the past, they are doomed to fall before the progressive forces of reason, liberty, and secularization.

Accompanying the temporal dichotomy is a spatial dichotomy between *us* in the West and *them*, the less enlightened peoples of the world. The spatial dichotomy tracks the temporal dichotomy because *they* are thought to be backward, resistant to modernity and to progress. The primary *they* in this dichotomy today is the Muslim community. Commentators frequently refer to aspects of Muslim culture or behaviors as "medieval." The principal way in which they differ from us is in their stubborn refusal to secularize, that is, to make a prudent distinction and separation of the Muslim "religion" from politics and the public square. They insist — like medieval Christians — on allowing their religion to intrude on every aspect of public life, and the result can only be the perpetual interruption of the rational by the irrational, the infringement of liberty by hidebound tradition, and the confusion of the discipline of the soul with the discipline of the body.

This dichotomy is typified by Samuel Huntington's famous thesis of a "clash of civilizations" between the West and the Muslim world. This thesis was first put forward by Bernard Lewis in an article entitled "The Roots of Muslim Rage": "It should by now be clear that we are facing a mood and a movement far transcending the level of issues and policies and the governments that pursue them. This is no less than a clash of civilizations — the perhaps irrational but surely historic reactions of an ancient rival against our Judeo-Christian heritage, our secular present, and the worldwide expansion of both."[3] Lewis identifies the West as a monolithic reality identified with reason, secularization, and modernity, and the Muslim world as an equally monolithic reality that is irrational, religious, and antimodern.

We may rightly cherish the advances of the modern era that put an end to the Inquisition. What disturbs me about the triumphal tale of modernity, however, is the possibility that, ironically, the dichotomies I have described establish the conditions under which torture can take place in the modern world. The clash of the West versus barbarism has a tendency to create stereotyped enemies. If the enemies in this clash are essentially

3. Bernard Lewis, "The Roots of Muslim Rage," *Atlantic Monthly*, September 1990, p. 13. The page number refers to the online version: http://www.theatlantic.com/doc/print/199009/muslim-rage.

irrational, then they cannot be reasoned with, but only dealt with by force. The "othering" of the enemy is on plain display in the Abu Ghraib photos. Chained to cages, hooded, covered with excrement, attached to electrodes, dragged around on leashes, stacked naked, the prisoners — who the Schlesinger Report admitted were not even intelligence targets — were made to play the part of the subrational "others" that they occupy in the popular Western imagination. What General Fay in his report on Abu Ghraib called the "escalating 'de-humanization' of the detainees" is an essential precondition for the practice of torture.

The recent debate over the use and justification of torture by the U.S. government displays a dual aspect. On the one hand, we claim that we do not torture; on the other hand, we imply that we must. Official discourse repudiates torture as archaic, barbaric, opposed to the reason and liberty and modernity for which the United States stands. At the same time, Bush administration attempts to broaden the definition of torture and circumvent the McCain anti-torture bill imply that — precisely as the standard bearer of liberty in the fight against a subhuman, demonic enemy — our hands must not be tied in using "enhanced interrogation techniques," as the euphemism would have it. Both attitudes toward torture — that we don't and yet that we must — stem from the American exceptionalism I discussed in the preceding chapter: the idea that the United States has a messianic role to play in assuring that history moves forward against the enemies of progress, liberty, and reason.

In important ways, the United States has not really secularized at all. What has happened instead is that in the modern era the holy has migrated from the church to the state.[4] By this I do not mean that Christian evangelicals have an inordinate influence in the current administration. I mean that faith in the United States and in "secular" Western values can take on the status of a religious conviction, and the United States has assembled the largest military in history to propagate it. The clash of civilizations is a crusade from both directions. As Emran Qureshi and Michael Sells put it, "those who proclaim such a clash of civilizations, speaking for the West or for Islam, exhibit the characteristics of fundamentalism: the assumption of a static essence, knowable immediately, of each civilization, the ability to ignore history and tradi-

---

4. John Bossy, *Christianity in the West, 1400-1700* (Oxford: Oxford University Press, 1985), pp. 153-71.

tion, and the desire to lead the ideological battle on behalf of one of the clashing civilizations."[5]

Torture, in reality, does not belong to the past, nor is it confined to subrational, antimodern, religious non-Westerners. As much as Americans prefer to believe that the torture unmasked in recent revelations is aberrant, the work of a few "bad apples," the truth is that the United States has been actively involved in torture through proxies for decades — in Vietnam, the Shah's Iran, Egypt, Saudi Arabia, Israel, and throughout Latin America. The temporal and spatial dichotomies exemplified in the Black Legend of the Inquisition reassure us that we are essentially different from our enemies, and that we would never resort to such barbarism. But the truth is that we can only guard against the resort to torture by abjuring such absolute dichotomies between *us* and *them*.

Torture is a part of the Christian past. From a Catholic point of view, the church does indeed have penance to do for the Inquisition. But how? I propose that the way to do penance for the Inquisition is to speak out and resist torture as it is practiced now. The examination of conscience that would precede such penance would require rejection of the many ways that we try to distance ourselves from realization of our own sins. Chief among these in this case is the attempt to put distance between ourselves and torture by relegating it to the past or to the remote "other." Confession of our sin would require not simply the admission that torture has been done in our name, but the confession that only God is God, and not any nation-state that claims to save us from evil. Christians worship a God who was tortured to death by the empire; it is this God who saves by saying no to violence on the cross. Our penance, then, would take the form of resisting the idolatry of nation and state and its attendant violence. Catholicism should be particularly equipped for this, since it is a worldwide church that transgresses the artificial boundaries of all nation-states. Having popes who are Italian, Polish, German, and so on should be a salutary reminder that the sisterhood and brotherhood of humanity that we celebrate takes priority over national borders. We should be able to reach beyond the "clash of civilizations" to establish real dialogue among distant neighbors of all faiths. Our penance should involve speaking out against

5. "Introduction: Constructing the Muslim Enemy," in *The New Crusades: Constructing the Muslim Enemy*, ed. Emran Qureshi and Michael A. Sells (New York: Columbia University Press, 2003), pp. 28-29.

torture — in the classrooms and in the streets. Our penance should also involve the refusal to fight unjust wars and to use unjust means within those wars.

Torture is not just a relic of the past. It has emerged as a tool of state that will claim a place as long as the "War on Terror" divides the world between us and them. We should of course denounce terrorism in all its forms. But in doing so we should not demonize others, and thereby create new Inquisitions of our own.

CHAPTER SIX

The Liturgies of Church and State

—◦◦◦◦—

Today the most significant misunderstanding of the Christian liturgy is that it is sacred. Let me clarify. The problem is that "sacred" has been opposed to "secular," and the two are presumed to describe two separate — but occasionally related — orbits. The problem is not simply that this separation leaves the church's liturgy begging for relevance to the "real world." The problem is, further, that the supposedly "secular" world invents its own liturgies, with pretensions every bit as "sacred" as those of the Christian liturgy, and these liturgies can come to rival the church's liturgy for our bodies and our minds. In this chapter I want to briefly explore some particulars of the liturgies of the American nation-state. I will suggest, first, that such liturgies are not properly called "secular," and second, that the Christian liturgy is not properly cordoned off into the realm of the "sacred."

National Liturgy Is Not Secular

We are accustomed to speaking of "civil religion," but we are less accustomed to speaking of a national "liturgy," even though the original meaning of the word *leitourgia* is simply "an action by which a group of people become something corporately which they had not been as a mere collection of individuals."[1] Central to liturgy are ritual language and gesture, "memory-inducing behavior that has the effect of preserving what is indispensable to the group."[2] In a basic sense, liturgy enacts and maintains community by the ritual remembering or re-presentation of foundational narratives, thereby helping to construct the perceived reality in which each member of the community lives. In this general sense, then, it is not difficult to see why commentators point to the "liturgical" nature of patriotic rituals that reinforce American group identity and an American view of the world.

There is general agreement that we live in an unliturgical age, and in many ways that is true. The rites and customs that structured the hours, days, and seasons of traditional societies have largely faded in the face of Western individual freedoms. Where this generalization does not apply, however, as Eric Hobsbawm points out, is in the public life of the citizen. Here modern societies are every bit as "liturgical" as traditional ones. "Indeed most of the occasions when people become conscious of citizenship as such remain associated with symbols and semi-ritual practices (for instance, elections), most of which are historically novel and largely invented: flags, images, ceremonies and music."[3] Rituals that many assume to be ancient are in fact the product of the late nineteenth and early twentieth centuries, when rituals were invented in Europe and the United States to stoke a nascent sense of exclusive national loyalty, supplanting previously diffuse loyalties owed to region, ethnic group, class, and church. In time such rituals would become not simply expressions of a deeper reality but constitutive of reality. We would come to judge events by how well they conformed to the enacted myths of patriotic ritual. As Carolyn Marvin and David Ingle say of the American myth, "our criteria for judging and remembering history are liturgical."[4]

For anyone familiar with Benedict Anderson's famous definition of a nation as an "imagined political community," this should come as no sur-

1. Alexander Schmemann, *For the Life of the World* (Crestwood, NY: St. Vladimir's Seminary Press, 1988), p. 25.

2. Carolyn Marvin and David W. Ingle, *Blood Sacrifice and the Nation: Totem Rituals and the American Flag* (Cambridge: Cambridge University Press, 1999), p. 129.

3. Eric Hobsbawm, "Introduction: Inventing Traditions," in *The Invention of Tradition*, ed. Eric Hobsbawm and Terence Ranger (Cambridge: Cambridge University Press, 1983), p. 12.

4. Marvin and Ingle, *Blood Sacrifice*, p. 155.

prise. According to Anderson, "it is *imagined* because the members of even the smallest nation will never know most of their fellow-members, meet them, or even hear of them, yet in the minds of each lives the image of their communion."[5] Anderson shows how texts such as daily newspapers helped create a sense of communion among the scattered people of emergent nations. For Anderson, the fact that the nation is imagined does not imply that it is unreal, or somehow false. People do extraordinary things in the real world — most remarkably kill and die in war — because they imagine themselves as participating in the enacted drama of the nation. There is a close affinity to the liturgy here, for the liturgy is a passage into imagining the world in a certain way. As Alexander Schmemann says, liturgy is "the journey of the Church into the dimension of the Kingdom" such that "our *entrance* into the presence of Christ is an entrance into a fourth dimension which allows us to see the ultimate reality of life."[6] The community called forth in the liturgy is an imagined community, just as the nation is. As the Letter to the Hebrews says, those who approach the altar approach much more than meets the eye:

> You have not come to something that can be touched. . . . But you have come to Mount Zion and to the city of the living God, the heavenly Jerusalem, and to innumerable angels in festive gathering, and to the assembly of the firstborn who are enrolled in heaven, and to God the judge of all, and to the spirits of the righteous made perfect, and to Jesus, the mediator of a new covenant, and to the sprinkled blood that speaks a better word than the blood of Abel. (Heb. 12:18, 22-24)

If the nation and the church were merely parallel instances of communities imagined by ritual action, they would not necessarily challenge the division of labor between the sacred and the secular. In fact, however, the nation competes with the church on the same "religious" grounds. For as Anderson points out, the nation in Western civilization in many ways replaces the church in its role as the primary cultural institution that deals with death. According to Anderson, Christianity's decline in the West necessitated another way of dealing with the arbitrariness of death. Nations

---

5. Benedict Anderson, *Imagined Communities: Reflections on the Origin and Spread of Nationalism*, rev. ed. (London: Verso, 1991), p. 6.

6. Schmemann, *For the Life of the World*, pp. 26-27.

provide a new kind of salvation: my death is not in vain if it is for the nation, which lives on into a limitless future.[7]

According to Marvin and Ingle, the sacrifice of life on behalf of the nation not only gives death meaning; it is, in fact, the very glue that holds the social order together.

> Americans generally see their nation as a secular culture possessed of few myths, or with weak myths everywhere, but none central and organizing. We see American nationalism as a ritual system organized around a core myth of violently sacrificed divinity manifest in the highest patriotic ceremony and the most accessible popular culture.[8]

For Marvin and Ingle, death in war — what is commonly called the "ultimate sacrifice" for the nation — is what periodically re-presents the sense of belonging on which the imagined nation is built. Such death is then elaborately ceremonialized in liturgies involving the flag and other ritual objects. Indeed, it is the ritual itself that retrospectively classifies any particular act of violence as *sacrifice*.[9] Ritual gesture and language are crucial for establishing meaning and public assent to the foundational story being told. The foundational story is one of both creation and salvation. At the ceremonies marking the fiftieth anniversary of D-Day in 1994, for example, President Clinton remarked of the soldiers that died on that day both that "they gave us our world" and that "they saved the world."[10]

Whether one accepts Anderson's more textually based account or Marvin and Ingle's more bodily and bloody thesis, it is not difficult to see that national ritual is not adequately categorized as "secular." Carlton Hayes has written:

> Curious liturgical forms have been devised for "saluting" the flag, for "dipping" the flag, for "lowering" the flag, and for "hoisting" the flag. Men bare their heads when the flag passes by; and in praise of the flag poets write odes and children sing hymns. In America young people are ranged in serried rows and required to recite daily, with hiero-

---

7. Anderson, *Imagined Communities*, pp. 9-12.
8. Marvin and Ingle, *Blood Sacrifice*, p. 3.
9. Marvin and Ingle, *Blood Sacrifice*, p. 136.
10. Bill Clinton, quoted in Marvin and Ingle, *Blood Sacrifice*, pp. 138, 140.

phantic voice and ritualistic gesture, the mystical formula: "I pledge allegiance to the flag and to the country for which it stands, one nation, indivisible, with liberty and justice for all." Everywhere, in all solemn feasts and fasts of nationalism the flag is in evidence, and with it that other sacred thing, the national anthem.[11]

Francis Bellamy, author of the Pledge of Allegiance, commented on how the pledge was meant to sink in with schoolchildren through ritual repetition. He added, "It is the same way with the catechism, or the Lord's Prayer."[12] Examples could be multiplied. Even the late Chief Justice William Rehnquist acknowledged, in supporting a proposed amendment against "desecration" of the flag, that the flag is regarded by Americans "with an almost mystical reverence."[13]

Here the word "almost" is crucial, for American civil religion can never acknowledge that it is in fact religion: to do so would be to invite charges of idolatry. Here liturgical gesture is central, because gesture allows the flag to be treated as a sacred object, while language denies that that is the case. Everyone acknowledges verbally that the nation and the flag are not *really* gods, but the crucial test is what people do with their bodies, both in liturgy and in war. It is clear that, among those who identify themselves as Christians in the United States and other countries, there are very few who would be willing to kill in the name of the Christian God, whereas the willingness, under certain circumstances, to kill and die for the nation in war is generally taken for granted.

Christian Liturgy Is Not Sacred

Christian liturgy knows no distinction between sacred and secular, spiritual and material. To participate in the liturgy is to bless God as God blessed all of material creation, to respond to God's blessing by blessing God. Schmemann puts it this way: "In the Bible to bless God is not a 'religious' or a 'cultic' act, but the very *way of life*." As such, liturgy is the *natural*

11. Carlton Hayes, *Essays on Nationalism* (New York: Macmillan, 1926), p. 107.
12. Francis Bellamy, quoted in Cecilia O'Leary, *To Die For: The Paradox of American Patriotism* (Princeton: Princeton University Press, 1999), p. 178.
13. William Rehnquist, quoted in Marvin and Ingle, *Blood Sacrifice*, p. 30.

(not simply *supernatural*) act of humanity, to imagine the world as God sees it, and to return the world to God in praise. All of creation is "material for the one all-embracing eucharist," at which humanity presides as priest. It is only because of our fallen condition that it seems natural *not* to live eucharistically, to accept the reduction of God and God's blessing to a small reservation of life called "sacred."[14]

When this happens, what remains outside the sacred is not simply the "secular" or the "natural" — stripped of God, disenchanted, and functioning on merely material principles. For the Bible does not know the material as some self-sufficient substrate upon which is overlaid the spiritual. There is no such thing as "pure nature" devoid of grace. There is, of course, the denial of grace. But what remains when humans attempt to clear a space of God's presence is not a disenchanted world but a world full of idols. Humans remain naturally worshiping creatures, and the need for liturgy remains a motivating force, as we have seen, in a supposedly "secular" space. Christ came not to start a new religion but to break down the barrier between human life and God. To be redeemed from our fallen condition, therefore, means to resist the imagination that would bifurcate the world into sacred and secular. Casting away this division also means seeing that Christian liturgy and the liturgies of the world compete on the same playing field, as it were, and that a choice between them must be made.

There is a sense in which the Christian liturgy can properly be called "sacred," insofar as it facilitates the very presence of God, who is absolutely other than creation. Indeed, as the book of Hebrews makes clear, the liturgy is an ascension to heaven and therefore a separation from the world as it is. But the church does not simply forget the world but remembers it to God, offers it to God in the hope that God will transform it and we will partake in the world to come. Schmemann says: "This is not an 'other' world, different from the one God has created and given to us. It is our same world, *already* perfected in Christ, but *not yet* in us."[15] In ascending we are able to gain enough height, as it were, to see the world as a whole. In the liturgy we are able to see the world, to *imagine* it as it really is, which is to say, as it will be and already is in the eyes of God. This is why the Eucharist is understood as the eschatological anticipation of the heavenly banquet.

14. Schmemann, *For the Life of the World*, pp. 15-16.
15. Schmemann, *For the Life of the World*, p. 42 (italics in original).

The Christian liturgy unfolds a different imagination of space and time than do the liturgies of the nation. With regard to space, the liturgies of nationalism truncate the imagined community at the borders of the nation-state; one's fellow citizens are other Americans or French or Chinese. The nationalist seeks to exempt his or her nation from being bound by transnational bodies or statutes, thus establishing a permanent "state of nature" between and among nation-states. The Christian liturgy, by contrast, transgresses the borders of the nation-state and of the world through the participation of the worshiper in the transnational body of Christ both on earth and in heaven. In the liturgy, the imagined community exempts no one in principle, and stretches even to our fellow citizens in heaven (Phil. 3:20).

The conceptions of time are different as well. Patriotic liturgies are cyclical, constantly establishing the present reality by reference to past sacrifice that has triumphed over chaos. The present tries to re-present a link with the founding sacrifices through ritual. As Marvin and Ingle argue, however, this process is inherently anxiety-producing, since the present ritual can never really reproduce the bodily sacrifice on which it is based. Thus, D-Day celebrations were marked by guilt that the present generation is merely living off the sacrifices of those who died there. There is a fear that the "greatest generation" has passed and that the current generation has not undertaken sacrifices to equal those in the "Good War." Therefore, what is needed is a return to the original sacrifice, kicking the "Vietnam Syndrome," and new good wars to unite the country. "This is how the totem order regenerates itself, by endlessly seeking to close the gap between present bodies and the blood history that engenders them."[16]

Ritual enacts our debt to the past, which we cannot pay via ritual, but only via fresh sacrifice. In contrast, the Christian liturgy is not merely cyclical but points forward to the eschatological consummation of history in which violence and division are overcome. The Eucharist is the re-presentation of Christ's foundational sacrifice, but it does not resacrifice Christ, nor is new blood sacrifice demanded of us, for as Hebrews makes plain, Christ died "once and for all" (Heb. 7:27; 9:12; 10:10). Furthermore, there is no gap between ritual and reality, because Christ is really and fully present in the Eucharist. Thus we approach the altar, not marked with guilt but "with a true heart in full assurance of faith" (Heb. 10:22), for the

---

16. Marvin and Ingle, *Blood Sacrifice*, p. 136.

altar we approach is not bound by a bloody past, but is a foretaste of a perfect future. The Eucharist is, in John Zizioulas's fitting phrase, the "memory of the future."[17]

All of this sounds wonderful, but we must confess that it is the shriveling of this vision within the church that has allowed the flourishing of ersatz realities. There is a longing in nationalist ritual that bespeaks a desire for communion that is at the heart of Christian liturgy. Patriotic liturgies have succeeded in imagining communities because Christian liturgies have failed to do so in a fully public way. As the church expanded after Constantine, Christian worship was not centered on the parish but on the whole city. No Roman or Greek assumed a city could exist without a public cult. The church sought to replace the pagan cult of the city with the Christian liturgy. Therefore, Christian worship on the Lord's Day and other feasts generally took the form of a series of services in churches and public spaces, linked by public processions, totaling six to eight hours. Here was the church taking itself seriously as nothing less than "the embodiment in the world of the World to come."[18] Much of this way of imagining the world has been lost as the liturgy has shrunken to a short semiprivate gathering.

If the Christian liturgy is to reclaim its centrality to the imagination of a redeemed world, we must look with a critical eye on liturgies that compete for our allegiance. We must not quarantine the liturgy into a "sacred" space, but must allow it to shape the way we form our mundane communities, our goals, allegiances, purchases, and relationships. Aidan Kavanagh says:

> [I]n a Christian assembly's regular Sunday worship, a restored and recreated world must be so vigorously enfleshed in "civic" form as to give the lie to any antithetical *civitas*. . . . The assembly is not a political party or a special interest group. But it cannot forget that by grace and favor it *is* the world made new; that creation, *not* the state, is a theocracy; and that the freedom with which all people are endowed by the Creator is something which by our own choice is prone to go awry.[19]

17. John Zizioulas, *Being as Communion* (Crestwood, NY: St. Vladimir's Seminary Press, 1985), p. 180.

18. Aidan Kavanagh describes this series of services in his book *On Liturgical Theology* (New York: Pueblo Publishing Company, 1984), pp. 56-66 (quoting from p. 57).

19. Kavanagh, *On Liturgical Theology*, p. 175.

CHAPTER SEVEN

The Church as Political

———⁓———

In one way or another, all political theologies at the end of the twentieth century can be read as so many attempts to come to grips with the death of Christendom without simply acquiescing in the privatization of the church. Nevertheless, Christian political theology has strangely neglected the topic of the church. This neglect is curious from the point of view of theology, but perfectly understandable from the point of view of politics in the modern liberal nation-state. From the latter point of view, politics has been emancipated and properly differentiated from theology. Politics takes place in an autonomous, secular sphere, and is established on its own foundations. The church may or may not contribute to this process in various ways; but secular history and salvation history are two distinct processes. Even for most theologians who do not accept the Enlightenment story of secularization, the end of Christendom is to be accepted as the proper separation of the church from worldly power. The politics of the nation-state appears as a universal, encompassing all citizens regardless of their other affiliations. The church, in contrast, is a particular association, one of many that inhabit civil society. To base a politics in the church would be to set politics on a particularist and sectarian footing. Therefore, the church may make some contribution to the larger political life, but is not itself a political body.

In this chapter I contend that a full theological understanding of the church requires us to refuse this political marginalization of the church.

Any adequate ecclesiology must acknowledge the political implications of two crucial theological data: 1) there is no separate history of politics apart from the history of salvation; and 2) the church is indispensable to the history of salvation.

Israel and the Body of Christ

Unless we anachronistically read a Weberian definition of politics back into Scripture — that is, the idea that politics is defined as having to do with attaining and maintaining power over the apparatus of the state — then Israel and the church are clearly political entities in the general sense that they give order through law and ritual to the social life and everyday practices of a distinctive community of people. The political significance of the church cannot be told from a merely sociological viewpoint, however, but must begin from its theological significance in the history of salvation. At the heart of the modern reluctance to see the church as itself a type of politics is the inability to see the church as more than a gathering of individuals who are assumed to be the real subject of salvation. In the biblical witness, however, salvation is inherently social. The Jewish and Christian conviction about salvation is remarkable precisely in that *salvation has a history*. Salvation is a fully public event that unfolds in historical time before the watching eyes of the nations. Salvation is not a matter of pulling a few individual survivors from the wreckage of creation after the Fall, but is about the re-creation of a new heaven and a new earth (2 Pet. 3:13; Rev. 21:1). The history of salvation is not told separately from the history of politics. In Scripture the story of salvation takes flesh on a public stage and interacts with pharaohs, kings, and caesars. Salvation itself is imaged as a coming kingdom and a new city.

Indispensable to the history of salvation is Israel/church. God calls a community of people to be a foretaste of salvation, one concrete community called to live differently so that others may taste and see God's peaceful revolution and be blessed, too. Even political theologies that try to keep political history and salvation history together tend to neglect the centrality of the people of God to the history of salvation. "How odd of God/To choose the Jews" remains the unspoken refrain, for the idea of a chosen people is an affront to the universalism of modern politics. It is nevertheless a basic theological datum, one that in the recent past has often been elided by supersessionism; the church opens up and universalizes the particularism of Israel. As Gerhard Lohfink's important book *Does God Need the Church?* argues, however, the theo-logic of the salvation of the *whole world* through *one particular people* (Gen. 12:3) is implicit in the logic of a creation with freedom.

> [H]ow can anyone change the world and society at its roots without taking away freedom? It can only be that God begins in a small way, at one single place in the world. There must be a place, visible, tangible, where the salvation of the world can begin: that is, where the world becomes what it is supposed to be according to God's plan. Beginning at that place, the new thing can spread abroad, but not through persuasion, not through indoctrination, not through violence. Everyone must have the opportunity to come and see. All must have the chance to behold and test this new thing. Then, if they want to, they can allow themselves to be drawn into the history of salvation that God is creating. . . . What drives them to the new thing cannot be force, not even moral pressure, but only the fascination of a world that is changed.[1]

Some such explanation of the logic of election is necessary if we are to avoid supersessionism, given the basic scriptural datum that Israel/church is central to the history of salvation and thus to political history.

The Israelites, of course, most often did not in fact look much different from other communities. The Old Testament tells the history of salvation in a penitential key, highlighting the sin of the Israelites — from which salvation is promised. The claim of the Israelites to be the people of God is not a claim of moral superiority for the Israelites, but a claim that the very drama of sin and salvation is being embodied to the world in Israel. Central to this embodiment are covenant, liturgy, and law. As Walter Brueggemann writes, "Deuteronomy offers covenant as a radical and systemic alternative to the politics of autonomy, the economics of exploitation, and the theology of self-indulgence."[2] Indeed, theology and politics are inseparable, for the autonomy of royal power — in this context both

---

1. Gerhard Lohfink, *Does God Need the Church? Toward a Theology of the People of God*, trans. Linda M. Maloney (Collegeville, MN: Liturgical Press, 1999), p. 27.

2. Walter Brueggemann, "Always in the Shadow of the Empire," in *The Church as Counterculture*, ed. Michael Budde and Robert Brimlow (Albany, NY: State University of New York Press, 2000), p. 48.

Israelite and Assyrian — is an autonomy vis-à-vis God, and thus a form of idolatry. Liturgy is never merely "religious" or otherworldly, but is the enacted drama of the different kind of power and the different kind of political order that YHWH wills over against the oppressors of Israel: "This distinctive community is invited to affirm that *the world constructed in liturgy* is more reliable and more credible than the world 'out there.'"[3] Torah likewise is not "religious" law, but covers every aspect of life, from "civil" and "criminal" law to body hair, from governance to birds' nests.

Nevertheless, Israel, in its self-understanding, is not a political entity of the same order as other ancient political units. As I have observed above, Israel's experience of what we would call "statehood" is relatively brief, from David to the conquests by the Assyrians and Babylonians, and Israel's experience of statehood is not what gives it identity or continuity. The preceding period of tribal confederacy (1200-1000 B.C.) was not merely the "pre-national" period, as if it were just a primitive form preliminary to monarchy. Tribal confederacy may have been a deliberate countermodel to the monarchies of the Canaanite city-states.[4] When the Deuteronomist tells the story, he casts the shift to kingship in a negative light (1 Sam. 8). The social order codified by Torah reaches back behind kingship for its norms and avoids any connection with the Davidic "state." Both in the forms of its post-exilic Temple community and the federation of synagogues that follows, the people of Israel is a *tertium quid*. The synagogal community is neither a polis nor a *koinon*. (A *koinon*, or association, was a subset of the whole polis; it was a club formed around particular or special interests.) The concern of the synagogue, however, was for the whole of life, as mandated by the Torah. Synagogues maintained communication with each other and were concerned to remain connected to the land of Israel. The Roman Empire recognized their peculiar status and granted them exemption from military service and from the imperial cult.[5]

The church adopted this model from the synagogue and began to use the term *ekklesia* to denote the peculiar political status of the people of God. The *ekklesia* was the "assembly" of all those with citizen rights in a Greek city-state. The church's use of the term *ekklesia* may have its original

---

3. Brueggemann, "Always in the Shadow," p. 43.
4. Lohfink, *Does God Need the Church?* pp. 107-8.
5. Lohfink, *Does God Need the Church?* pp. 116-18.

roots in the Deuteronomic phrase "the day of the assembly" at Sinai (Deut. 9:10; 10:4; 18:16). In adopting the term *ekklesia*, the church was making a claim to being more than a mere *koinon*: it was not a mere part of a whole, but was itself a whole, its interests being not particular but catholic, embracing the fate of the entire world. The church saw itself as the eschatological fulfillment of Israel, and hence as the witness and embodiment of salvation to the world. The church was not polis, and yet it used the language of the kingdom of God to describe the very concrete and visible fulfillment of Israel that was "at hand" in the event of Jesus Christ (Mark 1:15). The church was not polis, and yet it used the language of citizenship to describe membership in it (Eph. 2:19; Phil. 3:20). In the church, citizenship was available through baptism to those excluded from such status in the polis, namely, women, children, and slaves.

The scholarly recovery of the Jewishness of Jesus over the last few decades has had important implications for the political significance of the church, because it puts to rest the (often anti-Semitic) spiritualization and interiorization of the gospel.[6] Jesus does not come to replace the crudely external law and make it a matter of personal faith and motivation; he comes not to abolish the law but to fulfill it (Matt. 5:17-18). Baptism and Eucharist now become the center of the ritual fulfillment of the law, enacting a liturgical drama that recalls the confrontation of Christ with the powers and calls the participants into the body of Christ. The eucharistic body and the body of the community are so closely connected that Paul is convinced that divisions in the community along socioeconomic lines threaten to turn the Eucharist into an occasion of condemnation (1 Cor. 11:17-34). The body of Christ was not a mystery cult but a new way of living reconciled lives in the world, and this way included all aspects of life. The church was to be the visible eschatological sign of God's plan of salvation for all of creation. That it often was not demanded, as Paul saw, was the story of the church that needed to be told penitentially.

It should be no surprise that the Romans treated the church as a political threat whose practices were subversive of good order in the empire. In Pliny's letter to Trajan (ca. A.D. 110) he reports that he applied Trajan's ban on political societies to the Christian communities of Asia Minor. In the Roman view, Christian failure to worship the pagan gods and their assumption that allegiance to Caesar conflicted with allegiance to Christ

---

6. See, for example, E. P. Sanders, *Jesus and Judaism* (London: SCM, 1985).

was not simply a religious matter, but concerned imperial political order. N. T. Wright notes that Christians did not attempt to defend themselves from persecution with the claim that they were merely a "private club" or *collegium* for the advancement of particular interests. They continued to proclaim the kingship of Christ, even if such kingship was not based on Caesar's model.[7] That Christ's kingdom is not of *(ek)* the world (John 18:36) was regarded as a statement of origin: the kingdom is not of this world, but it is in the world and deeply concerned with it.

Christendom and Church

If the history of salvation did not simply begin a long detour in the fourth century, we must be able to account for the continuity of the church before and after Constantine. We are accustomed to viewing the establishment of Christianity as the official creed of the Roman Empire as a radical break with the church's past, and it was. But there is a deeper continuity, insofar as the church had always thought of itself as a body with political significance. The Constantinian shift was not from otherworldly to worldly church, from Christ-against-culture to Christ-of-culture, from sect-type to church-type. Instead, the shift was in the way that Christians read what God was doing in salvation history. Oliver O'Donovan's work is helpful not merely because it makes a positive account of Christendom possible, but because it makes the Constantinian shift *explicable*. Fourth-century Christians did not simply become drunk with power and move the church off its foundations. Many Christians now imagined that God had finally brought the governmental powers under God's rule, and thus the church's political task had changed — perhaps temporarily — from martyrdom to government.[8] Constantine was not the beginning of political theology, but he represented a shift in Christian thinking and practice regarding how the kingdom of God was being made manifest in the world.

The long experiment with Christendom that followed Constantine finally and definitively crumbled in the twentieth century. The contempo-

---

7. N. T. Wright, *The New Testament and the People of God* (Minneapolis: Fortress, 1992), pp. 346-57.

8. Oliver O'Donovan, *The Desire of the Nations: Rediscovering the Roots of Political Theology* (Cambridge: Cambridge University Press, 1996), pp. 215-17.

rary ferment of political theology can be understood as an attempt once again to reimagine what God is doing with the principalities and powers in the present age. The separation of the church from the means of violence is — I think rightly — generally accepted as a good thing. If we are not to build an account of Christendom on the abandonment of the church by the Holy Spirit, however, we need to say more than that Christendom is a diversion in the search for the proper form of the church. Constantine does not represent the mere "fall" of the church from some pristine state of righteousness, nor does Christendom represent an unfortunate intermingling of two essentially distinct things — theology and politics, church and state — that we enlightened people of modernity have finally managed properly to sort out and separate. What is lumped together under the term "Christendom" is in fact a very complex series of attempts to take seriously the inherently political nature of the church and its instrumental role in the integral salvation of the world in Jesus Christ. After the fall of the Roman Empire in the West, the church was left holding the bag, as it were, and people turned to their local bishops as judges and protectors. As kingship developed, occasions for conflict between church and temporal rulers increased, primarily because kingship itself was theologically viewed as a scripturally and liturgically sanctioned office of order within the people of God. Conflicts between civil and ecclesiastical authorities were due not to the confusion of *essentially* distinct responsibilities but, on the contrary, to the inherent inseparability of church and politics.[9]

Nevertheless, though we cannot simply dismiss Christendom as some terrible mistake of the Holy Spirit, the ambiguities involved in Christian wielding of coercive power eventually brought the experiment of Christendom crashing to earth. In the Augustinian view that dominated the early Middle Ages, coercive government was not natural to human being, but with the Fall became necessary because of human sinfulness. As long as an eschatological focus could be maintained, it was possible to view the use of coercion by the temporal authorities as only temporarily necessary while we await the fullness of the kingdom of God to be realized in a new heaven and a new earth. Thus Augustine taught that the "earthly peace" enforced by coercion could be made use of by the *civitas dei* as something merely borrowed and temporary: "The heavenly city, or rather the

---

9. Brian Tierney, *The Crisis of Church and State, 1050-1300* (Englewood Cliffs, NJ: Prentice-Hall, 1964), pp. 1-11.

part of it which sojourns on earth and lives by faith, makes use of this peace only because it must, until this mortal condition which necessitates it shall pass away. Consequently, so long as it lives like a captive and a stranger in the earthly city, though it has already received the promise of redemption, and the gift of the Spirit as the earnest of it, it makes no scruple to obey the laws of the earthly city, whereby the things necessary for the maintenance of this mortal life are administered."[10] The difference between spiritual and temporal authority is a difference of time, not space: spiritual authority deals with the eternal, temporal authority with the provisional measures necessary between the first and second comings of Jesus Christ. Politics remains projected onto salvation history.

With the waning of the Augustinian view and the rediscovery of Aristotle and Roman law in the eleventh and twelfth centuries, however, there begins the process of turning the temporal into a space, one that will eventually be seen as standing outside the church. Coercive government is endowed with permanence; it is not an unfortunate necessity based on the contingent reality of human sinfulness that awaits the consummation of Christ's kingdom, but rather a natural and inevitable feature of human society based on the intrinsically social nature of human being. According to Aquinas, it is "natural" for human beings to live in the society of many, but such a multitude would disintegrate "unless there were a general ruling force within the body which watches over the common good of all members."[11]

This sense of the naturalness and permanence of coercive government is captured by the rise in the later Middle Ages of the terminology and reality of the "state," a static and permanent institution that stands separate from both ruler and ruled.[12] At the same time that temporal authority was thus losing its eschatological reference and becoming "spatialized," to use Catherine Pickstock's term, the temporal was also being redefined as a space essentially separate from the spiritual.[13] In the in-

---

10. Augustine, *The City of God*, trans. Marcus Dods (New York: Modern Library, 1950), pp. 695-96 [Book XIX.17].

11. Thomas Aquinas, *On Kingship* (Toronto: Pontifical Institute of Medieval Studies, 1949), pp. 5-6.

12. Quentin Skinner, *The Foundations of Modern Political Thought* (Cambridge: Cambridge University Press, 1978), 2:352-58.

13. Catherine Pickstock, *After Writing: On the Liturgical Consummation of Philosophy* (Oxford: Blackwell, 1998), pp. 135-66.

vestiture controversy, kingship was effectively stripped of its liturgical reference in order to safeguard the independence and superiority of the spiritual authority of the church. With the passage of time, however, this would prove to be a Pyrrhic victory for the church, because it set the stage for the rise of a self-sufficient and autonomous civil authority that would be sacralized on its own terms, quite apart from the church.[14]

The ambiguity and tension of the earlier Augustinian view of coercive power as an intra-ecclesial mode of restraining sin thus broke open into a complete split between coercive power and spiritual authority, or between power and love. In the modern era, the national state would arise as the autonomous bearer of lethal power over bodies, and the church would take its place as the caretaker of souls. Temporal and spiritual would come to occupy distinct spaces: the temporal referred to certain things — politics, business, and so forth — and the spiritual to others — conscience, sacraments, and so on. Christianity would become interiorized as a "religion," and the modern distinctions between religion and politics, church and state would become institutionalized in the secular nation-state. This process would only be fully completed in the twentieth century. Not coincidentally, the twentieth century produced a tremendous flourishing of theologies of the political, as Christians attempted to puzzle through the political implications of the gospel after Christendom. The church has finally been freed from Christendom, from the ambiguities of the wielding of coercive power. We have not, however, been freed from the question of the political nature of the church. Political theologies are built on the recognition that we cannot submit to the privatization of the church. What role they leave for the church, however, varies greatly.

Politically Indirect Ecclesiology

Most post-Christendom theologies of the political do not simply embrace the idea that salvation history has been privatized, but they nevertheless endorse the relative autonomy of politics from theology and make the influence of the church on politics indirect. Christendom saw various kinds

---

14. See Ernst H. Kantorowicz, *The King's Two Bodies: A Study in Medieval Political Theology* (Princeton, NJ: Princeton University Press, 1957); see also William T. Cavanaugh, *Torture and Eucharist: Theology, Politics, and the Body of Christ* (Oxford: Blackwell, 1998), pp. 212-21.

of claims of church authority over temporal power, some based on claims that the church possessed direct political authority, others based on the idea that the church's authority in the temporal was *potestas indirecta*. The latter theories were based on the spiritual power — typically possessed by the pope — to discipline any erring member of his flock, including and especially temporal rulers.[15] Post-Christendom political theology recognizes that the church cannot simply renounce politics and retreat to private concerns, but it tends to operate at one more remove of indirectness from the medieval conception of indirect power. In Christendom, questions of the direct or indirect power of the church over the temporal had to do with the power of the church to discipline Christian rulers. In modern secular societies, however, political theologies tend to operate at an additional remove from the state, staking a claim to influence the state only through the activities of Christian citizens in civil society. Furthermore, most assume that, when addressing a pluralistic society, theology cannot be directly politicized, but must first be translated into some more publicly accessible form of discourse in order to have an influence in civil society.

For Jacques Maritain, for example, the fall of Christendom has allowed a proper distinction between the temporal and the spiritual, which are spatialized as "planes." This is not merely a concession made by the church, but is the outworking of the gospel itself. Christ made clear that his kingdom is spiritual, not of this world. In contrast to the pagans, Christ interiorized the sacred, locating it in the human heart, removed from the vicissitudes of time. In a corollary move, Christ liberated us by making a sharp distinction between what is Caesar's and what is God's. The genesis and growth of the modern secular state is thus not the rejection of the Christian ideal but, on the contrary, offers the opportunity for the full flower of the Christian spiritual life properly untangled from its confusion with material culture.[16]

Though the temporal plane has its own relative autonomy, however, it remains subordinate to the spiritual plane. The merely natural virtues involved in political and social life — running businesses, governments, and wars — are meant to be "elevated" by the supernatural spiritual vir-

---

15. Tierney, *The Crisis*, pp. 2-5.

16. Jacques Maritain, *The Things That Are Not Caesar's*, trans. J. F. Scanlan (New York: Charles Scribner's Sons, 1931), p. 1.

tues. The church, nevertheless, unites souls outside of temporal space and time and is not directly involved in the realm of political ethics. The church, therefore, does not act as a body on the temporal plane, but it exerts an indirect influence through the individual. The individual Christian acting on the temporal plane of the political and the social is animated by the spiritual plane. On the temporal plane, the Christian acts "as Christian," but not "as a Christian as such."[17] In this way, a "new Christendom" is possible in which the state remains explicitly secular, but individual Christians bring the inchoate influence of the gospel to bear on public life, without speaking explicitly Christian language in the public forum.

John Courtney Murray provides another influential example of the indirect political influence of the church. In Murray's work the key distinction is between state and civil society: the state is to play a limited role within society, that of protecting public order; the realm of freedom and moral agency is civil society, and the pursuit of the common good is a matter for society as a whole. The church has no access to the coercive power of the state, but it contributes to the common good by attempting to "permeate all the institutions of society — economic, social, cultural, political — with the Christian spirit of truth, justice, love, and freedom."[18] Here Murray recasts the medieval notion of the "indirect power" of the church so that its subject is not the ruler or the state but the individual conscience of the Christian citizen of the nation-state. For Murray, the church itself is meant to be a vibrant and robust association at the service of society, but, like Maritain, he does not view the church as itself a political institution. The political implications of the gospel must be translated into a "spirit" that permeates material institutions. Furthermore, there is a bifurcation of the natural and the supernatural, such that, in the pluralistic public realm, the church must not speak theologically, but in the language of the natural law, which is in theory accessible to any reasonable person — Christian or not.[19]

It is this requirement to make the Christian message intelligible within the confines of a post-Christendom political liberalism that makes

17. Jacques Maritain, *Integral Humanism* (New York: Charles Scribner's Sons, 1968), p. 294.

18. John Courtney Murray, *Religious Liberty* (Louisville: Westminster/John Knox, 1993), p. 183.

19. John Courtney Murray, *We Hold These Truths: Catholic Propositions on the American Proposition* (Kansas City, MO: Sheed and Ward, 1960), pp. 295-336.

the church drop out of Reinhold Niebuhr's political theology almost entirely. Niebuhr is no less convinced than Murray that religion is necessary to sustain the ethos of a pluralistic democracy. But Niebuhr is much less confident than Murray is that the church has privileged access to some truths essential to the common good. For Niebuhr, religion's contribution to the proper functioning of a democratic social order is the recognition that such claims to privileged access are most often due to the sin of pride. Sin pervades the human condition, and conflicts of self-interest are inevitable. The genius of democracy is precisely that it balances such interests and refuses to allow any particular claims to achieve universal status.

Christianity, with its anthropology of human sinfulness, thus serves a democratic order by relativizing any claim to justice and truth. "Religious faith ought therefore to be a constant fount of humility; for it ought to encourage men to moderate their natural pride and to achieve some decent consciousness of the relativity of their own statement of even the most ultimate truth."[20] Such humility, of course, precludes the possibility that the church be given some kind of privileged position for mediating God's will for the ordering of society. Ecclesiology is simply absent from Niebuhr's political theology. He no doubt assumed that the church was sociologically necessary for Christianity to exist in organized form, but any claim that the church was the source of an alternative politics could only be treated as a manifestation of pride, and thus a threat to a democratic political order.

The above political ecclesiologies share an atomizing pathology. The emphasis is on the individual Christian citizen acting in the temporal realm; the church does not act as a body in the temporal. The new political theology of Johann Baptist Metz, on the other hand, sees the church acting as an "institution of social criticism" within modern secular democratic society. Nonetheless, Metz's ecclesiology still aims at an indirect influence of the church in political matters. Metz begins with the acceptance of the "proper" emancipation of the political from the religious. Indeed, the autonomy of the political in Metz is less encumbered by the kind of explicit subordination to the spiritual that is found in Maritain. For Metz, the Enlightenment signifies the achievement of the maturity of human freedom. The secularized political order is an order of freedom; political realities

---

20. Reinhold Niebuhr, *The Children of Light and the Children of Darkness* (New York: Charles Scribner's Sons, 1944), p. 135.

are no longer given but are subject to free human action. Like Maritain, Metz sees the outlines of salvation history only in the relative autonomy of the world from the church. Secularization is not the dethroning of Christ in the world, but rather "the decisive point of his dominion in history," for it is Christianity that sets the world free to be itself.[21]

Metz considers the old versions of political theology — Bonald, Donoso Cortés, Schmitt, and others — to be "precritical" because they do not accept the Enlightenment critique of religion, believing that theology can be directly politicized. At the same time, however, Metz is concerned that the legitimate separation of the church from the political sphere not result in the mere privatization of the church, the handing over of the gospel to the anemic embrace of bourgeois sentimentality. Metz's solution is that the church take its place in civil society as an "institution of social criticism" whose mission is defined as a service to the history of freedom unfolding since the Enlightenment. On the basis of the memory of Jesus' confrontation with the powers and his preference for the marginalized, the church will criticize all social forms as falling short of the kingdom of God. Even the church itself is put under the "'eschatological proviso,' which makes every historically real status of society appear to be provisional."[22] The criticism the church provides is not merely negative, but it is a challenge to make actual in the present the eschatological promises of the biblical tradition: freedom, peace, justice, and reconciliation. Because theology cannot be directly politicized, however, theology must be translated into "practical public reason" for consumption in the arena of civil society.

Metz's positive evaluation of secularization was taken over by much of liberation theology. The work of Gustavo Gutiérrez has the great merit of emphasizing that there are not two histories, one sacred and one profane, one of salvation and the other of politics: "The history of salvation is the very heart of human history."[23] However, this evaluation has the effect of deemphasizing ecclesiology. For Gutiérrez, the Maritainian model of political theology that preceded liberation theology in Latin America was still infected by a "certain ecclesiastical narcissism" because of its desire to

---

21. Johann Baptist Metz, *Theology of the World*, trans. William Glen-Doepel (New York: Seabury, 1969), p. 19.

22. Metz, *Theology of the World*, p. 114.

23. Gustavo Gutiérrez, *A Theology of Liberation*, trans. Sr. Caridad Inda and John Eagleson, rev. ed. (Maryknoll, NY: Orbis Books, 1988), p. 86. Hereafter, page references to this work appear in parentheses in the text.

create "a society inspired by Christian principles" (p. 36). Secularization demands that we recognize the full autonomy of the temporal, an "entirely worldly world" that operates on the assumption that human beings in their freedom are the agents of history. According to Gutiérrez, secularization is not an anti-Christian impulse but simply the outworking of the biblical idea that creation is separate from the creator, and that "God has proclaimed humankind lord of this creation" (p. 42). The world is autonomous, but it is also permeated by God's grace. Gutiérrez thus wishes to overcome the bourgeois privatization of the church by elevating the spiritual status of the mundane political world and by breaking down the barriers between theology and politics. The church is the explicit witness to the liberation of humanity from sin, including social and political sin of all kinds. However, the church is not epistemologically privileged in understanding social and political processes, which operate on their own worldly autonomy and are thus best understood by the social sciences:

> [R]ather than define the world in relation to the religious phenomenon, it would seem that religion should be redefined in relation to the profane.... [I]f formerly the tendency was to see the world in terms of the Church, today almost the reverse is true: the Church is seen in terms of the world. In the past, the Church used the world for its own ends; today many Christians — and non-Christians — ask themselves if they should, for example, use the influence of the Church to accelerate the process of transformation of social structures. (p. 42)

Despite criticisms of liberation theology for politicizing the faith, there is little room here for a directly political ecclesiology. The church contributes to the transformation of political and social structures, but the church plays an instrumental role, and it is not itself envisioned as a kind of politics. As an autonomous process, politics are in some sense "outside" the church, and so the application of the church to politics is once again indirect.

Church as Polity

As different as the above approaches are from one another, they share the assumption that the modern separation of theology and politics is proper and politics resides in a different autonomous space from that marked out by the church. Therefore, the church must approach politics indirectly, from afar. There is a different approach, however, that seeks to overcome this division by examining the politics embedded in core Christian theological themes, without need of translation from theology to politics, or vice versa. Key to this approach is reimagining the political as a direct response to God's activity in the world, a return to the Augustinian conviction that politics is truly politics only when mapped onto salvation history. God's acts and human acts are not to be identified, but both take place, as O'Donovan says, in the "one public history which is the theatre of God's saving purposes and mankind's social undertakings."[24] Central to this reimagining is the conviction that the church is at the heart of God's plan of salvation.

Oliver O'Donovan's work is unusual in this regard, because it regards Christendom as the most significant practical instance of the conviction that theology is politics. As O'Donovan sees it, Christendom is simply the unfolding drama of God's rule as manifested in the Old Testament and as fulfilled in the kingship of Christ. If Christology is given its due political weight, then after the ascension the nations could simply not refuse to acknowledge Christ. If Christ really is the fulfillment of the salvation history begun in Israel, then God must in fact be using the governing authorities for his own purposes in bringing about a new social order. Nevertheless, the government is not the church; the church exists to serve as a distinctive witness, to remind the government of its temporary status. As ruler, the ruler is meant to judge; as member of the church, the ruler is meant to judge with clemency; and the church is there to signal the inherent tension between the two obligations. The church thus plays a central role in the transformation of the social order. The church itself bears the fullness of God's politics through history. "Does the authority of the gospel word confer no social structure on the community which bears it? Does that community have no 'social space' determined by the truth?"[25] There can be no question of a disembodied Christianity that only serves, in a Gnostic fashion, to inform the consciences of individual citizens occupying an autonomous political space.

O'Donovan presents a serious challenge to Christian accommoda-

---

24. O'Donovan, *Desire of the Nations*, p. 2.
25. O'Donovan, *Desire of the Nations*, pp. 200, 208.

tion to liberal social orders. Nevertheless, O'Donovan, who locates himself in an established national church, depends on the state to be the police department of the church. His repositioning of politics within salvation history recovers the eschatological dimension missing from much of contemporary political theology, but his eschatology has a strong accent on the "already" of Christ's victory. As a result, he puts a great deal of emphasis on the biblical images of rule, to the exclusion of images of wandering, pilgrimage, exile, and resident alien status. These themes are taken up by Stanley Hauerwas, who has no doubt that God's reign will triumph, but he wants to be more reticent than O'Donovan about how God's reign is in fact manifested on the way. The lordship of Jesus, Hauerwas suspects, is nothing like the worldly rule of states, and is most often found in the signs of weakness and contradiction that mark the Christian way of the cross. The political task of the post-Christendom church is to suffer rulers as faithfully as possible, to the point of martyrdom if necessary, to wait upon the Lord and not to presume to rule in his place.[26]

Such a reticence about the reign of God seems to prompt Hauerwas to say more about the church, to identify the church fully as polis — as the subtitle of one of his books indicates — though it is a polis without a police department. Unencumbered by the need to rule, the church is called to be "a 'contrast model' for all polities that know not God."[27] The church's role in the history of salvation is precisely to bear God's politics through history. The hallmark of God's politics is that authority operates on the power of the truth, and not on violence. In the modern nation-state, the autonomy of politics from God's rule ensures that social order is based only on the arbitrary suppression of will by will. The role of the church is not merely to make policy recommendations to the state, but to embody a different sort of politics, so that the world may be able to see a truthful politics and be transformed. The church does not thereby withdraw from the world but serves it, both by being the sign of God's salvation of the world and by reminding the world of what the world still is not.

26. Stanley Hauerwas, *Wilderness Wanderings* (Boulder, CO: Westview, 1997), pp. 199-224.

27. Stanley Hauerwas, *A Community of Character: Toward a Constructive Christian Social Ethic* (Notre Dame, IN: University of Notre Dame Press, 1981), p. 84.

Questions

The most common objection to the suggestion that the church itself embodies a politics is that such a politics is sectarian. Such an objection depends on a relatively novel sociological use of the term "sect." In theological parlance, a sect was a group that put itself outside the authority of the church. The difference between the Waldensians and the Franciscans lay not in their attitudes toward "culture" or the "world," but in their relationships to church authority. In the twentieth century, however, "sect" came to indicate a group whose practices put it at odds with the dominant culture and political elites of the nation-state. The underlying assumption is that it is not the church but the nation-state that is "catholic"; the church, insofar as it is a political actor, is a particular association of civil society that is encompassed by the larger universal political sphere of the nation-state. Theologically speaking, this is a grave error. As even O'Donovan recognizes, the church was catholic even in the catacombs.[28] Salvation history is not a subset of world history, but simply is the history — not yet complete or legible — of human action in a grace-soaked world. As widely as O'Donovan's Christendom differs from Hauerwas's resident aliens, both agree that political theology cannot be done without an account of the directly political nature of the church and its role in salvation history.

If salvation is not of the church but of the world, however, there can be no question of a withdrawal of the church from the world. The church catholic is to live like the Jews of the Diaspora, "to seek the welfare of the city where I have sent you into exile" (Jer. 29:7), even if that city is Babylon.[29] Without seeking to rule, the church has more to contribute precisely because it is the bearer of God's politics, and because it is catholic, transnational, transcending the parochial borders of the nation-state.

Nevertheless, some difficult issues need attention for the development of a directly political ecclesiology. Though "church" is a crucial theological locus, it is by no means always clear in practice where the boundaries of the church lie. "Church" and "world" are often more prescriptive than descriptive terms; in practice, the church is full of the world. This is as it should be: the dialectical drama of sin and salvation implies a dialogical relationship between the church and its others, which include

---

28. O'Donovan, *Desire of the Nations*, p. 216.
29. John Howard Yoder, *For the Nations* (Grand Rapids: Eerdmans, 1997), pp. 1-5.

the world and God. Indeed, the Holy Spirit blows where she wills, and the activity of the Spirit is not limited to the church. The church is therefore a relational body, not a closed system. The church is not a polis; *ekklesia* names something closer to a universal "culture" that is assembled from out of the particular cultures of the world.[30]

The church is not only crossed by nonchurch elements, but also contains anti-Christ elements. The church is a *corpus permixtum,* full of both saints and sinners. As Nicholas Healy reminds us, ecclesiology must maintain both poles of Paul's dictum in Galatians 6:14: "[F]ar be it from me to glory except in the cross of our Lord Jesus Christ." On the one hand, we must not boast of the church, as if the church were already the answer to all the world's social ills; on the other hand, we must glory in Christ and regard the church as a key actor in the unfolding of the drama of salvation that Christ's cross has won.[31] The eschatological "not yet" means that the history of the drama so far needs to be told hopefully but penitentially, with room for marginal voices and conflicts. The story is not told in an epic manner, as if the church were made to rule. As the embodiment of God's politics, the church nevertheless muddles through. God is in charge of all of history. The church's job is to try to discern in each concrete circumstance how best to embody the politics of the cross in a suffering world.

30. Nicholas M. Healy, *Church, World and the Christian Life: Practical-Prophetic Ecclesiology* (Cambridge: Cambridge University Press, 2000), pp. 159-75.
31. Healy, *Church, World and the Christian Life,* pp. 1-24.

CHAPTER EIGHT

The Sinfulness and Visibility of the Church: A Christological Exploration

⟞⟞⟋⟋⟍⟝

In ecclesiologies that emphasize the concrete practices of the church, there is a strong emphasis on the visible holiness of the church. Stanley Hauerwas, for example, says: "The church is not the kingdom but the foretaste of the kingdom. For it is in the church that the narrative of God is lived in a way that makes the kingdom visible. The church must be the clear manifestation of a people who have learned to be at peace with themselves, one another, the stranger, and of course, most of all, God."[1] The same emphasis on the visibility of the church is found in John Milbank, according to whom the church "itself claims to exhibit the exemplary form of human community."[2] The emphasis on visibility has among its aims to root theological reflection in the concrete practices of real, living communities, to correct an overly individualistic view of Christianity, and to encourage Christians to take themselves seriously as a countersign to the evils of the world.

Emphasis on the church's visible holiness raises problems, however, when confronted with the reality of sin. Too often, when we see the church, we see not the foretaste of the kingdom but a poorly organized

---

1. Stanley Hauerwas, *The Peaceable Kingdom: A Primer in Christian Ethics* (Notre Dame, IN: University of Notre Dame Press, 1983), p. 97.

2. John Milbank, *Theology and Social Theory: Beyond Secular Reason* (Oxford: Blackwell, 1990), p. 388.

hobby club fully infected by the sins of the world. To hold up the church as the exemplary form of human community seems like chauvinism. In my own attempts to encourage the church to help resist political and economic idolatries, I have been charged with presenting a "whiggish history of the church" and replacing the hubris of the individual subject with the hubris of a collective subject.[3] In Catholic circles, overemphasis on the visible holiness of the church has been called "ecclesiological Monophysitism" — for the way in which human nature is absorbed into the divinity of Christ. In Catholic debates, the charge tends to be leveled at triumphalism and authoritarianism in the church hierarchy, whereby it is too easily assumed that divinity is fully visible in the juridical structure of the church. Yves Congar, for example, found a danger of "ecclesiological monophysitism" in Pope Leo XIII's statement in *Divinum Illud Munus* that "[i]f Christ is the Head of the Church, the Holy Spirit is its soul."[4] The church as the body of Christ is treated as though it is wholly divine in its nature, even though the human actors that populate it act, it is admitted, in humanly sinful ways.[5] Whether the kingdom is said to be visible in the church's ju-

---

3. Christopher J. Insole, "Discerning the Theopolitical: A Response to Cavanaugh's Reimagining of Political Space," *Political Theology* 7, no. 3 (July 2006): 329.

4. According to Congar, Augustine did not say that the Holy Spirit is the soul of the church, but that the Holy Spirit does in the church what the soul does in our bodies. Augustine's point is functional, not ontological. Yves Congar, *I Believe in the Spirit*, trans. David Smith (New York: Crossroad, 1997), 1:154. See Bradford E. Hinze, "Releasing the Power of the Spirit in a Trinitarian Ecclesiology," in *Advents of the Spirit: An Introduction to the Current Study of Pneumatology*, ed. Bradford E. Hinze and D. Lyle Dabney (Milwaukee: Marquette University Press, 2001), p. 375n18. According to Hinze, the charge of "ecclesiological monophysitism" first surfaces in nineteenth-century critiques of Johann Adam Möhler. In the twentieth century, Congar would raise the danger of "ecclesiological monophysitism" in relation to Möhler's notion of the church as "a continuing Incarnation," wherein the divine overtakes the human, "according to which, as the Church is Christ's body so its mouth would be Christ's own, and all that it says would come from Christ." Yves Congar, quoted in Bradford E. Hinze, "The Holy Spirit and the Catholic Tradition: The Legacy of Johann Adam Möhler," in *The Legacy of the Tübingen School: The Relevance of Nineteenth-Century Theology for the Twenty-First Century*, ed. Donald J. Dietrich and Michael J. Himes (New York: Crossroad, 1997), pp. 78-79.

5. For more contemporary charges of ecclesiological Monophysitism, see John Beal, "'It Shall Not Be So Among You!': Crisis in the Church, Crisis in Canon Law," in *Governance, Accountability, and the Future of the Catholic Church*, ed. Francis Oakley and Bruce Russet (New York: Continuum, 2003). Gerard Mannion discusses Michael Himes's use of the term "ecclesiological monophysitism" in Mannion, *Ecclesiology and Postmodernity: Questions for the Church in Our Time* (Collegeville, MN: Liturgical Press, 2007), pp. 189-91.

ridical structure or in the concrete practices of Christian communities, emphases on the visible holiness of the church run aground if we do not properly acknowledge the sinful humanity of the church or wholly subsume it into the divinity of Christ's body.

It would be simple enough to respond to these objections by lowering our expectations of the church, to restore the proper balance or tension between the divine and the human elements in the church. This balance or tension, however, tends to treat human nature in the church as if it were static, a perpetually recurring standoff between the grace of God and the stubborn recalcitrance of human nature. Whenever expectations of the church get too high, we remind ourselves that, human nature being what it is, we can only expect so much as we muddle through. But as Christians, we believe that Christ has decisively broken through the standoff, that human sin is no longer just a counterbalance to divinity, but that the comedy of salvation is playing out in the life of the church. Must we give up on the visibility of the church, and simply hope and trust that somehow God is working despite the sinfulness of the church? Is there a way to integrate the visibility of the church with its sinfulness, without simply seeing them as two countervailing tendencies in a perpetual tug-of-war?

To address this question, we will first need to ask why visibility is such an important ecclesiological theme. I will examine Gerhard Lohfink's argument that the church as exemplary community is demanded by the very logic of the drama of creation and salvation found in Scripture. I will then examine some problems raised by Lohfink's account, and some attempts to avoid ecclesiological Monophysitism. Next, I will attempt to give an account of the church's visibility that fully recognizes its sinfulness. To do so, I will look to post-Chalcedon Christologies — especially those of Maximus the Confessor and Hans Urs von Balthasar, his later interpreter — that explore how Christ became sin, thereby countering both Monophysitism and Nestorianism. Finally, I will explore some ecclesiological consequences of the idea that Christ became sin, and suggest that the church's visibility lies in its repentance for its sin.

Does God Need the Church?

The story of the church begins with the story of creation. As the account of creation in Genesis makes plain, creation will unfold gradually as history. The creation itself is described as *toledot*, the "generations" of the heavens and the earth. Lohfink argues that creation unfolds over time precisely to make room for freedom. A creation alien from history, complete as given and unchangeable, would not allow for the exercise of freedom in change. God makes creation capable of being greater and freer than it is. In doing so, however, God risks a history tainted by sin.[6] Sin takes hold, and in the wake of Babel "the LORD scattered them abroad from there over the face of all the earth" (Gen. 11:8). But God points the way forward to the salvation of the world by the election of a peculiar people of God. Genesis begins with the story of universal creation, but very quickly descends to the local in the election of Abraham and his people. But the local is for the salvation of the universal; in Abraham all the nations of the earth will be blessed (Gen. 12:3).

The calling of a particular people, Israel, is the calling of the church. But why does God work in this way? What is the theo-logic of universal salvation worked through one particular people? According to Lohfink, God's salvation of the whole world contrasts with the way that revolutionaries want to change the world. Revolutionaries are short on time, and they must use violence to move the inert masses to act. God, on the other hand, wants to work a radical change without eliminating the freedom God bestowed on creation. So salvation is allowed to work itself out through history. God begins in a small, local way, with one people in one place.

> There must be a place, visible, tangible, where the salvation of the world can begin: that is, where the world becomes what it is supposed to be according to God's plan.... Everyone must have the opportunity to come and see. All must have the chance to behold and test this new thing. Then, if they want to, they can allow themselves to be drawn into the history of salvation that God is creating. Only in that way can their freedom be preserved. What drives them to the new thing cannot be force, not even moral pressure, but only the fascination of a world that is changed. (p. 27)

If Lohfink is right, the visibility of the church is the key to understanding how God saves in history. "Israel's task, given by God, is to show

---

6. Gerhard Lohfink, *Does God Need the Church? Toward a Theology of the People of God*, trans. Linda M. Maloney (Collegeville, MN: Liturgical Press, 1999), pp. 7-21. Hereafter, page references to this work appear in parentheses in the text.

to all nations how a just society would look" (p. 127). God attracts with beauty, and does not coerce; however, it is not Israel for its own sake that attracts, but God. The people of God does not work salvation through its own efforts, but only shows forth what God is doing in history. The great love affair as portrayed in the Old Testament is not between the people and Israel, but between Israel and God. The Song of Songs has long been interpreted as an allegory of the love between God and the people of God. And just as one falls in love with a particular person — not men or women in general — so the love affair between God and God's people is local. The most common way that people are attracted to God is by seeing other people living redeemed lives in community and being able to envision themselves living like that.

The theme of visibility is carried to its fulfillment in Jesus Christ, who is God in visible human incarnation. Jesus is the representative of Israel; all Israel is gathered in Jesus, the new Temple (John 2:21). The entire history of salvation is gathered into a single figure. But the kingdom of God still requires a concrete community of people. The people of God is thus identified with the body of Christ, the visible continuation of the incarnation in history. The task of the church is to proclaim that salvation has been fulfilled and to embody that salvation for the world. "What is decisive, after all, and everything depends on it, is that the community knows that God has called it to make the divine plan visible and to be a place of reconciliation in the world as the body of Christ. It is already that body, anterior to any of its own efforts" (p. 264).

Lohfink adds, "Nevertheless it must know that its task is still to become that body" (p. 264). The activity of God in history is often obscured and hidden by human sin, as Jesus' parables of the kingdom of God make clear. But as Lohfink points out, Jesus compares the kingdom of God not just to a mustard seed but to the whole process by which the tiny mustard seed grows into a great bush. In the end, the world is to be transformed; the story is to have a comic, not a tragic, ending. Jesus does not naively believe in the inevitability of human progress. Nevertheless, Lohfink contends that the transformation is to be of *this world*. The kingdom of God is not otherworldly, nor will this world have to be destroyed and a new world created — as the apocalypticists thought — in order to usher in the kingdom of God (pp. 39-49). The visibility of salvation in this world is the heart of Jesus' ministry.

In spelling out the theo-logic of salvation, Lohfink reinforces his emphasis on the local with the theme of unity. According to Lohfink, gathering the many into one is the form that salvation takes in the world. Scattering is not only the consequence of sin, as in the Babel story, but scattering defines sin — sin is the breakup of the original unity of creation. Lohfink cites dozens of Old Testament texts to show that "gathering" was a crucial term in Israel's theology since at least the Babylonian Exile. The psalmist pleads: "Save us, O LORD our God, and gather us from among the nations" (Ps. 106:47). The theme of gathering is continued in the New Testament, where the promises are fulfilled in Jesus Christ, who declares, "Whoever is not with me is against me, and whoever does not gather with me scatters" (Matt. 12:30). Christ is not only the gatherer but the gathered: the people are to be gathered into Christ's very body, which as Paul says, drinks of the one Spirit (1 Cor. 12:13). Unity, therefore, is not an accidental quality of the church, but is essential to the church, not simply in the general sense that any body performs its purpose better when it is unified, but because gathering the many into one is the very mission of the church. Salvation does not happen to individuals, who subsequently gather in the church. Salvation *is* the gathering. As Lohfink puts it, salvation "consists precisely in incorporation into the Church as a social body. Only in that way is it possible to participate in the history of liberation that began with Abraham" (p. 255).

What Lohfink's analysis of Scripture does for ecclesiology, then, is help us to see that visibility is not an accidental feature of the church, but is essential to God's plan of salvation as it unfolds in history.

> It is the will of God to have a people in the world so that one can clearly see, by looking at that people, how God proposes that human society should be, so that the world can see the unanimity and peace that is possible in such a people and thus come to peace for itself. It is the will of God to lead the whole world to liberation and redemption through the redemption and liberation that happens in one people. (p. 302)

Lohfink argues that a maximalist approach to the importance of the church is not simply the post hoc invention of ecclesiastical elites, but is embedded in the scriptural narrative and the very logic of salvation history. Rather than treat the church as a structural means to the Christian life, Lohfink sees the gathering of a visible community as the very healing of the wounds of history that God set out to accomplish.

Although one could certainly take issue with any number of Lohfink's individual exegeses, and although Lohfink often gives the mistaken impression that Scripture always speaks with one voice, one cannot help being impressed with the sense Lohfink has made of the whole. Despite modern efforts to carve up the biblical text, those who canonized the Bible thought there was an overall story to tell, and Lohfink has told it persuasively. Not only does he make sense of election and the church in the biblical story, but Lohfink's work also accords well with the high ecclesiologies of Paul and the fathers, who saw the church as both body and bride of Christ. Lohfink does not allow us to construct a Christianity devoid of concrete social embodiment. He sees that the lack of faith in God in contemporary Europe is largely due to the disappearance of the church, and not the other way around. The privatization of the church has destroyed "the place of God's physical presence" (p. 319) in the world, so belief in God has consequently faded.[7]

Ecclesiological Monophysitism and Ecclesiological Nestorianism

Nevertheless, to make God's presence depend so thoroughly on the visibility and unity of the church raises serious problems. What becomes of God's promises when sin obscures that visibility? Lohfink emphasizes that the salvation made visible in the church is the work of God, not the fruit of human striving. The sin that obscures the visibility of the church, however, *is* attributable to human effort. To make salvation dependent on the visibility of the church seems to put salvation in human hands. Despite what Lohfink says about the unfolding of God in history, too much emphasis seems to be put on what *we* do or do not do. And one does not have to search too far to find negative examples of the behavior of the church. If God attracts by implanting a community in human history that shows what salvation looks like, then it must be acknowledged that the

---

7. Lohfink quotes from Vilma Sturm's memoir, in which she recounts the dying of the faith in her family in Germany as typical of her generation. For Lohfink, her key insight is that God is "never and nowhere to be discovered." The fundamental movement of salvation is that God becomes accessible to people in history through Israel/church. When that concrete presence in history fades, so does the presence of God (pp. 317-19).

church often repels rather than attracts, and does not display anything like the unity that the eschatological gathering is meant to be.

Nicholas M. Healy has pressed this kind of critique with regard to ecclesiologies that put a great deal of emphasis on the visibility of church practices. Though Healy's main targets are Stanley Hauerwas and Reinhard Hütter, his critique applies to Lohfink as well. Healy objects to any overly idealized account of church practices that does not take account of the way that such practices are routinely neglected or misperformed because of human sin. To make the presence of God dependent on the visible unity of the body furthermore tends to identify the message with an idealized medium; the gospel becomes about *us*, not about God. The Holy Spirit is thus bound to the church's practices in such a way that the Spirit is not free to blow where she wills. Finally, such an ecclesiology is a recipe for despair.

> We know we are often unattractive to those outside, sometimes for good reasons, sometimes not. But we hope that the truth of the gospel and the effectiveness of witness to it do *not* depend upon what we look like or upon our being trained and disciplined and formed properly. For we know that if it did, the gospel would not be good news, at least not for us.[8]

According to Healy, we need a theological account of the fact that sometimes the church really is unattractive. We need an account of how the Holy Spirit is not bound to our practices, but can overcome them when required.

Healy suggests briefly how such a theological account can be derived from the work of Thomas Aquinas. In the *exitus-reditus* pattern of creation and redemption, the church on earth is a wayfarer, on its way back to God, but radically different from those *comprehensores* who have reached their goal and now see God in heaven. The church on earth is not the whole body of Christ, but part of it; Christ is the head of all humanity because Christ wills the salvation of all. The body of Christ is complex, with members and potential members relating differently to Christ de-

---

8. Nicholas M. Healy, "Practices and the New Ecclesiology: Misplaced Concreteness?" *International Journal of Systematic Theology* 5, no. 3 (Nov. 2003): 303. Hereafter, page references to this essay appear in parentheses in the text.

pending on the extent to which they have been united to Christ by the Holy Spirit in the virtue of charity. According to Healy, what sanctifies us for Aquinas are not external actions as such, but "right dispositions and intentions" (p. 305), which are the work of the Holy Spirit in us. And dispositions and intentions cannot be judged by observing external actions. "Some in the church *in via* are united in charity; some are not. Who are, and who are not, cannot be known now, certainly not by looking at what someone does" (p. 306). We can, of course, hope and trust that the Spirit of Christ is working in the church's midst, but we cannot claim more. "Membership in the public church and performance of its practices do not, of themselves, signify anything at all vis-à-vis one's relationship with God. What counts is the internal movement of the Holy Spirit, which issues in the intentional actions by which we obey Jesus Christ" (p. 306). Obedience to Christ is a matter of participation in Christ's life. "But for us *in via*, our participation in Christ is in his passion rather than his resurrection, as Thomas's understanding of the eucharist and other sacraments makes clear" (p. 306). This means that we should expect suffering, loss, confusion, and betrayal to be our lot; but the good news is that God justifies us anyway through Christ's merits. "But the church is not the kingdom, nor is its perfection the condition of anything at all. The church *in via* is a thoroughly human, and therefore a sometimes confused and confusing guide and helper for its members as they journey towards their Lord" (p. 307).

Surely Healy is right to object to idealized, "Monophysite" accounts of the church that do not take the church's sinfulness with sufficient seriousness. To say that the purpose of the church is to show what human society is supposed to look like is to hold the church to a standard of unity and purity that it has rarely, if ever, accomplished in history. To bind the Holy Spirit to well-performed practices in human history is in effect to banish the Holy Spirit from much of that history. Salvation is visible in a few local instances of faithful churches, mere flotsam on the waves of historical unfaithfulness. Healy is right to reject this approach. Faced with the manifest sin of the church throughout history, we should confess our sinfulness in sackcloth and ashes, while simultaneously putting our hope in the fact that God is not bound or defeated by our sin, but is working in us despite our weakness.

Nevertheless, what appears to be proper Christian humility can be problematic as well. First, Healy tends to make the church a medium or means to the end of the Christian life, a "guide and helper," in his words. Healy complains that ecclesiologies that emphasize the visible church conflate medium (church) with message (gospel). But if Lohfink is right, the church in the biblical and patristic witness is not just a medium or means. Of course, the church is not simply equated with Christ; it does have a mediating function, which it can perform well or badly. But if the church really is the body of Christ, as Paul says, then it is not merely a means to the end of unity in Christ. Jean-Marie-Roger Tillard says that, for Paul, "[b]elonging to the union between sisters and brothers in the ecclesial body is part of the new economy created by salvation. . . . It is not only a life *in the church* but — the nuance is of crucial importance — a life *from and by the church*."[9] If salvation is the gathering of what has been scattered into the unity of Christ, then the church is not merely a means to salvation or a place for the saved to gather, but is itself meant to be the first fruits of the appearance of salvation in human history. Lohfink's reading of Scripture in this light is not idiosyncratic; as Henri de Lubac has shown, it was in fact the reading that predominated among the fathers of the early church.[10] The church participates in the whole Christ, who has come into history to make us whole. The church is "thoroughly human," as Healy says, but in Chalcedonian fashion the fathers did not hesitate to say that the church is also thoroughly divine.[11] Healy, of course, does not deny the divinity of Christ's body, but his emphasis on the church's participation in the passion "rather than" the resurrection of Christ seems to defer the full participation of the church in the divine life, which lends itself to a temporal separation of divinity and humanity in the church. While it is true that the church now is not what it will be in the eschaton, the distinction between the church *in via* and what will happen "when we rise in Christ after our death" should not be overdrawn, since the holiness of the church is already given in Christ's triumph over death and the Holy Spirit's inauguration of the church (see Eph. 5:27).[12] It is problematic to say, as Healy does,

9. Jean-Marie-Roger Tillard, *Flesh of the Church, Flesh of Christ: At the Source of the Ecclesiology of Communion*, trans. Madeleine Beaumont (Collegeville, MN: Liturgical Press, 2001), p. 6.

10. Henri de Lubac, *Catholicism: Christ and the Common Destiny of Man*, trans. Lancelot C. Sheppard and Sr Elizabeth Englund (San Francisco: Ignatius Press, 1988), pp. 25-40; see also Tillard, *Flesh of the Church*, pp. 33-82.

11. For examples, see Tillard, *Flesh of the Church*, pp. 33-133.

12. Healy, "Practices and the New Ecclesiology," p. 307.

that in this life we participate in Christ's passion "rather than" his resurrection,[13] for as Paul tells the Colossians, "When you were buried with him in baptism, you were also raised with him through faith in the power of God, who raised him from the dead" (Col. 2:12).[14]

The second problem with Healy's account is that it runs the risk of an internalizing of the church. He clearly does not reduce the Christian life to interior dispositions; he presents his account as a balancing corrective to any overemphasis on external practices. Practices are necessary and important, but only as they are performed with appropriate intentions and dispositions. This much is certainly correct. The problem is that Healy makes it virtually impossible to judge intentions, and therefore judge practices. If practices tell us nothing at all about one's relationship to God, if we cannot know anything about a person's internal dispositions by looking at what someone does, as Healy says, then the church has been rendered invisible. Healy only hopes to correct an overemphasis on the visibility of church practices, but if we can tell nothing at all about the faithfulness of the church by looking at practices, then the church's visible witness is severely curtailed.

Surely we are able to make some judgments, albeit fallible ones, based on looking at what someone does. Intention for Aquinas is not the occult movement of the ghost in the machine, but an *embodied* "tending to something."[15] Virtues and vices are not purely interior dispositions but habits that are built up over time by repetition of practices. We judge intention just as intention is judged in a court of law: not just by what a person says she intended, but by her actions. The fact that someone is hanging around a bus station at 3 a.m. without a ticket gives us important clues about that person's intentions. Judgments based on such clues are

13. Healy gives two examples from Aquinas (*ST* III.68.1 ad 2 and III.83.1) to support his contention that *in via* we participate in the passion rather than the resurrection. These passages, however, do not support Healy's claim. Neither of these passages mentions the resurrection at all. In the first, Aquinas contends that those who are baptized are renewed in spirit, while their bodies remain subject to the "oldness" of sin. In the second, Aquinas argues that Christ is sacrificed in the Eucharist, and "we are made partakers in the fruit of our Lord's Passion," but he does not deny that we participate in Christ's resurrection in this life. To do so, he would need to contradict the Pauline witness. See Eph. 2:4-6 and Col. 2:11-14 and 3:1, where Paul speaks of already participating in Christ's resurrection.

14. Whether or not the Letter to the Colossians was actually written by Paul is not important to my argument.

15. Thomas Aquinas, *Summa Theologiae* I-II.12.1.

151

not infallible, but they need to be made, lest we abandon all possibility of judgment.

Likewise, the faith — or lack thereof — of the church is not completely opaque to the outside observer. We are not able to establish with certainty *in via* who is inside and who is outside the boundaries of the church. Indeed the establishment of such boundaries is usually an invitation to pride. In cases of excommunication a boundary is recognized, such as in the excommunication of torturers in General Pinochet's Chile that I have discussed elsewhere, but such cases are rightly rare.[16] The full boundaries of the church are never available to us. But just because the boundaries of the church are invisible, it does not mean that the center is invisible as well. The canonization of certain texts and people by the church is precisely the declaration that the center *is* visible, that you *can* know what Francis of Assisi's intentions were by looking at his actions, that salvation *is* visible in his life.

The Holy Spirit is not bound to the practices of fallible human beings, but neither does the Holy Spirit leave us in the dark, with no ability to see and recognize the salvation that Jesus Christ has made possible in the concrete social worlds in which we live. If ecclesiological Monophysitism and triumphalism is a danger to the church, the disappearance of the visible church is also a danger. As the case of Chile makes clear, a church that appears to include torturers and tortured alike without judgment has lost its ability to witness to the world. In such a case, God's plan for the visible unity of the world has simply been defeated by human sin. We can only lament the sin of all at the same time that we refuse to judge even where evil cries out for judgment.

Many of us, I suppose, would be willing to judge the extremes: General Pinochet at one end, Francis of Assisi at the other. But are only the extremes visible? What about the rest of the murky middle, the vast bulk of mediocre human persons like us that make up the majority of the empirical church? The tug of war between grace and sin tends to land ecclesiology somewhere in the middle. The divinity of the church needs to be balanced by the humanity of the church; the "already" of the kingdom of God needs to be balanced by the "not yet," and so on. Ecclesiological Monophysitism is a real danger, but so is what we might call "ecclesio-

---

16. William T. Cavanaugh, *Torture and Eucharist: Theology, Politics, and the Body of Christ* (Oxford: Blackwell, 1998).

logical Nestorianism," that is, the separation of the divinity and humanity of the church. We acknowledge that the church is the body of Christ, but it is also a merely human institution. Such separation of divinity and humanity in the church can either be temporal or spatial. In the temporal form, divinity is deferred: theosis or divinization of the people of God will only happen in the afterlife or in the eschaton. Participation of the church in Christ as we muddle through history is largely invisible. In the spatial form, a dualism is established between the church, in its pure and holy essence, and the sinful human beings that actually make up the concrete people of God in history.

As Karl Rahner has written, neither of these approaches to the sinfulness of the church suffices. It does not suffice to say that the church is holy, "without spot or wrinkle," only by way of anticipation, because Scripture, tradition, and church teaching have ascribed the quality of holiness to the earthly church. Neither does it suffice to separate the "objective" holiness of the institution and doctrines from the "subjective" sinfulness of the church's members. *Lumen Gentium* recognizes the subjectivity of both the holiness and the sinfulness of the church. A tendency in official theology since Vatican I — Rahner cites Pius XII's *Mystici Corporis Christi* — has been to posit an abstract "church" that stands almost as a separate entity over against the concrete people of God.[17] This concept is not only deficient sociologically but theologically. The dogmatic concept of church does not depict her as an ideal, an "ought-to-be," "something which is meant to be reached only asymptotically, as it were, by slow approximation."[18] The church is something real, and her members are really part of the church. While the validity and efficacy of the sacraments are independent of the sinfulness of their ministers, and the church claims infallibility for certain of its dogmatic pronouncements, acts that can truly be called acts of the church are not immune to the sins of those who administer the church.

> There exists no dogma according to which the assistance of the Holy Spirit which always remains with the Church would limit the effect of the sinfulness of the men who administer the Church to their purely

17. Karl Rahner, "The Sinful Church in the Decrees of Vatican II," in *Theological Investigations VI: Concerning Vatican Council II* (New York: Seabury, 1974), 288-89.
18. Rahner, "The Sinful Church," pp. 276-77.

private lives and not permit it to have any influence on those events which must be characterized as unmistakably acts of the Church, if the concept of the Church is not to evaporate into the abstract ideal of an invisible Church.[19]

Rahner is arguing for a concept of the church that is visible, holy, and sinful at the same time.

How is this possible? Theologically, we must do better than merely balance God and sin, divinity and humanity, to keep them parallel but separate. The persistence of sin in the world must be confronted with the fact that Christ has triumphed over sin definitively. If Christ has already disarmed the rulers and authorities (Col. 2:15), then there must be a way to see sin not simply as the negation of God's plan of salvation, but as incorporated somehow within the divine plan. To integrate both Lohfink's and Healy's insights, we would need to account for the visibility of salvation in the church in such a way that sin is incorporated into the visibility of the church. In christological terms, we need to recognize how Christ takes on sinful humanity in a way that neither negates it (Monophysitism) nor leaves it separated from his divinity (Nestorianism). We must acknowledge that what people see when they look at the church is *not* purity, the perfection of unity, the way the world is supposed to be. They see sin. But is there a way that sin does not simply negate the visibility of salvation in the church?

Christ Was Made Sin

If we need to avoid both Monophysitism and Nestorianism in ecclesiology, I suggest that we should look for clues on how to proceed from the original christological controversies over these two heresies. If the church is the body of Christ, then all ecclesiology must be Christology. Of course, it has to be pneumatology and patrology as well, but the particular ecclesiological problem of the relationship between humanity and divinity finds its most direct expression in the Chalcedonian problem of the two natures of Christ. Here we may begin to see how the humanity of the church may not simply be absorbed by, compete with, or be separated

19. Karl Rahner, "The Church of Sinners," in *Theological Investigations VI*, pp. 260-61.

from God's presence in the church. I will examine how certain Christologies that emerge from Chalcedon find a way to include sin "within" Christ without thereby diminishing his divinity.

Both Monophysitism ("without confusion, without change") and Nestorianism ("without division, without separation") were rejected in the definition of the Council of Chalcedon. In rejecting them, the council rejected any attempt to spare God from the full humiliation of being united to a sinful humanity. Cyril of Alexandria had insisted against Nestorius — and Leo the Great had insisted against Eutyches — that not only the cross but the incarnation itself was an emptying out of the Word into sinful humanity. For Cyril, the Word remained free in his own nature, even though "he appropriated the poverty of humanity to himself."[20] For Leo, "we are translated from earthly degradation to heavenly dignity through His unspeakable mercy, Who descended into our estate that He might promote us to His, by assuming not only the substance but also the conditions of sinful nature, and by allowing the impassibility of Godhead to be affected by all the miseries which are the lot of mortal manhood."[21] What both the Nestorians and the Monophysites had failed to grasp fully was that the Word became flesh not merely to repudiate sin, but to take it on, to assume it. That which is not assumed is not saved.

Maximus the Confessor elaborates on this theme. For Maximus, the cosmic Christ must assume the whole legacy of human fallenness in order to redeem it. This includes the passions. Maximus distinguishes between the natural passability (*pathos*) of creatures, that is, the capacity to be moved by God toward a final end, from the deviant passions (*pathē*) like lust that lend themselves to the dissolution of the soul. According to Maximus, Christ takes on even the liability to deviant human passions that produce sin, so that these "gentiles" of the soul, as Maximus calls them, can be redeemed rather than simply annihilated.[22] Christ converts such passions so that, for example, *eros* might propel us toward union with God.

It is important for Maximus that, in the incarnation, God does not

20. Cyril of Alexandria, *Scholia on the Incarnation* 5, in John McGuckin, ed., *Saint Cyril of Alexandria and the Christological Controversy* (Crestwood, NY: St. Vladimir's Seminary Press, 2004), p. 298.

21. Leo the Great, *Sermon* 71, translation found at www.newadvent.org/fathers/360371.htm.

22. Maximus the Confessor, *On the Cosmic Mystery of Jesus Christ*, ed. Paul Blowers and Robert Wilken (Crestwood, NY: St. Vladimir's Seminary Press), pp. 30-31.

simply repudiate sin but assumes it. Maximus addresses the statement in Colossians that Christ "put off" the powers and principalities (Col. 2:15), and reasons that he must have put them on to begin with. While recognizing that the Word was begotten without sin (Heb. 4:10), Maximus declares that the Word was only taking on the condition of the first man, Adam, who was created free from corruption and sin. When Adam broke God's commandment, however, humanity became subject to procreation based in lust and sin. Human nature was thus subjected to the deviant passions, and "retained the energies of all opposing forces, principalities, and powers." Christ reverses this process by assuming the original condition of Adam, by which he was "sinless but not incorruptible," and also taking on the liability to passions that were introduced into human nature as a consequence of sin. Thinking he was a mere man, the evil powers assailed him. "He submitted to it so that, by experiencing our temptations, he might provoke the evil power and thwart its attack, putting to death the very power that expected to seduce him just as it had Adam in the beginning."[23]

The agony in the garden is important in this regard, because both resistance and obedience are found within Jesus' prayer: "My Father, if it is possible, let this cup pass from me; yet not what I want but what you want" (Matt. 26:39). According to Maximus, who championed the dyothelite cause, the existence of two wills — human and divine — in Jesus is necessary so that the resistant human will can be taken up and healed. Though the two wills are irreducible by nature in Jesus, they are united in a personal union that turns the passion of fear into an act of filial adoration.[24]

Paul's dictum that "[f]or our sake, God made him become sin who knew no sin" (2 Cor. 5:21) is also important for Maximus. In *Ad Thalassium* 42, he explains this passage by making a distinction between the culpable sin of Adam, which was willed, and the consequences of that sin, by which "human nature unwillingly put off its incorruption."[25] Adam's sin was cul-

---

23. Maximus, *Ad Thalassium* 21, in Blowers and Wilken, *On the Cosmic Mystery*, pp. 110-11.

24. See Aaron Riches, "After Chalcedon: The Oneness of Christ and the Dyothelite Mediation of His Theandric Unity," *Modern Theology* 24, no. 2 (April 2008): 204-6. Riches argues that dyothelitism was needed to overcome any lingering separation in the definition of Chalcedon by making the unity of humanity and divinity concrete in the union of Christ's wills. The liturgy of the church is the extension of the dyothelite prayer of the Son (p. 217).

25. Maximus, *Ad Thalassium* 42, in *On the Cosmic Mystery*, p. 119.

pable, but its consequences were not. In Maximus's words, Christ did not become "my sin," but became "the sin that I caused." Christ, without culpability, assumed the corruption of human nature and its liability to deviant passions. In his early work, Maximus even attributes to Christ a "gnomic" will (*gnōmē*), that is, the will that must deliberate in seeking the good, rather than simply follow its natural passion for the good.[26] "He *became* the 'sin' that I caused, in terms of the possibility, corruptibility, and mortality, and he submitted voluntarily to the condemnation owed me in my nature, even though he himself was blameless in his freedom of choice, in order to condemn both my deliberate 'sin' and the 'sin' that befell my nature."[27]

Hans Urs von Balthasar observes this about Maximus's Christology:

> The deepest reason that Christ must possess a creaturely freedom belongs to salvation history: the healing of nature demands a descent to that tragic point in man, where sin, as opposition to God, has come into its own. For sin to be overcome from within, it had, in some way or other, to be found "within" Christ.[28]

For Maximus, Christ had to share all our human "vulnerabilities" (Balthasar's translation for *pathē*), including the human terror of death, as in the Garden of Olives, and even "the secret depth of the human soul, its revolt against God."[29] The obvious question is how Christ can contain both rebellion and divinity without rebellion being negated by divinity (Monophysitism) or without Christ being torn into two persons (Nestorianism). Maximus addresses this problem by distinguishing between "appropriation by relationship" and "appropriation by nature." Christ appropriates the punishment for our *pathē* by nature, but appropriates the guilt thereof by relationship. Maximus explains:

> Our vulnerabilities have two aspects: that of punishment and that of guilt. The former is characteristic of our nature as such; the latter sim-

---

26. Maximus attributed a gnomic will to Christ in his early work, *Commentary on the Lord's Prayer*; and in *Ad Thalassium* 42, he attributes "free choice" (*proairesis*) to Christ. Maximus would later retract those ideas at the height of the Monothelite controversy. See the editors' note in Maximus, *On the Cosmic Mystery*, p. 120n1.

27. Maximus, *Ad Thalassium* 42, in *On the Cosmic Mystery*, p. 121.

28. Hans Urs von Balthasar, *Cosmic Liturgy: The Universe According to Maximus the Confessor*, trans. Brian E. Daley (San Francisco: Ignatius Press, 2003), p. 263.

29. Balthasar, *Cosmic Liturgy*, p. 266.

ply disfigures it. The former was freely and ontologically taken on by Christ along with his human existence; through this act, he gave strength to our nature as it is and freed it from the curse that lay on us. But he made the latter aspect his own in the course of salvation history, through his love for humanity, in that he took it up to destroy it, as fire consumes wax or the sun the mists of the earth, so that in its place he might bestow on us his own blessings.[30]

Though Christ is not culpable, here Maximus says, more clearly than in *Ad Thalassium* 42, that Christ makes our guilt his own. As Balthasar points out, for Maximus this "relational" appropriation is also ontological, because original sin is a part of the universal reality of the human nature with which God unites ontologically in Christ. Thus Christ is able to subject not only his own will to that of the Father, but also the will of humanity in general — "even and especially that element in it which had not been subjected already." Balthasar uses the metaphor of drama to explain this movement in Maximus; the one person of Christ is the "stage" on which is enacted the struggle between God and human rebellion against God. Christ does not succumb to this struggle, but submits to contradiction in his very self in order to overcome this contradiction by submitting the will of humanity to the Father.[31]

The metaphor of drama should not lead us to think that Christ was merely play acting, merely appearing in some Docetist way to participate in the human drama of sin. Balthasar, in his own work, uses dramatic metaphor to display how it is that finite freedom is not simply swallowed up in infinite freedom. The metaphor of playwright, director, and actors shows how, within certain limits imposed by the script, directors and actors exercise a true, though finite, freedom without which the drama cannot succeed. The metaphor does not reduce Christ to play acting or pretending; rather, it envisions all of reality as a cosmic theo-drama of creation, sin, and redemption. Balthasar is noted for his insistence that Christ really did die and did not spend Holy Saturday hard at work in the netherworld. Likewise, human actors are not simply going through the motions of a predetermined script; salvation history is a drama because there is real freedom and real sin in the church.

---

30. Maximus, *Opuscula* 237B (PG 91), quoted in Balthasar, *Cosmic Liturgy*, p. 267.
31. Balthasar, *Cosmic Liturgy*, pp. 267, 268.

According to Balthasar, in the incarnation and the cross, God shows that God's sovereignty manifests itself not in clinging to what is its own, but in self-abandonment. God does not thereby cease to be God, but shows that divine power can make room for "self-exteriorization," even to the utmost.[32] "In his being 'made to be sin' and bearing the 'curse', infinite freedom shows its ultimate, most extreme capability for the first time: it can be itself even in the finitude that 'loses itself.'"[33] In the extreme of the cross, says Balthasar, God shows that the abyss of human refusal of God has been entirely bridged: "God is solidarity with us not only in what is symptomatic of sin, the punishment for sin, but also in co-experiencing sin, in the *peirasmos* of the very essence of that negation — though without 'committing' (Hebrews 4,15) sin himself."[34] This solidarity extends even to the descent of Jesus Christ to hell. Contrary to interpretations of Holy Saturday that have Christ actively preaching to or liberating those in hell, Balthasar insists that the second person of the Trinity is really and truly dead, and must await being raised by the Father on Easter Sunday.[35] This death is not merely a physical death, but a spiritual death as well. The interrelationship of sin and death is so pervasive in Scripture that Balthasar will not allow us to separate Christ's physical death from spiritual death (pp. 154-55). According to Balthasar, Thomas Aquinas agrees that the reason for the descent into hell is not some lack in the suffering of the cross, but because Christ has assumed all the *defectus* of sinners. Since sin is the soul's work, Christ's solidarity with sinners includes not just the death of his body but the death of his human soul — still hypostatically united to his divine person — and consequent descent into hell (p. 164).

In the drama of redemption, it is absolutely crucial that Jesus Christ

32. Hans Urs von Balthasar, *Mysterium Paschale*, trans. Aidan Nichols (Grand Rapids: Eerdmans, 1990), pp. 28-29.

33. Hans Urs von Balthasar, *Theo-Drama: Theological Dramatic Theory*, vol. 2, trans. Graham Harrison (San Francisco: Ignatius Press, 1990), p. 244.

34. Balthasar, *Mysterium Paschale*, p. 137. Hereafter, page references to this work appear in parentheses in the text.

35. Alyssa Lyra Pitstick has essentially accused Balthasar of heresy for his ideas on Jesus' descent into hell in her book *Light in Darkness: Hans Urs von Balthasar and the Catholic Doctrine of Christ's Descent into Hell* (Grand Rapids: Eerdmans, 2007). I cannot provide a thorough analysis of the book here, but I find the indictment of Balthasar overdrawn, and I find Pitstick's own limitation of Christ's descent to the "limbo of the fathers," whose residents have already been purged of sin, to be an unnecessary attempt to protect Christ from the contact with sin that his *kenosis* implies.

take on the entirety of human existence in order to heal it. But what becomes of the visibility of God's promise of salvation in this kenotic humiliation? Does human sin cover up the manifestation of the divine plan, or is sin vanquished by the brilliance of the divine glory? Balthasar does not accept either of these alternatives, for he believes that, in radically assuming what is contrary to the divine, God "discloses himself in the very act of his self-concealment. It is precisely the unsurpassable radicalness of this concealment which turns our gaze to it, and makes the eyes of faith take notice" (p. 52). This dynamic began already in Israel, in which the Word revealed itself in history to human beings while simultaneously abandoning itself to them "ever more defencelessly."[36] This process culminates in the incarnation of the Word, in which the most extreme manifestness of God is revealed in the deepest concealment. It is manifest because God appears to humans as a human; God explains God to humans by means of their own being and life. How could humans then not understand? At the same time, the incarnation is the deepest concealment, because God is revealed as one individual man in the crowd. If God is to speak to humans by means of humanity, then the incarnate one cannot be a superhuman, standing out from the crowd. He will have to "exhibit his uniqueness precisely through his ordinariness. . . . The insignificant must be the appearance of what is most significant" (pp. 457-58).

The cross, says Balthasar, puts an end to all worldly aesthetics, and marks the emergence of the divine aesthetic. That an instrument of torture should signal the emergence of the divine aesthetic should alert us to the fact that what is seen is not simply God in glory. Neither worldly nor divine aesthetics can simply exclude the ugly, the tragically fragmented, the demonic. Any attempt to exclude these is simply a form of what Balthasar calls "aestheticism." In the divine aesthetic, the beautiful does not simply appear despite sin, but in sin itself. "It is not only the limitation and precariousness of all beautiful form which intimately belongs to the phenomenon of beauty, but also fragmentation itself, because it is only through being fragmented that the beautiful really reveals the meaning of the eschatological promise it contains" (p. 460). In other words, in the drama of salvation, sin does not simply obscure the visibil-

36. Hans Urs von Balthasar, *The Glory of the Lord: A Theological Aesthetics*, vol. 1, trans. Erasmo Leiva-Merikakis (San Francisco: Ignatius Press, 1982), p. 457. Hereafter, page references to this work appear in parentheses in the text.

ity of the divine glory, but helps make it manifest in the form of the humiliated God.

> His bearing of the world's sin (Jn. 1.29), his being made sin for us (2 Cor. 5.21) is understandable only as a function of the glory of love, before and after and, therefore, also during his descent into darkness: what we have before us *is* pure glory, and even though it is really a concealment and really an entering into darkness (embracing even the descent into hell), it is always a function of its opposite. (p. 460)

Balthasar will not allow us to defuse this dynamic with a simple contrast of before and after, Christ crucified superseded by Christ risen, humanity superseded by divinity, sin superseded by salvation, earth superseded by heaven — lest the cross of Christ be "emptied of its power" (1 Cor. 1:17).[37]

What do we see when we see Christ? We see not only the second person of the Trinity, who has come to vanquish sin, nor only the perfect man who provides us a model of redeemed humanity to follow. What we see when we see Christ is the entire drama of sin and salvation acted out on the stage of his one person. A properly Chalcedonian Christology resists the Monophysite and Nestorian attempts to protect the divinity of Christ from contamination by sinful humanity. The drama of salvation lies entirely within the full assumption of our sinful humanity by Christ. What we see in Christ is that this kenotic movement is not the self-alienation of God but the realization in history of the very life of the Trinity.

The Church Is the Cross on Which Christ Is Crucified

Let us now explore some possible implications of Chalcedonian Christology for ecclesiology.[38] Ecclesiology is not a simple matter of transferring the

---

37. Balthasar, *Mysterium Paschale*, p. 52. Balthasar even thinks that the dynamic of concealment and revelation applies to the beatific vision, in which the content of the vision is the ever-greater incomprehensibility of God. Kenosis will be revealed not as the self-alienation of God, but as belonging to the very being of God as love, a love that, as kenotic, remains incomprehensible to us. See Balthasar, *The Glory of the Lord*, 1:461-62.

38. To do so may require us to move beyond Balthasar, who does not always integrate his christological insights into his ecclesiology; the latter is based on a — to my mind — problematic gender-based figural reading of the roles of Peter, Mary, John, and Paul. For a balanced and subtle critique of Balthasar on gender, see Barbara Sain, "Through a Different

attributes of Christ to the church. The church is not Christ, but the sacramental presence of Christ on earth. The church is Christ's body, not his divinity, and the divinization of the church is a dynamic process. The church is the body of Christ, but not because of its obedience to Christ, which is so often lacking. The claim that holiness is one of the marks of the church is not a moral claim, but a claim that God has elected the church to be both body and bride of Christ. Divine election does not erase the sin of the church, but neither does sin negate divine election. Any account of the visibility of the church that does not take account of the church's sin is inadequate both empirically and theologically. At the same time, any ecclesiology that is not simultaneously Christology is in danger of being merely sociological.

What is visible when we look at the church? We see Christ, but Christ as the stage for the entire drama of sin and salvation. Christ in the church does not simply obliterate sin (Monophysitism), nor is the divinity of Christ kept separate from sinful humanity (Nestorianism). What the church makes visible to the world is the whole dynamic drama of sin and salvation, not only the end result of a humanity purified and unified. In the drama, the church plays the part of sinful humanity. Ambrose declares: "The Church . . . rightly took on the appearance of a sinner [*merito speciem peccatricis*], because Christ too took upon himself the form of the sinner."[39] This "appearance" is not play acting, not a Docetic "seeming to be," but how the church is rightly seen. But the church also plays the part of that humanity that lives in the hope of redemption. The church, to put it another way, plays out the tragedy of sin while living in the hope that, in the end, the drama is in reality a comedy and not a tragedy. Sin, then, is not simply to be contrasted with the visibility of the church. The sin of the church is manifest, but it is incorporated into a larger drama of salvation.

However, the larger context must not be allowed to empty the cross of its power. The church is never far from the cross. It is a common patristic theme that the church is born of the cross; the water and blood flowing from the dead Jesus' side is commonly interpreted as representing baptism and Eucharist, given as constitutive elements of the church. The relationship of the church to the cross has a dual nature. On the one hand, if

Lens: Rethinking the Role of Sexual Difference in the Theology of Hans Urs von Balthasar," *Modern Theology* 25, no. 1 (Jan. 2009): 71-96.

39. St. Ambrose of Milan, *In Luc.* 6,21, quoted in Balthasar, "Casta Meretrix," *Spouse of the Word: Explorations in Theology II* (San Francisco: Ignatius Press, 1991), p. 270.

the church truly is the body of Christ, then the church is "co-crucified" with Christ. The church, precisely *as sinner*, hangs on the cross of Christ, and Christ dies humanity's "death of sin."[40] On the other hand, the church as representative of sinful humanity is itself the cross on which Christ is crucified. Romano Guardini suggestively observes: "Paradoxical as it may be, it is an historical fact that imperfection is an essential part of the temporal church. Christ lives on in the Church, but he lives as crucified. One almost ventures to use a parable and to say that the imperfections of the Church are the Cross of Christ. What would become of us if human nature vanished from the Church?"[41]

The sin of humanity puts Jesus to death. But that sin is not just something that obscures the true nature of the church, any more than the cross was just an unfortunate thing that happened to Jesus in the course of his salvation of the world. Sin is an inescapable part of the church *in via*, just as the cross is an essential part of the drama of salvation. The existence of sinful humanity in the church does not simply impede the redemption that Christ works in human history, but is itself part of the story of that redemption told over and over in the life of the church. As the fruit of the cross, however, the story can only be told in a penitential key.

The church fathers often supplement the image of the church as bride of Christ with the image of the church as prostitute. In the Hosea story especially, Hosea is a type of Christ: he takes on the full humiliation of marrying a "wife of whoredom" (Hosea 1:2), only to see her bear the children of three different fathers, then leave Hosea. Hosea pursues her and brings her back, just as God pursues an unfaithful humanity. Irenaeus says: "It pleased God to take his Church from the mass of sinners. She was to be saved through union with his Son, just as this harlot was sanctified through union with the prophet."[42] The Hosea story is read not just in terms of the historical relationship of God to God's people, but also with respect to the hypostatic union of divinity with sinful humanity in the person of Christ.[43] What is visible in this unconventional love story is the great love of God, who will stoop to self-humiliation in order to save us.

40. Balthasar, *Mysterium Paschale*, p. 134.

41. Romano Guardini, quoted in Gerard Noel, *The Anatomy of the Catholic Church: Roman Catholicism in an Age of Revolution* (New York: Doubleday, 1980), p. 13.

42. Irenaeus, *Against the Heretics*, 4, quoted in Balthasar, "Casta Meretrix," p. 229.

43. As, for example, in Hilary and Pseudo-Ambrose. See Balthasar, "Casta Meretrix," pp. 232-33.

Among the fathers, the Hosea (and Rahab) stories are often read in a supersessionist way, such that the unfaithfulness of Israel is contrasted with the redeemed faithfulness of the church. In this telling, there is a straightforward before and after in the transition from prostitute to spotless bride. A different line of interpretation, however, took the woman's affirmation from the Song of Solomon 1:5 — "I am black, but I am beautiful" — to indicate the simultaneous sinfulness and visible beauty of the church. Setting aside the problematic racial overtones of this interpretation (modern translations read "I am black *and* beautiful" [NRSV]), it rightly affirms that the church always stands within the transition from the old to the new. Salvation is not a past event, nor merely a far-off future event, but an ongoing drama in which the church is both whore and bride. The church fathers also rejected any attempt to separate "black" and "beautiful" into the "material" and "formal" aspects of the church, such that the church is pure in its sacramental and institutional manifestations but sinful in the material element — that is, the people contained in the institution. What the fathers meant by using this figure from the Song of Solomon was to convey the idea that the visible beauty of the church was not obscured or destroyed by its sinfulness. For the fathers, the church is closest to Christ when it assumes the same kenotic form. This form is not accidental, but essential to the church. Balthasar puts it this way:

> There is something about the essential form of the Church (and this is not her most inconspicuous feature) that is reminiscent of sin, conditioned by sin, something that in the present context always means infidelity and fornication. And yet it is not guilt but assimilation to the form of the sinner assumed by her Head.[44]

What are the practical effects of the view of the church's sin that I am exploring here? It could be taken as an invitation to resignation. We could declare the church *simul justus et peccator* and understand that formula in a purely forensic or eschatological way: we are fated to sin, but God overlooks our sinfulness, or sanctification is a purely future event, realizable

---

44. Balthasar, "Casta Meretrix," p. 271. It is not clear where Balthasar ultimately stands on the question of the sinfulness of the church. He seems to make a distinction between the church and its members when he says, "All Christians are sinners, and if the Church does not sin as Church, she does sin in all her members, and through the mouths of all her members she must confess her guilt" (p. 245).

only beyond history.[45] We cannot expect much, therefore, from communities of holiness that witness to what God is doing in history, because the drama of salvation has in effect been removed from real history. Holiness cannot be visible in the church except in anticipation, and we can only throw ourselves on the mercy of God to accept us despite our sin.

If, however, we adopt a Chalcedonian ecclesiology, in which sin does not simply negate the visible holiness of the church, then we are able to say that the holiness of the church is visible in its very repentance for its sin. The church is visibly holy not because it is pure, but precisely because it shows to the world what sin looks like. That is, humanity is able to name sin because it has been confronted with the Word of God. The cross is the condition of possibility of sin. It is possible to overemphasize the church's sinfulness; the church also makes grace visible, in its sacraments and its saints and its social presence among the poor. But the point is that, though sin and grace are countervailing movements in the church, repentance and sanctification are not. Rahner says:

> If the Church is holy not only institutionally but also "subjectively" and her holiness is a reality already present here and now, and not a mere juridical claim or an eschatological hope for future credit, then God gives this holiness to the Church *in so far as* he grants to her and her members the possibility and the reality of constantly fleeing from their sinful state to the mercy of God which alone makes holy.[46]

The church's proper response to being taken up into the life of God is not smug assurance of its own purity, but humble repentance for its sin and a constant impulse to reform. In so doing, it must listen to voices from outside the church as well. The church is visible in penance, not in the purity of an ideal social order. As John Webster has written, "Holiness is visible as faith's penitent cry for forgiveness and mercy, its appeal for God to do what

---

45. Barth reworks the *simul justus et peccator* formula so that it reflects the Christian situation of the transition from past sin to future justification: "Our sin has taken place, our justification is coming." The Christian lives in this process of conversion. Nonetheless, Balthasar criticizes Barth for removing both past and future to an eternity where there is no real progress or relapse in the Christian's life. Nothing really happens in history because it has already taken place in eternity. See Hans Urs von Balthasar, *The Theology of Karl Barth*, trans. John Drury (New York: Doubleday, 1972), pp. 253-60.

46. Rahner, "The Sinful Church," p. 292.

the Church cannot do for itself, namely, to keep it without sin and to gather it into the company of the saints in glory."[47] We cannot lay claim to God's holiness or even God's forgiveness. Repentance is not a strategy we choose, but a cry that comes up from the historical experience of sin. The church can show God's salvation of the world by confessing that God has not yet abandoned us, no matter how unfaithful we are. This is only possible if our sin has not simply been repudiated, but taken up into Christ himself in order to redeem it. We know what sin is because we know what the true nature of the church is. As John Zizioulas says, the higher the ecclesiology, the deeper the repentance.[48] A Christoform ecclesiology should result not in triumphalism but in the kenotic movement of repentance. As the saints seem to know, holiness is never something that can be claimed as one's own; holiness paradoxically can only be known in the real conviction that one is the worst of sinners. In the axiom of the desert fathers, "the beginning of salvation for everyone is to condemn himself."[49]

Both sin and holiness are therefore shared in the church. Zizioulas points to the way the desert fathers insisted on taking evil seriously by transferring it from the other to the self, thus advancing the emptying of the self and the loving of the other for who she is, without regard to moral qualities. Zosimas even urges us to regard the evildoer as a benefactor for allowing us to blame ourselves for the act done by the other.[50] This extreme act of kenosis is not just an exercise in humility, but a recognition of the deeply social nature of sin and the social nature of what Christ has done on the cross, in taking all sins to himself and creating a church out of them. The distinction between my sin and your sin is relativized. Christ himself has obliterated this distinction, choosing to take on the sins of others in his suffering on the cross. Those who would follow this act of kenosis must do likewise, and recognize the solidarity of all sinners. To do so is simultaneously to recognize the social nature of holiness, which is visible precisely in the penitence of the church. Such a view must invariably complicate the appeal to the church as a *corpus permixtum*, if such is taken to indicate a sharp — though presently invisible — division between the righteous and the sinners.

---

47. John Webster, *Holiness* (Grand Rapids: Eerdmans, 2003), p. 74.

48. John Zizioulas, *Communion and Otherness: Further Studies in Personhood and the Church* (Edinburgh: T. & T. Clark, 2006), p. 4.

49. According to Zizioulas, this saying is attributed to Nilus of Ancyra (p. 82).

50. Zizioulas, *Communion and Otherness*, p. 83.

If the visibility of the church lies in its repentance, however, we must ask whether and where the church is in fact capable of repentance. If the presence of sin is the condition of possibility for repentance, does not the presence of sin also make repentance difficult or impossible? For example, Ephraim Radner argues that repentance is only possible in a united church. The division of the church in modernity is evidence that the Holy Spirit has in fact abandoned the church, making true repentance impossible. Radner notes that the divided church has in many places lost the will to repent its divisions, preferring to see them instead as signs of a legitimate diversity of gifts in the church. We have lost the ability to repent precisely because we do not think that the Spirit has abandoned us. Radner says: "To lose God is to deny the loss."[51]

Radner is speaking specifically of denominational divisions in the church, but his comments apply more generally to the loss of visibility of the church. We return to Lohfink's quandary: the church in Europe and much of the West is dying because its practices have been rendered invisible. The church is no longer a visible social order, a visible way of life. But if salvation depends on the visibility of the church, has God simply abandoned us? Radner's approach is to affirm the Holy Spirit's abandonment of the church. Using the figure of Israel in exile, we can only give ourselves over to weeping over the church and to hope for repentance. Our hope for repentance lies in clinging to the figure of Jesus Christ. The church is bound in time to the body of Christ, and its sin cannot destroy these bonds. In fact, the sinfulness of the church joins it to the form of its being, Jesus Christ, who became sin. The dead Christ, abandoned by the Spirit to the sacrifice of the Father, is therefore the figure of the church, which has died its death of sin. The Spirit's work is accomplished in taking its distance from the church, to open a space of self-questioning and repentance. Sin is not regarded as something normal or inevitable, but is regarded with fear and trembling. Penitence is available to the church after all, but only by conforming to the body of Christ in its full humanity and full divinity. Radner puts it this way:

> The judgmental aspects of pneumatic withdrawal, then, ought to be acknowledged as such and suffered as such; but they ought also to be seen

---

51. Ephraim Radner, *The End of the Church: A Pneumatology of Christian Division in the West* (Grand Rapids: Eerdmans, 1998), p. 281. On the loss of repentance, see pp. 277-333.

as assumed by Christ Jesus as fully as all sin, and thus suffered by the Christian not only as a sentence, but as a sentence whose prior breadth of embrace by God's Son holds out a participatory invitation.[52]

Radner's conclusion that the Holy Spirit has abandoned the church is problematic, for then any kind of sacramental sanctification would be impossible. The sharp division he makes between the work of the Spirit and the body of Christ does not seem sustainable. Nevertheless, his point about the church's repentance as a participation in the death of Jesus Christ, who became sin, opens the possibility of a comic, not a tragic, resolution to the drama of salvation.

Conclusion

In the course of his analysis of creation and freedom, Gerhard Lohfink relates several postbiblical Jewish legends about God's hesitation before creating. In one, God debates with Torah, who warns that if God creates human beings, they will surely sin. God replies that, long ago, before creating anything at all, God had created repentance.[53]

I have argued that the unity of the church necessary to give witness to the world does not consist in maintaining the purity of the church. The visibility of the church consists in its transparency as the body of Christ, who did not remain pure, but became sin in order to redeem sin. The church's proper response as the body of Christ is to repent; indeed, the visibility of the church lies in its repentance. As the Jewish legend intimates, repentance is somehow prior to sin, just as God's grace is prior to any violation of God's law, and peace is ontologically prior to violence.

We need an ecclesiology that is robust enough to counter the powers that be, but humble enough not to reproduce the exclusions and pride of those powers. If the church is not in some way a visible countersign to the powers, then it simply opens the way for other allegiances — to the state or the market, especially — to take hold. Some apparently more humble ecclesiologies risk using a purported "realism" about sin to diminish the church's witness against a tragic view of the world. The reason the

---

52. Radner, *The End of the Church*, p. 350; see also pp. 339-43.
53. Lohfink, *Does God Need the Church?* p. 20.

church should reject violence, however, is not from a prideful conviction that we are the *cathari*, the pure, in a world full of evil. The church's call to nonviolence comes from the realization that we are not pure enough to direct history through violence. At the beginning of World War II, the pacifist Catholic Worker newspaper ran a headline: "We Are Responsible for the War in Europe." Christian nonviolence issues from an imitation of Christ's nonviolence, but also on a waiting on God's repentance to be worked in us. It is in this repentance that the church may make Christ and the drama of sin and redemption visible.[54]

54. I would like to thank Chris Ruddy and Brad Hinze for helpful comments on an earlier draft of this chapter.

CHAPTER NINE

A Politics of Vulnerability

—⟋⟋⟍⟍—

S tanley Hauerwas, one of the most important theological critics of the politics of modernity, has been persistently critical of liberal democratic polities. Recently, however, Hauerwas has entered into serious and sympathetic dialogue with the democratic theorists Jeffrey Stout and Romand Coles. Although Stout's book *Democracy and Tradition* (2004) is framed in part as a critique of Hauerwas, it articulates an attractive vision of democratic virtue and dialogical engagement that has evoked Hauerwas's praise. In his endorsement of the book, Hauerwas hails a "fresh conversation" between advocates of democracy and Christians. Stout, for his part, has the lead endorsement on the back of Hauerwas and Coles's 2008 book *Christianity, Democracy, and the Radical Ordinary:* "This book gives me hope. It takes the conversation over Christianity and democracy in a most welcome direction: away from ism-mongering and abstractions, down to earth, where instructive and inspiring examples can be found." Has Hauerwas finally come to his senses, in Stout's view? Has Hauerwas changed from the antidemocratic figure that Stout criticized so thoroughly in *Democracy and Tradition?*

In this chapter I will consider Hauerwas's views of democracy by way of his engagements of Stout and Coles. In the first section I will consider how the terms "democracy" and "liberalism" operate in Stout and Hauerwas, and how they find common ground in certain meanings of "democracy." In the second section I will show how Hauerwas and Stout part company in their construal of political space. In the third section I will show how Coles's radical democracy can help Hauerwas overcome some of the ambiguities in his previous attempts to articulate political space. In the fourth and final section I show the tensions between Hauerwas's and Coles's articulations of politics. Overall, this chapter is an attempt to show that Hauerwas's recent close and sympathetic conversations with two non-Christian democrats has the potential to lead to a more satisfying articulation and practice of a radical Christian politics than we have had heretofore. What follows is not just a reporting on these conversations; it is my attempt to horn in on them. I should acknowledge from the start that when I say what Hauerwas thinks, I sometimes mean what I think Hauerwas ought to think.

Democracy and Liberalism

Stout's book is as persuasive a defense of democracy as we are likely to see. It is a carefully reasoned and generous work that derives much of its rhetorical power from Stout's positioning himself between two extremes. On the one side are liberals such as John Rawls and Richard Rorty, who would severely curtail the admissibility of religious language in public democratic speech. On the other side are those whom Stout dubs "new traditionalists," such as Hauerwas, Alasdair MacIntyre, and John Milbank, who see nothing but threats to the integrity of Christianity by the liberal policing of the democratic order. Stout's position is attractive not only because he situates himself in the reasonable middle of this shouting match and tries to carve out a theoretical space for Christians and other "religious" people to participate in a secular democracy without compromising their basic theological convictions, but especially because Stout claims that such a reasonable middle already exists and is the majority position.[1]

In other words, Stout claims that Hauerwas reacts against a type of liberalism that exists mostly on the pages of books by Rawls, Rorty, and their followers, and not in actual practice. As Stout says of the two sides,

---

1. The term "religious" is problematic because it tends to identify certain kinds of beliefs, such as Christianity and Islam, as inherently different and less rational than other kinds of belief, such as faith in the market or the nation. For a thorough treatment of the invention and uses of "religion," see my book *The Myth of Religious Violence: Secular Ideology and the Roots of Modern Conflict* (New York: Oxford University Press, 2009), esp. chap. 2.

"they both hold, as I do not, that the political culture of our democracy implicitly requires the policing or self-censorship of religious expression in the political arena."[2] Stout points to the abolitionists, Abraham Lincoln, Martin Luther King, Jr., Dorothy Day, Rosemary Radford Ruether, and Wendell Berry as evidence that religious speech is not and has never been systematically excluded from public political speech in the United States. For this reason, Stout asks Hauerwas to take a decade off of talking about "liberalism" in American society. Critiques of Rawls's proposals might be useful, but assuming that Rawls's theory of justice actually describes how American democracy works is simply not helpful. At best, Stout would allow the use of the term "liberal society" to describe the "configuration of social practices and institutions" we are currently living with, but there never has been a single "liberal project," and "liberalism" is nothing but an "obsolete ideology" invoked by both critics and defenders who mistakenly thought there was such a "liberal project" (p. 130).

In place of liberalism, Stout prefers to talk about democracy, thereby drawing Hauerwas into a different kind of conversation. Stout hopes to meet Hauerwas and others on the ground of tradition by claiming that American democracy is itself a kind of tradition, not one of the acids of modernity that destroys tradition. Not only does American democracy not exclude religious speech, but it is not destructive of virtue. Like MacIntyre, Hauerwas has long accused liberalism of being antithetical to tradition, virtue, piety, and community. Liberalism prioritizes freedom over the good, thus recognizing that the basic unit of society is the individual pursuing his or her self-interest: "[T]he individual is the sole source of authority."[3] Liberalism assumes that shared tradition and common goods are not necessary for a social order; all that is required is a system of procedures for adjudicating conflict. Hauerwas says, "Liberal polity is the attempt to show that societal cooperation is possible under conditions of distrust" (p. 83). American founding fathers such as James Madison assumed that such a system of limited government could only work amongst virtuous people. Hauerwas argues, however, that such a system lacks the resources necessary to produce virtuous people. "Liberalism

2. Jeffrey Stout, *Democracy and Tradition* (Princeton, NJ: Princeton University Press, 2004), p. 84. Hereafter, page references to this work appear in parentheses in the text.

3. Stanley Hauerwas, *A Community of Character: Toward a Constructive Christian Social Ethic* (Notre Dame, IN: University of Notre Dame Press, 1981), p. 78. Hereafter, page references to this work appear in parentheses in the text.

thus becomes a self-fulfilling prophecy; a social order that is designed to work on the presumption that people are self-interested tends to produce that kind of people" (p. 79).

Stout wants to empty this critique of its persuasiveness by speaking of democracy as a lively tradition of virtue that produces self-reliance, piety toward "the sources of our existence and progress through life," and disciplined, open dialogue with others (p. 30).[4] Key figures for Stout are Ralph Waldo Emerson and Walt Whitman, in whose writings — unlike those of Rawls and Rorty — questions of character, virtue, and piety are treated with great seriousness. Emerson and Whitman did not see democracy as leading to self-assertion, social fragmentation, and the destruction of piety. On the contrary, Stout shows that the character of the democratic person was of utmost importance to such figures, precisely because certain virtues, such as independence of mind, are necessary for a democracy to function. The virtuous democrat must be capable of giving and asking for reasons in the public arena that do not rely merely on deference to either aristocratic or ecclesiastical authority. The reason that some traditionalists believe that democracy is antithetical to piety is that they define piety as deference to the hierarchical powers that be. What Stout calls "self-reliant piety" is taking responsibility for one's own highest commitments, as something for which reasons can be requested and given (pp. 30-31). Authority is not done away with, but it is dispersed into individuals who must earn it. "Moral authority belongs not to a class of ordained experts, but rather to anyone who proves his or her reliability as an observer and arguer in the eyes of the entire community" (p. 221).

In responding to Stout's book, Hauerwas has acknowledged that liberals can give accounts of why virtues are important, but the real question is what virtues are being recommended. For example, Hauerwas says that "one of the primary intellectual virtues for liberalism is cynicism," the assumption that one can step back from one's engagements.[5] Hauerwas clearly thinks that some engagements do not acquire authority by proving themselves before the bar of individual judgment. We need to be freed from the tyranny of our own wills. This is one obvious point on

---

4. Stout uses this locution repeatedly, apparently to substitute for "God" or some other such object of piety that would restrict "piety" to "religious" people.

5. Stanley Hauerwas, "Postscript: A Response to Jeff Stout's *Democracy and Tradition*," in *Performing the Faith: Bonhoeffer and the Practice of Nonviolence* (Grand Rapids: Brazos, 2004), p. 225.

which Hauerwas and Stout will not agree. Stout's own autobiographical remarks show that he regards his "stepping back" from his earlier attachment to Martin Luther King, Jr., and Jesus as a necessary stage in his moral maturation.

> In the days of my adolescent sublime, Martin Luther King, Jr., was the hero of my humanitarian cause, and Jesus was one of three personifications of my loving divinity. Nowadays things have become more complicated, because I have come to know more about these figures of virtue than their hagiographers and publicists wanted me to know. Now that I am less innocent of the complexities, I am no less moved by love and justice, no less cognizant of the place such traits have in a virtuous character, and no less able to put these concepts to work discursively than I used to be. . . . To the extent that King and Jesus exemplify virtues in my imaginative life, they now do so imperfectly and defeasibly. I therefore need an open-ended way to think the relation through: as it were, from both sides at once. (p. 173)

Hauerwas would object, of course, that such defeasibility in Jesus is not something that a Christian could accept. But Stout would respond that his pragmatic account of democracy does not require that Christians be shaken loose of their most deeply held convictions. Stout thinks that Hauerwas's attacks on doctrinal "liberalism" simply do not apply to the mainstream reality of democracy in America. Part of the appeal of Stout's analysis is that he aims to be more discriminating than Hauerwas, advocating a "surgical" critique of society and its political system rather than issuing broadsides against abstractions like "liberalism" (pp. 59-60). Hauerwas himself, as Stout notes, has confessed that he has "grown tired of arguments about the alleged virtues or vices of liberalism," though he can't quite bring himself to avoid them.[6] Stout wants to take the conversation away from discussion of political theories such as those of Hobbes, Locke, and Rawls, and address instead the concrete reality of American democracy.

> I find the social-contract model of political community — and especially its conception of public reason — insufficiently historical and

---

6. Hauerwas, *A Better Hope*, p. 10, cited in Stout, *Democracy and Tradition*, p. 140.

sociological. As a student of religion, I am inclined to approach these topics more concretely. That means beginning with the religious visions and perfectionist projects that have actually mattered to most Americans, and only then constructing a philosophical account of the promise and dangers implicit in our political culture. (p. 21)

From here Stout goes on to examine the writings of Whitman and Emerson, but one wonders why this should count as a more historical or sociological way to proceed. Stout might wish to hold up Whitman and Emerson as exemplars of democratic thought, but it is by no means clear that their projects are those "that have actually mattered to most Americans." Who besides a few scholars reads Whitman and Emerson today? Likewise, Stout's chapter on moral examples is a discussion of some scholarly works on moral examples, and not an empirical examination of American society.

Who can legitimately claim to be presenting a more accurate, empirically based portrait of virtue in American society, Stout or Hauerwas? Stout accuses Hauerwas of painting an idealized portrait of the church while caricaturing American society. The result is an overly sharp dualism between church and world and an inability and unwillingness to engage with the society at large (pp. 154-57). Hauerwas has responded to similar charges many times before, by acknowledging the church's failures, giving a kind of Fall narrative ("we have almost forgotten that the church is also a polity that at one time had the confidence to encourage in its members virtues sufficient to sustain their role as citizens in a society whose purpose was to counter the unwarranted claims made by other societies and states" [*Community of Character*, pp. 73-74]), and distinguishing between *is* and *ought* ("theologically the question is not what Christians do think, but what they ought to think given their basic convictions" [p. 108]).[7]

Stout makes the same moves in defending democracy. He is capable of quite scathing critiques of American society, but he also appeals to a Fall

7. Similarly, "my strategy is to try to help us recover the everyday practices that constitute that *polis* called church that are every bit as interesting and exciting as baseball. What we Christians have lost is just how radical our practices are, since they are meant to free us from the excitement of war and the lies so characteristic of the world." Hauerwas, *In Good Company: The Church as Polis* (Notre Dame, IN: University of Notre Dame Press, 1995), p. 8.

narrative (on the question of character, Stout says "we have largely forgotten how to pose it in Whitman's democratic way. Indeed, we have largely lost sight of the tradition of reflection that *Democratic Vistas* represents" [p. 19]), and to a distinction between *is* and *ought* ("the so-called democratic societies . . . are in fact severely deficient when judged from the perspective implied by their own best thinking" [p. 289]).[8] It should be said, however, that neither Hauerwas nor Stout makes the distinction between *is* and *ought* consistently. Both make idealized statements about the virtues of the church or the habits of a democratic people that seem to contradict other statements about the dire state of the church or the *demos*.[9]

What exactly does the *is* — as opposed to the *ought* — look like according to Stout?

> As I survey the day-to-day lives of my fellow citizens, it seems reasonable to fear that we have largely:
> - ignored the plight of the poor everywhere;
> - permitted the American state to prop up countless tyrants abroad;
> - neither adequately prevented nor mourned the civilian casualties of our militarism;
> - failed to hold professional elites responsible to the people;
> - acquired a habit of deferring to bosses;
> - preferred pecuniary gain and prestige to justice;
> - ceased to trust ourselves as competent initiators of action;
> - retreated into enclaves defined by ethnicity, race, and lifestyle;
> - and otherwise withdrawn from politics into docility, apathy, or despair. (p. 24)

8. *Democratic Vistas* refers to the book published by Whitman in 1871. Stout faults MacIntyre for not recognizing his own indebtedness to a Romantic appeal to a story of ruin and fall (p. 135), but Stout is capable of using the same trope.

9. For example, a few sentences after Hauerwas says "because the church rarely now engenders such a people and community, it has failed our particular secular polity," he says, "For the Christian, therefore, the church is always the primary polity through which we gain the experience to negotiate and make positive contributions to whatever society in which we may find ourselves" (*Community of Character*, p. 74). Stout, for his part, juxtaposes his indictments of American society with statements like this one: "It is a remarkably widespread and steady commitment, on the part of citizens, to talk things through with citizens unlike themselves. This commitment is there, prior to all theorizing, in the habits of the people" (p. 297).

It would be difficult for Hauerwas to outdo this list for devastating indictments of American society. The difference between Stout and Hauerwas is really not in their portrayals of the empirically observable state of virtue in American society. The difference is that, according to Stout, Hauerwas thinks the problem is too much democracy, and Stout thinks the problem is not enough. He says that Hauerwas thinks democracy undercuts the kinds of tradition and community that make it possible to produce virtuous people (pp. 24-25). On the other hand, he argues that democracy is a tradition that does produce communities of virtue, even if it is a tradition in grave danger of being lost.

Given the degree of agreement between Hauerwas and Stout on the empirically observable ills of American society, can they not come to an agreement on democracy? Part of the problem is that they use "democracy" equivocally in this discussion. Immediately after Stout gives the above list, he asks: "If some or all of these fears are indeed justified, is not our political economy in immediate danger of ceasing in practice to be a democracy in any but a purely formal sense?" (p. 24) What "democracy" seems to mean for Stout (despite the centrality of the concept to his book, he never defines it) is not primarily a formal, institutional system of state government, but something like a tradition of virtuous self-reliance, social justice, and free exchange of ideas. It is hard to escape the impression that what counts as "democracy" are the things that Stout likes about American society. At the end of his book, Stout responds to Jean Bethke Elshtain's fear that the streams of religious and ethical virtue that feed American democracy are running dry. Stout responds: "We should not imagine the life-giving sources on which we depend as something essentially alien to American democratic modernity. That stream is in us and of us when we engage in our democratic practices. Democracy, then, is misconceived when taken to be a desert landscape hostile to whatever life-giving waters of culture and tradition might still flow through it. Democracy is better construed as the name appropriate to the currents themselves in this particular time and place" (p. 308).

If "democracy" means what is life-giving and virtuous in American society, then it is understandable why Hauerwas is happy to endorse Stout's book. In his response to the book, Hauerwas has written: "Put bluntly, this is a position with which we Christians not only can, but should want to, do business. Stout does try to give an account of democratic life that is not in the first place state theory. I am extremely sympathetic with that project."[10] Hauerwas is especially open to Stout's presentation of democracy insofar as it illuminates John Howard Yoder's advocacy of a church of dialogue and patient listening to the least members of the community. "It is extremely important to understand that Yoder understood that nonviolence requires the kind of conversation Stout associates with democracy."[11] In 1981, Hauerwas had himself endorsed a qualified view of the church as "democratic" in this sense, provided it does not mean that truth is simply unavailable to the community as a whole.[12]

The question is what one means by "democracy." "Democracy" is what Stout calls traditions of self-reliant piety, independent thinking, and reasoned dialogue in American society. He has no general name for the kinds of self-interested violence, greed, fragmentation, and despair that he lists as "largely" characterizing American society. Hauerwas calls those latter types of dynamics "liberalism," because he thinks these vices are not unrelated to the prioritizing of freedom (libertas) over the good. The problem with Hauerwas's talk of "liberalism" is that, as Stout says, "his heavy-handed use of the term 'liberalism' as an all-purpose critical instrument continually reinforces the impression that total rejection is in fact required" (p. 148). If total rejection of American society as a whole is called for, then Hauerwas brings the charge of sectarianism upon himself.

10. Hauerwas, *Performing the Faith*, p. 219.

11. Hauerwas, *Performing the Faith*, p. 229.

12. "The challenge of the political today is no different than it has always been, though it appears in a new form. The challenge is always for the church to be a 'contrast model' for all polities that know not God. Unlike them, we know that the story of God is the truthful account of our existence, and thus we can be a community formed on trust rather than distrust. The hallmark of such a community, unlike the power of the nation-states, is its refusal to resort to violence to secure its own existence or to insure internal obedience. For as a community convinced of the truth, we refuse to trust any other power to compel than the truth itself. It is in that connection that the church is in a certain sense 'democratic,' for it believes that through the story of Christ it best charts its future. We rejoice in the difference and diversity of gifts among those in the church, as that very diversity is the necessary condition for our faithfulness. Discussion becomes the hallmark of such a society, since recognition and listening to the other is the way our community finds the way of obedience. But the church is radically not democratic if by democratic we mean that no one knows the truth and therefore everyone's opinion counts equally. Christians do not believe that there is no truth; rather, truth can only be known through struggle. That is exactly why authority in the church is vested in those we have learned to call saints in recognition of their more complete appropriation of that truth." Hauerwas, *Community of Character*, p. 85.

Hauerwas may be happy to engage Stout's presentation of democratic virtues as a way of affirming what is good in American society and avoiding the charge of sectarianism.

Nevertheless, the term "liberalism" does allow Hauerwas to identify pathologies in American society that link the things Americans most value and defend with the things that threaten to destroy them. A significant absence in Stout's analysis is that he has no explanation for the coincidence of democracy and the evils of American society that he lists. Such evils simply appear as an extrinsic force that has somehow gotten mixed up with democracy and threatens to ruin it. Stout laments American militarism no less than Hauerwas does, but offers no explanation for how the nation at the center of the democratic experiment came to spend more on its military than all the other nations of the world combined. Hauerwas can point to a connection between liberal universality and the Wilsonian urge to make the world safe for democracy — by military means, if necessary. Hauerwas could appeal to George W. Bush's words: "Every nation has learned, or should have learned, an important lesson: Freedom is worth fighting for, dying for, and standing for — and the advance of freedom leads to peace."[13]

Andrew Bacevich's book *American Empire* (2002) shows how the impulse to "openness" in politics and markets has provided the ideological fuel for American military adventures from the late nineteenth century to the present.[14] As Colin Dueck's study of American foreign policy has shown, Americans tend to favor military action "either for liberal reasons, or not at all."[15] Likewise, Hauerwas's use of "liberalism" allows him to account for the connection between a society that values freedom above all and the existence of an enormous, bureaucratic state that oversees and penetrates society at every juncture. Without common goods to which to appeal, legal procedure is necessary to keep self-interested individuals

---

13. George W. Bush, "Remarks by the President at the 20th Anniversary of the National Endowment for Democracy." Available online: http://www.whitehouse.gov/news/releases/2003/11/20031106-3.html.

14. Andrew Bacevich, *American Empire: The Realities and Consequences of U.S. Diplomacy* (Cambridge, MA: Harvard University Press, 2002). Bacevich's account is given extra weight by the fact that the author, currently a professor of political science at Boston University, is a retired Army colonel.

15. Colin Dueck, *Reluctant Crusaders: Power, Culture, and Change in American Grand Strategy* (Princeton, NJ: Princeton University Press, 2006), p. 26.

from interfering with each other's freedoms. Hauerwas says: "The bureaucracies in our lives are not simply the result of the complexities of an industrialized society, but a requirement of a social order individualistically organized."[16] Stout will rightly object that there is more to American society than self-interest and individualism, and Hauerwas in his more charitable moments would agree. But Stout has not yet offered a way to connect what he identifies as the core of American thinking on public life with the destructive dynamics that he acknowledges so largely characterize American public life.

In this respect, it is Stout's account of democracy that will need to deal with the charge of being too abstract. Hauerwas praises Stout for offering an account of democratic life that is not just state theory, but the almost complete absence of any recognition of the actual role of the state is in fact a weakness in Stout's account. When Stout occasionally mentions the state or nation-state, it is always to criticize its antidemocratic tendencies. Stout clearly wants a more limited government and wants to promote more truly participatory forms of political action. But he has not accounted for the existence and growth of the state in the twentieth century, nor does he offer any positive comments about how his ideal democracy would inhabit, oppose, dissolve, or use the state as it currently exists.

Hauerwas has wondered why Stout is so worried about Hauerwas's critiques of democracy when in fact they are critiques of the nation-state that both agree is anything but democratic.[17] What Stout is really worried about, however, is that Hauerwas is helping to drain the energy from the religious left, which he believes is needed to oppose the corporate takeover and fragmentation of American democracy.[18] Stout sees Hauerwas as discouraging participation in democracy. This is true if democracy is

16. Hauerwas, *Community of Character*, p. 79. Likewise, Hauerwas observes: "It is now an old, but still compelling, insight that the irony of the American conservatives is that the social policies they support in the name of the freedom of the individual necessarily result in the growth of the state. The state becomes the only means we have to perform those functions that liberal values and strategies destroy." Hauerwas, *Against the Nations: War and Survival in a Liberal Society* (Minneapolis: Winston Press, 1985), pp. 124-25.

17. Hauerwas, *Performing the Faith*, p. 237n46.

18. "The new traditionalism portrays the religious Left as *a mutation of secular liberalism* that is infecting the churches like a deadly virus. . . . If the religious Left does not soon recover its energy and self-confidence, it is unlikely that American democracy will be capable of counteracting either the greed of its business elite or the determination of many whites to define the authentic nation in ethnic, racial, or ecclesiastical terms" (Stout, p. 300).

defined in terms of the state. Stout seems to see the state as a neutral tool that can be brought back to serve the people. But this does not seem like a satisfactory place from which to criticize the state that he sees as so detrimental to the current practice of democracy in America. At the very least, Stout has much more work to do to provide a rudimentary account of the relationship between democracy and state, and not simply ignore the state as if it were an extrinsic factor in considering the failures or hopes of democracy in America, or as if the antidemocratic dynamics of the state were accidental.

The almost complete absence of capitalism from Stout's account is also problematic. He does include a few scathing indictments of multinational corporations as opponents of capitalism, striking deals with dictators, exploiting workers, buying elections, controlling the flow of information, destroying the environment, and turning our children toward greed, envy, and mindless consumerism (p. 225). Again, however, Stout refuses to connect this kind of behavior with democracy, seeing it instead as an extrinsic force that threatens democracy. It may be that, in his aversion to "ism-mongering," Stout is unwilling to cast aspersions on large abstractions such as "capitalism," preferring instead to target specific actions by businesses that are detrimental to society. This kind of surgical strike is laudable. But the danger is that Stout's account of democracy will be a rarified one, cleansed of any association with free-market ideology and practice. It then becomes just a coincidence that democracy and capitalism arose together in the same places at the same times. Stout is right not to engage in sweeping denunciations or defenses of capitalism as a whole. I have argued elsewhere that there is no point in Christians declaring themselves either for or against "the free market" as such.[19]

The question is: "When is a market free?" What is needed is careful discernment about what kinds of economic practices produce true freedom and what kinds do not. But to avoid blessing or damning capitalism as a whole, it is not necessary or helpful to ignore it. The plain historical fact is that the ideology and practice of "free" markets is closely related to the ideology and practice of "free" elections. The term "liberalism" allows Hauerwas to make connections between the never-satiated desire of corporations for freedom and the consequent erosion of the real political freedoms

19. William T. Cavanaugh, *Being Consumed: Economics and Christian Desire* (Grand Rapids: Eerdmans, 2008), chap. 1.

of people. For example, Hauerwas quotes C. B. Macpherson's contention that the "liberal-democratic society is a capitalist market society, and the latter by its very nature compels a continual net transfer of part of the power of some men to others, thus diminishing rather than maximizing the equal freedom to use and develop one's natural capacities which is claimed."[20] Stout's complaints about the corporate erosion of democracy, however fierce, lack teeth because he offers no explanation as to how or why the evils of capitalism happened to get mixed up with democracy.

Any serious discussion of nationalism is also lacking in Stout's account of American democracy. Stout accuses the "neo-traditionalists" of railing against the secularization of liberal society at a time when the secularization thesis of early twentieth-century sociology has been so thoroughly discredited. America is secular not in the sense that people cannot use religious reasons in public, but only in that they cannot assume that their fellow citizens make the same religious assumptions (Stout, p. 97). What Stout overlooks is the critique of civil religion in American society. What many theological critics of America warn against is not the mere absence of "religion" but the presence of idolatry, the replacement of the biblical God with the god of American civil religion. Stout thinks John Milbank, for example, has greatly exaggerated the dominance of "secular reason" in liberal societies; but Stout misses the point of Milbank's *Theology and Social Theory,* which is that "secular" social theory is in fact a type of (bad) theology.[21] Milbank's approach is not new, nor is it confined to theological critics. From Carlton Hayes's *Nationalism: A Religion,*[22] to Robert Bellah's work on civil religion,[23] to Carolyn Marvin and David Ingle's observation that "nationalism is the most powerful religion in the United States,"[24] many

20. Hauerwas, *Performing the Faith*, p. 228.

21. Stout likewise criticizes my essay "City: Beyond Secular Parodies" (in *Radical Orthodoxy: A New Theology*, ed. John Milbank, Catherine Pickstock, and Graham Ward [London: Routledge, 1999], pp. 182-200), for ignoring the demise of secularization theory, completely missing the point of the essay, which is that the political theory of Hobbes, Locke, and Rousseau is a kind of false theology in service to a false god (Stout, pp. 100-102).

22. Carlton J. H. Hayes, *Nationalism: A Religion* (New York: Macmillan, 1960).

23. Robert N. Bellah, "Civil Religion in America," in *American Civil Religion*, ed. Donald E. Jones and Russell E. Richey (San Francisco: Mellen Research University Press, 1990), p. 21. This article originally appeared in the Winter 1967 issue of *Daedalus*, the journal of the American Academy of Arts and Sciences.

24. Carolyn Marvin and David W. Ingle, "Blood Sacrifice and the Nation: Revisiting Civil Religion," *Journal of the American Academy of Religion* 64, no. 4 (Winter 1996): 767.

have noted, as Stout does not, that Christian theological convictions in the public sphere can easily give way to the substitution of America for the Christian God. Hauerwas has long noted the dangers of Christians giving over their most constitutive loyalties to the nation-state, for which they are expected to die and kill. Stout likewise decries mindless nationalism and militarism, and he upholds individual independence and a limited state as his ideal. He defends the freedom of the individual conscience against any attempt to entrust a modern nation-state to define the ultimate object of piety (pp. 40-41). But again, Stout seems unable to give an account of how American democracy happened to get mixed up with a sometimes virulent nationalism. Hauerwas's appeal to dynamics that he labels "liberalism" allows him to make connections between the nation-state that is limited in theory and the one that commands intense and lethal loyalty in practice. Where individual freedoms trump any shared vision of the good, a kind of Romantic attachment to the nation-state as itself the highest good rushes in to fill the vacuum. Hauerwas, following MacIntyre, believes that the nation-state is too large to be an authentic community, and can be only dangerous when it tries to masquerade as one.[25]

The Whole and Its Parts

The only kind of nationalism Stout discusses is Black Nationalism, to which the second chapter of his book is devoted. Although he finds Black Nationalism understandable in the light of the historic injustices inflicted on African Americans, he worries that the kind of separatism advocated by the movement undermines the virtues that are "essential to identification with the civic nation as a whole" (p. 42). In contrast to Hauerwas, Stout refers to the United States as a community that is threatened by falling apart into separate communities. Stout refers repeatedly to "the civic nation" (e.g., pp. 42, 56), "the democratic community" (e.g., p. 43), "the people" and "the body politic" that are threatened with dismemberment (p. 59). According to Stout, "a democratic critic, who serves the people as a whole, should leave the people whole at the end of the day" (pp. 59-60). It is problematic that "Black Nationalism, like the new traditionalism, re-

---

25. Hauerwas, *In Good Company*, pp.25-26. Hauerwas borrows this insight from MacIntyre.

duces the possibility of building large-scale coalitions of the kind needed to achieve large-scale reforms" (p. 56). Therefore, Stout recommends the approach of James Baldwin, who established an "ironic distance" from both Black Nationalism and his own upbringing in the Christian church, advocating instead a greater sense of individuality in African Americans (pp. 50-51).

Thus does Stout emphasize the civic nation on the one hand and the individual on the other. He is concerned that appeals to more local forms of community, if exaggerated, will tear the larger national community apart. The ideals of democracy "can achieve political expression only when people learn to think of themselves as individuals while identifying with a broader ethical inheritance and political community" (p. 293). Local communities discussing local goods are valuable. "But at the national level it must be the people as a whole, attending to the concerns and well-being of the people as a whole" (p. 293). Stout hastens to add: "The phrase 'as a whole' here is not intended to reify the people into something that will itself become the object of mystical attachment or awe" (p. 293). He rejects the identification of the civic nation with "the massive institutional configuration of the nation-state, of which we should always remain suspicious. . . . I am not recommending that we become *preoccupied* with our identities as members of a civic nation" (p. 297). He is simply concerned that people will retreat into enclaves and not be capable of identifying with those who are different from themselves. What he does not explain is how the democratic deliberation of "the people as a whole" is to be expressed, if not through the mechanisms of the nation-state.

Stout clearly does not want the ugly side of American nationalism, but he offers no explanation for it, and can only gesture at an ideal "civic nation" as a remedy. Local community is important for Stout. One of the most interesting and moving parts of his book, in my opinion, is his discussion of his neighborhood and city in his conclusion to the book (pp. 300-305). Nevertheless, "America" is still an important project for Stout, because he needs a whole to which to appeal to keep local kinds of community from becoming ingrown and divisive. He is caught in an oscillation between the individual on the one hand and the whole on the other, a kind of simple space.

For Stout, there are parts, but one political whole: *e pluribus unum*. He is happy to allow Christians to participate fully as Christians in American society, as long as they accept that they are part of the whole that is American society. According to Stout, I might be deeply ambivalent about my membership in American society, even following Thoreau's example and going to prison for refusing to pay taxes. But even if this were the case, "I would intend the gesture as an act of communication, as a signal to other members of my community that I intend to hold them responsible for their injustices. So long as I am thinking along those lines, I am still identifying with that community, even as I express my alienation from it" (p. 299). All kinds of identification with a community involve ambivalence; Christians are constantly dissatisfied with various aspects of the church.

> Retreating from identification with the American people while intensifying one's identification with the people of God leaves a Christian with roughly the same dilemmas, the same ambivalence, with which he or she started. The only alternative is full-fledged separatism, which involves commitment to a group that is small enough and uniform enough to eliminate ambivalence altogether, at least for a while. But why would I want to confine my *discursive* community to the people who already agree with me on all essential matters? (p. 299)

For Stout, then, the choice is between a wider embrace of difference in the whole, or a narrow confinement to homogeneity in the part.

The charge of separatism leveled at Hauerwas is, of course, nothing new. He has attempted to refute the charge of sectarianism many times, but clearly not to his critics' satisfaction. Stout, one of Hauerwas's most perceptive and nuanced critics, acknowledges that Hauerwas wants not complete rejection of a society but "selective service," discerning when and where loyalty to Christ demands withdrawing support from any given social or political order. Stout thinks that Hauerwas's heavy-handed use of the term "liberalism" invites the charge of "sectarianism," because it seems to demand a wholesale rejection of American society (p. 148).[26] But I think the deeper problem for Hauerwas is that he often has implicitly accepted the terms of part and whole that Stout has offered. In his essay "The Politics of Charity," for example, he puts the problem in terms of participation or nonparticipation in society. "For the importance of participa-

---

26. Stout quotes from Hauerwas's book *Christian Existence Today* (Durham: Labyrinth Press, 1988).

tion can be appreciated only if there is significant nonparticipation on the part of Christians. The church must provide the space in society that gives the basis for us to be able to decide to what extent we can involve ourselves in support of our society — in effect, what kinds of citizens we should be." The idea that the church is a "space in society" sets up the problematic of part and whole to which Stout points. Although Christians are obligated to "have a concern about the societies in which they exist . . . our first object must be to form the church as the society where truth can be spoken without distortion."

This establishing of "the boundaries between the world and the people called Christian" is for the sake of the world to recognize itself as world, but we must seemingly not hope that the world will be changed, for to do so is to count on our effectiveness. Hauerwas attempts to wean Christians away from the Constantinian notion that we must be in charge of the whole of history, but in so doing he seems to relegate the church to minority status as a *normative* condition: "What we are offered in Christ is a story that helps us sustain the task of charity in a world where it can never be successful."[27]

In his later work, Hauerwas has tried to address the problems with this position, most notably perhaps in his embrace of a kind of Constantinianism in his 1995 essay "What Could It Mean for the Church to Be Christ's Body? A Question Without a Clear Answer." Upon seeing an entire Irish village called Sneem shut down businesses and turn out to celebrate its children's first communion in the public square, Hauerwas remarks, "If this is Constantinianism, I rather like it."[28] What Hauerwas likes most about it is the physical and visible nature of a Christianity that has not been spiritualized. But what separates Sneem from the Mennonite and Jewish communities that Hauerwas extols is the fact that the *whole* village is there. Hauerwas acknowledges this fact obliquely when he says that he wants to remind American Christians that the church is itself an "imperialistic polity" meant to resist the imperialism of the United States. The church is to be "a body constituted by disciplines that create the capacity to resist the disciplines of the body associated with the modern nation-state."

What Hauerwas does not acknowledge is that the snug relationship

---

27. Stanley Hauerwas, *Truthfulness and Tragedy: Further Investigations into Christian Ethics* (Notre Dame, IN: University of Notre Dame Press, 1977), pp. 138-43.

28. Hauerwas, *In Good Company*, p. 20.

between church and state in Ireland, currently unraveling, is what makes or made Sneem possible. Through its alliance with the state, the church was able to make many of its own practices obligatory in Irish society, and the church became part of the coercive apparatus of the state in some-times appalling ways, as the recently-released Ryan Report has documented.[29] Hauerwas is searching for ways to articulate how the church can neither retreat to a part nor rule the whole, but the example of Sneem creates more problems than it solves. The best Hauerwas can do in this essay is to say what the church is not: it is not communitarian, it is not spiritualized, it is neither polis nor *oikos* (though he does call the church a polis in the introduction to the book in which this essay appears).[30]

Complex Space

If neither of these two essays articulates a satisfactory "position" of the church with regard to politics, it is in part because Hauerwas has never wanted to stake out the church's "space" in the world. The logic of the cross is an unsettled and unsettling logic, running close to both the "Constantinian" urge to claim Jesus' lordship over all creation and the "sectarian" refusal to be implicated in the violence of making sure history comes out right. But Hauerwas has often lacked a way of articulating the complexity of space in such a way as to present a positive account of the church's political life; church as enclave or church as polis are equally unsatisfactory. I find Hauerwas's book of conversations with the non-Christian ("radical democrat") Romand Coles to be the most satisfying articulation of Hauerwas's politics to date, because Coles gives Hauerwas a way of talking about the church that refuses the oscillation between parts and the whole.

Coles defines radical democracy as "political acts of tending to common goods and differences."[31] These acts always exceed our presupposi-

---

29. The Ryan Report is the official document of the Commission to Inquire into Child Abuse in Ireland. The Report, released in May 2009, documents thousands of cases of abuse by clergy of children handed over to the care of Catholic religious orders by the state.

30. Hauerwas, *In Good Company*, p. 8. The subtitle of the book is also "The Church as Polis."

31. Stanley Hauerwas and Romand Coles, *Christianity, Democracy, and the Radical Ordinary: Conversations between a Radical Democrat and a Christian* (Eugene, OR: Cascade Books, 2008), p. 3n4. Hereafter, page references to this work appear in parentheses in the text.

tions and institutional forms, and especially exceed state formations, despite the latter's claim to be the exemplary form of democracy. The term "radical" is used only because "democracy" by itself has been so commonly used as an antidemocratic weapon by the nation-state. In this book, Hauerwas and Coles assume, as does Stout, that the nation-state is to be regarded with suspicion as an imaginary thing commonly used to block democratic aspirations. Radical democracy, however, goes beyond Stout's notion that there is a whole, a civic nation, to which democratic aspirations refer. There is not "the people as a whole," as in Stout's phrase, but rather "a multitude of peoples enacting myriad forms of the politics of the radical ordinary" (p. 8). There is no simple space in which to organize and adjudicate difference: "[D]emocracy has no stable 'table' around which differences can be gathered" (p. 19). The parts do not simply feed into the whole. For this reason, localism is not encouraged for its own sake, but must always be refracted through complex translocal connections. Drawing on the work of Sheldon Wolin, Coles calls for combining localism with "attentiveness to difference and insurgent publics on a variety of larger scales that oppose the megastate and global capital, and gradually seek institutions of 'rational disorganization' that might de-center, disperse, and devolve their gargantuan organizational powers" (p. 150). Coles gives a number of examples of how such plural spaces are being generated by worker-owned firms, community coalitions, the Industrial Areas Foundation, Community Development Corporations, and others. The aspiration is much more complex than appeals to the civic nation. Coles acknowledges that "America" has sometimes been used to name radical aspirations, as in some forms of abolitionism, labor organizing, and the civil rights movement. Nevertheless, such appeals to an ideal of America "greatly risk succumbing to the salvific dream of America, and many have, in ways that have gotten very ugly" (p. 339). Coles recognizes that "the more dominant 'America' is by its own definition a jealous and proprietary secular god that wants to exclude and/or subordinate all other attachments" (p. 338). Any attempt to resist and disperse the antidemocratic tendencies of the nation-state will thus also need to disperse the imagination of one whole national community.

As we saw above, Stout cites the abolitionists, Dorothy Day, Wendell Berry, Abraham Lincoln, Martin Luther King, Jr., and others as evidence that religious speech is not excluded from public political speech in American society. But it is doubtful that all these figures construed political space in the same way. Did Dorothy Day think that she was participating in something called "American society"? She did not deny Christians' complicity in the project called "America," but her primary social imagination was the body of Christ, which transgressed and ignored the boundaries of nation-states. Hers was an anarchist and internationalist vision based on eucharistic communities that were both local and simultaneously taken up into the universal sweep of Christ's body. It would be a violence to Dorothy Day's witness to co-opt her refusal to pay taxes and her protests against what she called "this filthy rotten system" into an identification with the American community, as Stout does with Thoreau. To see Dorothy Day (or Ella Baker or Robert Moses or Wendell Berry) as just one more colorful, cantankerous figure in the great diverse tapestry of American democracy is to misconstrue her politics. For Stout, she must either participate or not participate in the whole. For Day, however, America was not the whole. The body of Christ was the whole, not merely as a rival polis, but refracted through local eucharistic communities of hospitality linked only by loosely organized bonds of charity. This is much closer to Coles's vision of complex space than to Stout's insistence on the priority of the whole society.

According to Coles, after speaking on behalf of the grass-roots efforts of the Industrial Areas Foundation, Hauerwas told him, "What I've been trying to do all along is to *make the church worthy* of participating in the kind of political relationships sought by IAF."[32] Hauerwas might contend that he has been saying the same thing all along, but radical democracy does seem to have given Hauerwas ways of more adequately conceptualizing how the church might enact the politics of Jesus without needing to adopt any position at all vis-à-vis "wider society." Wider society, America, nation-state, civic nation — all are imaginative projects that oversimplify the complexity of political space. Hauerwas has long been concerned with local forms of church that resist the dominant myths of America. What he has sometimes struggled to articulate is how those forms of church can be seen as doing more than resisting or participating in the dominant society, and how they can be seen as participating in other networks of connectivity that leave the imagination of a dominant society behind. Coles helps

---

32. Stanley Hauerwas, quoted in Romand Coles, "Democracy, Theology, and the Question of Excess: A Review of Jeffrey Stout's *Democracy and Tradition*," *Modern Theology* 21, no. 2 (April 2005): 312.

Hauerwas see that church is not simply about "smaller politics." When Hauerwas makes such a contention in the conclusion of the book, Coles quickly urges him to acknowledge that the politics both seek is in fact more expansive than the nation-state, and Coles cites Mennonite cross-border missionary work as an example.

> What we are saying, it seems to me, is that specificity and enduring relationships of tending, and a sense for the complexities and nuances of distinct places and histories, are elemental aspects of the kind of politics we endorse. These are most often less difficult in localities. But they can be cultivated in painstaking ways on other scales too. And they should not be conceived as a barrier against larger scales but rather as the sites and practices without which people will likely lack the experiences, relationships, and knowledge necessary to inhabit larger scales without succumbing to "seeing like a state," or like a Walmart, or like an NGO that has lost receptive contact with people beyond its staff. (p. 341)[33]

If Hauerwas could write like this consistently, the charge of "sectarianism," which depends on a simple view of political space, might disappear.

The Church and Radical Democracy

This is not to say, however, that Hauerwas need only sign up as a radical democrat and all his problems will be solved. Significant differences remain between Hauerwas and Coles. Coles worries that Hauerwas, in trying to build up the church's politics, has not done enough to embody habits of receptive generosity. Hauerwas claims that he learns from radical democrats, but, Coles asks, what has he really received from them if what he has learned is that Christians were radical democrats all along? (p. 35) Hauerwas says that the church is at the service of the world and is open to learning from the world, but Coles worries that Hauerwas has not done enough to cultivate a sense of the radical insufficiency of the church. The

---

33. "Seeing like a state" refers to the title of James Scott's book on how states simplify and read political space. James C. Scott, *Seeing Like a State: How Certain Schemes to Improve the Human Condition Have Failed* (New Haven, CT: Yale University Press, 1998).

church seems to have its identity constituted prior to its encounter with the world, instead of being constituted in part by its very encounters with others (pp. 35-42, 210-12). Hauerwas tries to answer Coles's worries about lingering Constantinianism by saying: "I have long argued that neither Yoder nor I are 'sectarians.' We are rather theocrats. It is just very hard to rule when you are committed to nonviolence. But we are willing to try. 'Try,' however, means that politics is always a matter of persuasion" (p. 22n5). Coles, however, does not think that the problems with ruling, of having "handles on history," go away with renouncing violence. Shopping malls are not violent, but they nevertheless seek total rule over human desire for baleful ends (pp. 39-40). Again, Hauerwas is not entirely successful in struggling to escape the dichotomy of sectarianism and rule.

Coles acknowledges that Hauerwas, especially in his calls for nonviolence and his writings about the mentally handicapped, has stressed the importance of vulnerability, but Coles is concerned that Hauerwas's vulnerability is sometimes based on a conviction that there is a prior orthodoxy that ensures that we get the story straight. But radical democracy meets the other unsure of what will become of one's story in the encounter. Coles imagines a true encounter between Christians and Native Americans in which one story does not try to incorporate the other. "What if the development of the Christian story ends up being the development of one among other things — say, the Nez Perce/Lakota/Christian story — such that each of these narratives is profoundly *thrown out of joint*, out of narrative structure, even out of an improvisational narrative structure, and what develops comes to be seen as essentially unexpected newness born of an unexpected encounter?" (p. 43).

Hauerwas, however, thinks some account of orthodoxy is necessary. "I have assumed that 'orthodoxy' but names the developments across time that the church has found necessary for keeping the story of Jesus straight. Therefore, rather than being the denial of radical democracy, orthodoxy is the exemplification of the training necessary for the formation of a people who are not only capable of working for justice, but who are themselves just" (p. 30). Formation and habits is a crucial theme in the book, as in all of Hauerwas's work. He is worried that, without strong communities capable of forming character, there will be none of the saints that both Coles and Hauerwas hold up as examples throughout the book. "I emphasize the significance of the church because I fear that the devastated character of the church in our time will be unable to produce the Will Campbells, the Ella Bakers, the Martin Luther Kings, the Bob Moseses" (p. 111).[34] Although he doesn't say so explicitly, Hauerwas is worried that the radical vulnerability that Coles wants can easily slide into the kind of ironic distance from all traditions that is already the hallmark of the postmodern subject. Christians who enter every encounter with others ready to throw orthodoxy out of joint lack the steadfastness and fierceness of the saints. St. Benedict included a vow of stability in his rule because he saw the shallowness of the gyrovagues, who went from one monastery to another, never subjecting their wills to the direction of an abbot.[35] Stability and vulnerability go hand in hand, because the monk must allow the tyranny of his or her own will to be broken in community. Saints are those who are entirely vulnerable to the will of God, but those kinds of people are produced in communities that are able to keep the faith steadfastly and pass it down over time.

The difference between Hauerwas and Coles on these questions is not absolute, but more a matter of emphasis. I am tempted to see the difference in the fact that Coles writes from an urban context, and Hauerwas often has rural examples in mind when he thinks of the church. Coles's prose is mobile, always reaching beyond the last paradox, always seeking a new layer of openness. When Hauerwas writes of the church, he seems to think in terms of people who have brought the same casserole to every funeral luncheon for the last twenty-six years. Coles recognizes the importance of habit for resisting the tyranny of power, though he tends to situate habit within a kind of fugitive revolution, habituating where things are working better, but disrupting habit where mobilization is called for (pp. 153-54, 160).[36] Hauerwas holds habit in high esteem, but backs away from claims of narrative completeness. "So it's not like the gospel is some grand story that helps me get the world straight. It is a story that helps me discover who I should worship" (p. 342).

Worship perhaps marks the most significant difference between Hauerwas and Coles. Coles acknowledges the importance of liturgies for

34. In the same vein, Hauerwas writes, "What bothers me a bit about the Wolinian fugitive character of democracy is that I don't know who is going to carry that story across time."

35. *The Rule of St. Benedict in English*, ed. Timothy Fry, OSB (Collegeville, MN: Liturgical Press, 1982), 1:10-11.

36. Coles takes this from Wolin, though later in the book he says, "My Wolin is not quite as fugitive" (p. 345).

radical democracy, by which he means body practices that express gifts and habituate people to generosity, patience, courage, and so on (p. 323). But worship is not in Coles's vocabulary. Coles is suspicious of the proclamation of Jesus as Lord, fearing that there may be a link between the pre-Constantinian "fidelity to the jealousy of Christ as Lord" and post-Constantinian modes of rule (p. 22). Hauerwas, however, insists that we begin and end with the reality of God, and he worries that radical democracy "can become an end in itself, an end to which God becomes an afterthought" (p. 111). When Rowan Williams says, "real life in Christ requires us to look death in the face," Coles adds "real life in radical democracy" (p. 193). For Hauerwas, however, Christ and radical democracy cannot be symmetrically related, because Christ is the goal and radical democracy is a process.

Coles mitigates his concern with the language of Christ as "Lord" and "Victor" by construing Christ in an antiteleological way, through an analysis of Rowan Williams's reading of Mark. According to Williams, Mark undoes any attempts to make Jesus Christ the guarantee of success: "There can be *no* simple assurance of final victory" (p. 180).[37] Coles takes this to mean that what we see in the incarnation, crucifixion, and resurrection of Christ is "not the *object* of our hope (an ordered and secure topography in the form of his resurrected body) but the vulnerable *way* of radical hope (in which his body is disordered in crucifixion and is disordered in new ways with his resurrection)" (pp. 180-81). What Coles is trying to do with this distinction between object and way is to deny any sense of closure that would cut off Christian receptiveness to the other. Even a far-off eschatological imagining of peace as harmonious difference does not satisfy Coles, for whom "the radical-democratic ordinary is inherently tensional in a way that not only opposes antidemocratic powers that transcend it, but is endlessly agonistic in relation to itself" (p. 171). The church, too, must be hospitable to conflict if it is to remain penitent and therefore faithful to Christ. Those who want to follow the way of Christ must always recognize that Christ is an exile from their own communities. Therefore, any eschatological imagining of peace must remain tensional. Peace is not an end state but a peacemaking in and as conflict and tension, forged in generous receptivity (pp. 186-89).

It is not clear how far a Christian can go with Coles here. Coles says

---

37. The quote is from Williams; Coles italicizes the "no."

that, for him, "joy is intensified by immanence" (p. 344). Imaginings of other worlds must always return one to this world, where there is no final end, only the joy of living out the generous play of difference. Although Coles avoids any appeal to tragedy as a way of resignation to conflict, he is equally wary of comic appeals to history neatly wrapped up in the triumph of Christ. In Hauerwas, however, a comic note does appear in his appeal to rest. "Because we believe that the end has come, through the death and resurrection of Jesus we see what God would have us to be; it means that as Christians, we can live eschatologically. To so live means that we don't have to live in a way to make sure that God's purpose comes out all right. We can rest easy in God's creation . . ." (p. 342). Rest is as central to Hauerwas's conception of peace as tension is to Coles's. Because we can rest assured that God has triumphed, we don't have to try to triumph over others. This is the kind of rest that resists closure: we don't have to know *how* God has triumphed, how the story will come out.

It is not clear how Coles's denial that Christ is the object of our hope could allow for the worship of Christ. For Hauerwas, however, worship is key to knowing, as he puts it, that "God is God, and I ain't" (p. 342). But knowing that God is God, and that Christ is God, is not the same as knowing *how* God is God. Worship is a posture of unseeing trust, the ultimate vulnerability of acknowledging the difference between Creator and creature — and thus the reality of one's own death. When and where worship has not simply become debased self-worship, it has the potential of awakening a person to his or her radical dependence on the source of being. It is there that a politics of vulnerability begins. But the other side of the vulnerability of worship is the confidence that someone is ruling the universe, and peace is not accomplished by human striving. Hence the words of the psalm: "Be still, and know that I am God" (Ps. 46:10). It is God who "makes wars cease to the end of the earth" (Ps. 46:9). Violence is a function of forgetting that God is God, and I ain't.

Conclusion

Stanley Hauerwas has tended to avoid democratic language largely because of the way it has been associated with imperialism and with identifying the will of an elite with the will of the people. Jeffrey Stout and Romand Coles have done a great deal to rescue the language of democracy

194

from the nation-state, and they associate it with virtues of dialogical engagement and receptive generosity. Hauerwas's engagements with Stout and Coles have allowed him to find common ground between the political aspirations of non-Christians and the politics of Jesus that he has long sought. Insofar as "democracy" indicates the rule of the *demos*, however, a gap remains between democrats and those who believe that God rules. The good news, however, is that worshiping the God who rules in the Crucified One can and should make Christians vulnerable to those who don't.

Index